Moctezuma's Children

Moctezuma's Children

Aztec Royalty under Spanish Rule, 1520–1700

Donald E. Chipman

University of Texas Press, Austin

Requests for permission to reproduce material from this work should be sent to Permissions, University of Texas Press, P.O. Box 7819, Austin, TX 78713-7819.

∞ The paper used in this book meets the minimum requirements of ANSI/NISO Z39.48-1992 (R1997) (Permanence of Paper).

Library of Congress Cataloging-in-Publication Data

Chipman, Donald E.

    Moctezuma's children : Aztec royalty under Spanish rule, 1520–1700 / by Donald E. Chipman.

    p. cm.

    Includes bibliographical references and index.

    ISBN 978-0-292-72597-3

    1. Montezuma II, Emperor of Mexico, ca. 1480–1520—Genealogy. 2. Moctezuma, Isabel, 1509–1550—Genealogy. 3. Aztecs—Kings and rulers—Genealogy. 4. Kings and rulers—Mexico—Genealogy. 5. Families of royal descent—Mexico. I. Title: Aztec royalty under Spanish rule, 1520–1700. II. Title.

    F1230.C54 2005

    929'.2'0972—dc22

                           2004027640

To the memory of Ann Prather Hollingsworth and my parents,
Albert and Olive Chipman

Contents

Acknowledgments

IN THE SUMMER OF 1975, having compiled a bibliography of
printed materials relating to the descendants of Moctezuma II, I
carried out my first archival research in the Archivo General de la Nación (AGN) in Mexico City. Joining me there was Ann Prather
Hollingsworth, my doctoral student, who had chosen Pedro Moctezuma
and his descendants as her dissertation topic. Ann collected information
on the Aztec emperor's principal male heir while I focused on Isabel and
Mariana Moctezuma.

During the summer months of 1976, I conducted additional research
in the Archivo Histórico Nacional (AHN) in Madrid and the Archivo
General de Indias (AGI) in Seville. Most of my efforts centered on locat-
ing pertinent documentation for our topics, which I flagged for micro-
filming.

Over the next four years, I assisted Ann's research and supervised her
dissertation to completion. We then decided on a collaborative effort on
selected members of Moctezuma's progeny. Through no fault of Ann's,
that work did not come about. My research interests shifted to the Spanish Borderlands, with emphasis on colonial Texas, while Ann studied
Pedro Moctezuma in greater depth. She hoped to revise her dissertation
for publication, but she and her husband, Bob, retired to Morelia,
Michoacán, in the late 1980s.

Meanwhile, the Texas State Historical Association launched the largest
publication project ever attempted in Texas: a fifteen-year effort that
resulted in six massive volumes, *The New Handbook of Texas* (1996). My

responsibilities as co-advisory editor for all entries on Spanish Texas and writer of approximately sixty entries ended, but a co-authored work on the Moctezumas was not possible, because Ann was battling a serious illness that took her life in November 1999. Following Ann's death, Bob Hollingsworth generously offered me her notes and microfilm, as well as permission to use her copyrighted dissertation. This book, then, is dedicated in part to her memory and scholarly contributions to it.

I also owe a debt of gratitude to Luis López Elizondo, an independent researcher and scholar in Múzquiz, Coahuila, Mexico. Luis read the chapters, provided information on a number of useful Web sites, and served as a valuable contact with scholars in Mexico and Spain. It is Luis's intention to carry the story of Moctezuma II's descendants from 1700 to the present—an undertaking that I have encouraged and will assist by making my research materials available to him. Additionally, Luis hopes to receive permission to translate this book into Spanish, thereby making it more accessible to a broader readership. I am indebted to María Castañeda, who located a copy of Juan Cano de Saavedra's will in the AGI and sent a photocopy to me.

F. Todd Smith, my colleague and fellow Spanish Borderlands scholar in the department of history at the University of North Texas, read the entire manuscript and made valuable suggestions for improving it, as did his wife, Helen Sophie Burton, now a doctoral degree recipient in Latin American history from Texas Christian University. Sophie, a Fulbright Scholar in residence at Seville from January to July 2002, and Todd have been generous with their time and expertise. They helped me fill lacunae by checking documentation in the AGI, and they facilitated my brief stay in Seville in May 2002.

As he has done with other of my publications, my friend and colleague Randolph B. (Mike) Campbell read the manuscript, made valuable suggestions, and lent his sharp eye to the improvement of my prose. The manuscript also profited from a careful reading by Robert S. Weddle of Bonham, Texas, and by Doris and Jason Chipman of Denton, Texas.

I am especially grateful to Rollie R. Schafer and Art Goven, both former vice-provosts for research and chairs of the University of North Texas (UNT) Faculty Research Committee (FRC). The FRC has consistently supported my research and publication efforts throughout my thirty-eight years at UNT. Lloyd Chesnut, vice-president for research and technology, provided financial assistance that aided in the preparation of maps, genealogy charts, and illustrations, which were expertly prepared by Chad Maloney of UNT's Center for Media Production.

During my years at UNT, I have frequently traveled from Denton to Austin to take advantage of materials housed in the incredibly rich Nettie Lee Benson Latin American Collection at The University of Texas. In more recent times, Michael O. Hironymous, in the rare books and manuscripts section, and Adán Benavides, assistant to the head librarian for research programs, have been invariably kind and helpful. Their associates, Ann Lozano and Jorge Salinas, deserve recognition for their good humor, tolerance of an off-campus researcher, and professionalism.

At the University of Texas Press, I would like to thank the incomparable Theresa J. May, assistant director and editor-in-chief, who has piloted several of my books through the rocks and shoals of publication. Thanks are also extended to Leslie Doyle Tingle, my manuscript editor at the press.

As usual, all omissions, weaknesses, and errors are my responsibility.

Introduction

MANY BOOKS ON NEW SPAIN mention the descendants of Moctezuma II, the ninth Aztec emperor, often in relation to whom they married or their *encomienda* holdings (grants of Indian vassals), but heretofore the story of these children of the emperor has not been told uniformly or comprehensively. Thus a detailed study of the principal heirs of Moctezuma II adds to an understanding of the nature and long-term impact of the conquest of Mexico. Specialists, informed general readers, and students alike will find the story both interesting and educational. For example, three-fourths of Moctezuma's principal descendants were women. Their accomplishments make this work especially useful for gender studies in Latin American history. And because important descendants of the Aztec emperor relocated to Spain in later generations but depended on New World income, these children of the emperor fit into trans-Atlantic studies. By the 1600s many of Moctezuma II's heirs resided in Spain, making this book of interest to historians of that nation. Finally, students in college and university courses on colonial Mexico and colonial Latin American history will learn much about Spanish political and cultural assumptions from the way the conquerors and the Spanish crown treated Aztec royalty.

As the initial draft of this manuscript neared completion, I was struck by the synchronicity of an article appearing in the April 12, 2002, issue of the *Chronicle of Higher Education*. The story recounts the efforts of Alejandro González Acosta, a Cuban-born historian living in Mexico, to help the modern-day descendants of Moctezuma II "receive millions of dollars in back payments from the Mexican government, which cut them off without a penny in the 1930s." Entitled "The Scholar as P.I.: A Historian Takes on the Case of Moctezuma's Heirs," this article explains how the Mexican government paid a pension to the heirs of Moctezuma II for more than a century after independence but then stopped on January 9, 1934, during the interim presidency of Abelardo Rodríguez. Almost certainly, Dr. González Acosta and contemporary Moctezuma family claimants in Mexico will welcome the research contained in this volume, as will members of the titled nobility in Spain. Among contemporary Spanish peers who trace their family origins to Moctezuma II are the Dukes and Duchesses of Moctezuma and Tultengo, the Dukes and Duchesses of Atrisco, and the Counts and Countesses of Miravalle.

Chapter 1 provides essential background on the indigenous side of the later lives and careers of the Moctezuma descendants. The second chapter presents an account of the Spanish conquest that weaves details about Isabel Moctezuma and her first five marriages, as well as vicissitudes of the early period of Fernando Cortés's rule and challenges to it, into the mix. Thus, the story of the Moctezuma offspring is placed within the more general political history of the early conquest era.

Literature, both primary and secondary, on the subject of pre-Spanish Indians in Central Mexico and the Spanish conquest is vast and often interpreted differently. It is simply impossible to find scholarly consensus on many subjects. Anthropologists, ethnohistorians, and historians, for example, do not even agree on what to call the native people who occupied Tenochtitlan—were they Aztecs, Mexica, Nahuas, or Tenochcas? Why did these same people carry out human sacrifice on such an extensive and horrifying scale? How important was the alleged confusion of Fernando Cortés with Topiltzin Quetzalcoatl? Were Spaniards viewed as "white gods"? How should the emperor's name be spelled? How did Moctezuma II die? And how did Cortés determine the principal heirs of Moctezuma, who make up the core of this study?

The reader needs to know my approach to these questions and others. Many years ago, as I prepared to enter graduate school, it occurred to me that my interests in colonial Latin America would require a knowledge of both history and anthropology. So I majored in history and chose a minor field in Mesoamerican anthropology.

When approaching the controversial issues mentioned above, words penned by anthropologist Alfred L. Kroeber seem especially appropriate.

One needs to make a clear distinction between historical "facts" and historical "interpretations." There is no question, for example, that the Aztecs once controlled a substantial portion of Central Mexico and that the Spanish conquest toppled their empire in 1521. But when it comes to interpretations, historians can never "prove" anything. Instead, as Kroeber observes, we infer "greater or lesser probabilities—probabilities of fact, of relation, or significance. . . . [The] whole business, beyond the assemblage of materials, is a judicial weighing of possibilities and a selection and combination of these into the most coherent whole or pattern."[1] For this very reason, there can never be a truly definitive treatment of any subject. We must also be mindful of "how new insights can compel us to reexamine inherited arguments about past events."[2]

One can best hope to obtain dependable facts by looking at original sources—both published and unpublished. My choice of materials in the first category for Chapters 1 and 2 deserves comment. I rely in part on the writings of Diego Durán, Bernardino de Sahagún, Fernando Cortés, and Bernal Díaz del Castillo.

Three mendicant orders were responsible for imparting the Christian doctrine to the natives of New Spain in the early postconquest era. The Franciscans arrived in 1524; the Dominicans, in 1526; and the Augustinians, in 1533.[3] Diego Durán was not a member of the original twelve Dominicans in the New World; he came later, as a young boy, and soon thereafter began to learn Nahuatl, the language of the Aztecs. His formal schooling came in Mexico City, and he entered the Dominican Order as a novice in 1556. Because he spoke the language of the Aztecs, which he mastered thoroughly, Durán profited by learning firsthand their customs and beliefs, which later appear in his writings.[4] It became an article of faith with Fray Diego that one could not properly instruct natives in the precepts of Christianity without knowledge of their language and ancient customs, and he criticized both clerics and colonists who lacked this expertise. Durán appears to have won the confidence and trust of his informants so completely that they spoke openly and freely in his presence. Of his published works, I have used the *Historia* to good advantage.

Bernardino de Sahagún was a Franciscan who also mastered Nahuatl. Many regard Fray Bernardino as the New World's first ethnographer. His major contribution was to take a leading role, along with fellow Franciscans Alonso de Molina and Andrés de Olmos, in transliterating a spoken but not alphabet-based written language into Spanish orthography.[5]

Using the Spanish alphabet to approximate and record the syllabic sounds, or oral components, of Nahuatl, Sahagún began an exhaustive study of Aztec history, customs, and religion that is preserved in a twelve-volume work entitled *General History of the Things of New Spain*. Translated by Arthur J. O. Anderson and Charles E. Dibble (between 1950 and 1982), Sahagún's great work now appears as the *Florentine Codex*. Like Durán, Sahagún is a valuable source.

Secular and religious authorities argued that Sahagún's intense interest in every detail about a pagan, indigenous culture inevitably lent the impression that such concern by a member of a "superior" society meant that the former must be of value and therefore worth preserving, and they often challenged him for his comprehensive study of the Aztecs. This contention drew a consistent, analogous response from Sahagún, who argued that, before a physician can treat an illness, he must first know as much about it as possible. Nevertheless, Sahagún, like Durán, never saw his work in print.

Of the many editions of Fernando Cortés's letters to the Emperor Charles V, the most valuable for this study have been *Cartas y documentos* (1963) and *Letters from Mexico* (1986). The first contains copies of the conqueror's *encomienda* grants to Isabel and Mariana Moctezuma, as well as other related documents; the second presents the best translation of the letters into English. Designed to cast himself in the most favorable light possible in the eyes of the Spanish king, Cortés's highly personal account of the conquest must be weighed against other sources. For example, his assertion of Moctezuma's steadfast willingness to cede his empire to Charles V, his rationale for the massacre at Cholula, and his account of the circumstances leading to the death of the Aztec emperor are all suspect. On the other hand, his letters were often closely contemporaneous with events described within them.

Two valuable editions of Bernal Díaz's classic account of the conquest of New Spain are an English translation by A. P. Maudslay, *The Discovery and Conquest of Mexico, 1517–1521* (1956), and a superior two-volume work in Spanish, *Historia verdadera de la conquista de la Nueva España* (1955). Although he composed it late in life, Bernal Díaz's work displays the author's remarkable memory for detail and masterly style in communicating it. No one, whether historian or anthropologist, can write about the conquest without consulting the firsthand recollections of this shrewd old soldier-colonist-chronicler.

My secondary sources for the two initial chapters cannot be confined to so small a number. Furthermore, those that I have used and cited hardly scratch the surface of available literature. Lacking any knowledge whatsoever of Nahuatl, I have relied primarily on specialists who have that expertise or on those whose scholarship impresses me most.

Miguel León-Portilla stands tall as Mexico's great savant and a brilliant scholar. Of his publications, *The Aztec Image of Self and Society* (1992) presents a succinct "introduction to Nahua culture," as the subtitle implies. León-Portilla relies on ancient codices and makes good use of both Sahagún and Durán. One of his most widely read edited works is *The Broken Spears* (1992). The translation by Lysander Kemp is intended for the general reader, but the thrust of the narrative is a poignant relation of the conquest as viewed by the vanquished Aztecs—certainly a departure from the norm.

James Lockhart is also an unquestioned master of Nahuatl. He and his doctoral degree recipients at the University of California at Los Angeles have continued to make contributions in the field of colonial Latin American history, in part by demonstrating command of that elegant language. I have also used *The Nahuas after the Conquest* (1992) and *We People Here* (1993) to good advantage. Among Lockhart's mentees whose publications have proved valuable are Robert Haskett, Susan Schroeder, and Stephanie Wood.

Books by Nigel Davies—*The Aztecs* (1973), *The Toltecs* (1977), *The Toltec Heritage* (1980), and *The Aztec Empire* (1986)—provide invaluable information on Tula (or Tollan), Hidalgo, part of which became the patrimony of Moctezuma's son Pedro. Davies also gives the most satisfactory explanation among many for the escalating scale of human sacrifice practiced by the Aztecs.

Although published more than forty years ago, Charles Gibson's *The Aztecs under Spanish Rule* (1964) proved to be more useful than any other secondary source. Its value lies in his detailed treatment of *encomienda* history in the Central Valley, and it helped me target materials housed in the AGI. However, for post-Gibson insight into such matters as *encomienda* and *altepetl* (ethnic unit), I acknowledge Lockhart and his use of Nahuatl-language sources.

I commend the University Press of Colorado for issuing H. B. Nicholson's *Topiltzin Quetzalcoatl* (2001), based on his long-ago completed dissertation at Yale University, and for publishing the revised edition of Davíd Carrasco's *Quetzalcoatl and the Irony of Empire* (2000). If one wishes to pursue the possible existence and importance of the human priest/deity Topiltzin Quetzalcoatl, which I do not do in this book, Carrasco's works are indispensable.

I have shamelessly used Susan D. Gillespie's *The Aztec Kings* (1989) and Camilla Townsend's "Burying the White Gods" (2003). Townsend's article in the *American Historical Review* summarizes cutting-edge studies on the conquest of Mexico since the late 1980s.

Ethnohistorian Ross Hassig's *Aztec Warfare* (1988), *Mexico and the Spanish Conquest* (1994), and his chapter in *The Oxford History of Mexico* ("The Collision of Two Worlds," 2000) guided my comments on the military arm of the imperial Aztecs. Hassig provides one of the most plausible explanations of Moctezuma's actions from the first news of Spaniards touching his empire in 1517 to his death in 1520.

I found parts of Hugh Thomas's *Conquest* (1993) to be very useful. Why? Because Thomas, assisted by his staff of researchers at the AGI, is the only published scholar to have made extensive use of the massive *residencia*, or trial, of Fernando Cortés. Having plowed my way through Nuño de Guzmán's *residencia* as governor of Pánuco for a doctoral dissertation and skimmed his *residencias* as president of the first Audiencia of New Spain and as governor of New Galicia, I know that these end-of-term-in-office inquests are maddeningly repetitive and often irrelevant. But as Thomas observes, on the plus side, the six thousand manuscript pages of the Cortés trial increase the number of eyewitness accounts of the conquest from about ten to more than a hundred.[6] Given that very few accounts of the conquest date from the 1520s, Thomas has tapped previously unused sources of men who testified in the first decade after the conquest.

I owe a continuing debt of gratitude to France V. Scholes, my mentor at the University of New Mexico. Scholes spent the better part of his adult life studying the life and career of Cortés. Sadly, his proposed three-volume study of the conqueror did not come to fruition. However, his lectures on Cortés and the conquest have continued to influence my writing. Scholes and the late Eleanor B. Adams compiled and edited seven volumes of *Documentos para la historia del México colonial* (1955–1961), which are cited herein, as well as other works listed in the bibliography.

Chapters 3, 4, and 6 are largely carved from archival materials. Even so, I am aware that no one will ever read every document pertaining to the descendants of Moctezuma II. I have carried out research in Spain on four occasions (in 1976, 1990, 1998, and 2002). The indispensable materials in the AGI are contained in various *ramos* of Patronato 245, in five *legajos* of Audiencia de México (762–764, 1088), and in Justicia (165, 181, and 938). In the Archivo General de la Nación, the same may be said of documentation found in Vínculos y Mayorazgos (69, 76, and 80).

Chapter 5 largely relies on, in addition to my publications on the northern frontier of New Spain, seminal studies of the region by other scholars. Peter J. Bakewell's *Silver Mining and Society* (1971) provides excellent background information on the region from the mid-sixteenth century to the end of the Hapsburg era. Philip W. Powell's *Soldiers, Indians, and Silver* (1952) serves as a dependable source on wars with the Chichimec Indians in the second half of the sixteenth century. That conflict had to conclude before the Spaniards could advance into New Mexico. Marc Simmons's biography of Juan de Oñate (*The Last Conquistador*, 1991), husband of a Moctezuma descendant, is an excellent study of this famous governor of colonial New Mexico and founder of Santa Fe. I am especially indebted to Don T. Garate's fine article on Juan de Oñate, published in the *Colonial Latin American Historical Review* ("Juan de Oñate's *Prueba de Caballero*, 1625" [1998]), for information on the Basque background and family ties of the Oñates, Zaldívars, and Tolosas—all of whom are related by marriage to Moctezuma heirs. Archival materials contained in AGI, Patronato 80, N. 5, R. 1, supplement published sources on the silver-mining aristocracy of colonial Zacatecas and its environs.

Readers will immediately see the need to refer to the notes that accompany each chapter, because I have tried to make the narrative as readable as possible by placing many details and place names, as well as historiographical matters and differing interpretations of the Spanish conquest, in endnotes. Notes, like those referencing AGI, Patronato 80, have precise folio citations in nearly every instance, except for those materials contained in Audiencia de México (762–764). Documentation in those *legajos* is exceedingly repetitious, and in some cases archival personnel have conveniently rearranged the *expedientes* (files of papers bearing on a particular case) in chronological order.

While commenting on scholarly accouterment, I should also note my decision to use the almost universal rendering of the emperor's name in the Spanish-speaking world—Moctezuma. I have applied diacritical marks to Spanish words and names that appear in the text but omitted them on names and nomenclature of Indian origin. In the further interests of readability, I have endeavored to avoid specialized vocabulary. At times, as above in this paragraph, the reader will find terminology followed by a brief explanation in parentheses. I have also added a glossary of Spanish and Nahuatl words.

Finally, I have included a number of maps and illustrations, as well as five genealogy charts that delineate the family relationship of the Aztec emperors and the principal descendants of Moctezuma II. Unfortunately, the complexity of this topic made it necessary to use a topical approach, at times resulting in more repetition than is stylistically desirable.

The overarching theme in this book is a case study of Indian royals in New Spain, the descendants of Moctezuma II who survived the conquest, who did not just curl up and die in the face of "superior" Spanish culture. They engaged it, at times got the better of it, and, in doing so, profited from it. Their methods included lawsuits, often encouraged by their Spanish spouses; persistent appeals when judgments went against them; repeated importunities made to the king and the Royal Council of the Indies; entrance into strategic marriages with the Spanish peerage; and successful competition for the highest office in New Spain. As Susan Schroeder has commented about other indigenous women in early Mexico, two daughters and a granddaughter of the Aztec emperor are remarkable for their "extraordinary capacity . . . for accommodation, cultural conservatism, and survival in the face of catastrophic change and seemingly insurmountable obstacles."[7] The same can be said of Pedro Moctezuma and his heirs, especially female descendants in the seventeenth century who carried on the struggle for family rights, privileges, and titles of nobility that continued through their bloodlines. Moreover, the Moctezuma heirs are good examples of what Lockhart cites as the "particular modality of contact . . . measured in distance, frequency, or hours spent, as the vehicle for interaction." The emperor's offspring were thrown among Spaniards from the beginning, forcing them to adapt rapidly to Hispanic culture. Their experience was one of "both conflict and cooperation," of both "struggle and survival."[8]

According to Spanish concepts of legitimate marriage and parentage, which are critical to this study, it appears that no male descendant of Moctezuma II and his wife, Teotlalco, survived the conquest of New

Spain (1519–1521). All died before or during the disastrous retreat from Tenochtitlan, labeled "La Noche Triste" (Sad Night, June 30–July 1, 1520) by Spaniards, or were later executed by Cuauhtemoc in an effort to remove potential challengers. The only son of the emperor who figures prominently in sixteenth-century documentation (Tlacahuepan) was the offspring of a union between Moctezuma II and Miahuaxochitl, a princess in the ruling house of Tollan. Tlacahuepan, known to Spaniards as Pedro Moctezuma, and his principal descendants were the most politically successful of the emperor's descendants. They are the primary subjects of Chapters 4 and 6.

Spaniards regarded one daughter of Moctezuma (Tecuichpotzin) as his principal heir. Tecuichpotzin, later christened Isabel, was probably born in 1509. Her Nahuatl name has been translated as "little royal maiden," and as fate would have it, there is little doubt that this child held preeminent status among both Aztecs and Spaniards. Her marital odysseys alone speak to her importance. Tecuichpotzin appears to have had three indigenous consorts or husbands, and she may have served briefly as empress in 1520. She assuredly married three Spaniards in the decade that followed the conquest. In all, Isabel Moctezuma gave birth to seven children (four sons and three daughters), and five of that number had children of their own. As *encomendera* of Tacuba, one of the cities of the Aztec Triple Alliance, this daughter ranks among the most important Indian women in the history of New Spain. Doña Isabel's life history and that of her descendants is one of vast complexity, because of repeated attempts to increase her rights of inheritance and legal challenges to her will launched by her third Spanish husband, Juan Cano, and her sons. These and other topics are examined in Chapters 3, 5, and 6.

Two additional daughters of Moctezuma and a favored secondary wife (Acatlan) survived into the postconquest era. The first, doña Ana, had a short life and apparently died in the mid-1520s. It is certain that this child of the emperor left no descendants who are recorded in sixteenth-century documentation. Her full sister, early on known as doña Mariana and later as doña Leonor, became *encomendera* of the important town of Ecatepec. Like her half-sister, Isabel, Mariana married more than once—twice, in her case. Also like Isabel, Mariana's offspring engaged in a flurry of petitions and lawsuits, fewer in number but not in intensity, because she gave birth to just one daughter. These descendants, however, did not fare well in the long run. Castilian law, the bad judgment of a son-in-law, and a fragmented family doomed the legacy of the Ecatepec encomienda by the early 1600s. This relatively brief segment of Moctezuma family history is detailed entirely in the first part of Chapter 4.

Chapter 5 addresses the marriage of Leonor Cortés Moctezuma, the product of a liaison between Fernando Cortés and Isabel Moctezuma, to Juan de Tolosa, the discoverer of rich silver veins at Zacatecas in 1546. The progeny of this doña Leonor and her amply bearded husband, dubbed "Barbalonga"—two daughters who married and produced offspring and a son who did neither—created a Gordian knot of family ties with the Zaldívars and the Oñates of northern New Spain.

For historians who are not specialists in colonial Latin American history and for the general reader, I think it is important to note that the Spanish crown chose to honor three heirs of Moctezuma II as *reyes naturales* (natural kings or monarchs), who possessed certain inalienable rights as Indian royalty. These descendants benefited as members of Aztec society, which was a mirror image of Spain's in its overall social arrangement. Both civilizations divided their populations into nobility and commoners but provided only limited opportunity for upward social mobility to the latter. In Aztec society all categories of nobility applied equally without regard to gender, as was the case in Spain.[9]

By 1519 both Charles V and Moctezuma II carried the title of emperor. However, by August 1521, the Aztec empire had fallen to Spanish forces and Indian allies commanded by Cortés. One might assume that a conquered people forfeited all rights to their conquerors, but that did not happen. As Lucas Alamán observed in the nineteenth century, there are few examples in history where the victors have given so many privileges to the vanquished—pensions, rights of entailment, admission to military orders, and titles of nobility.[10] How this came about is a major subtheme in the chapters that follow. In recounting the family history of these descendants of Moctezuma II, I also hope to help gray the so-called Black Legend, a distorted view that, in comparison to other colonial powers, Spaniards were extremely cruel in their treatment of the native people who were unfortunate enough to fall within their New World empire.

AUTHOR'S NOTE

Spanish Currency in the Hapsburg Era

The Spanish used two pesos of differing value. The *peso de oro de minas* (gold peso) was valued at 450 *maravedís*; the *peso de oro común* (silver peso) was valued at 272 *maravedís*. The silver peso contained eight *reales*, each valued at thirty-four *maravedís*. The *maravedí*, also a coin, was the smallest unit of currency. Often, the value of an item would be given in hundreds of thousands of *maravedís*, rather than in pesos. A *ducado*, or ducat, equaled 375 *maravedís*.

One

The Aztecs and Moctezuma II, to 1519

THE ORIGINS OF AN EPIC JOURNEY that would result in the
Aztecs becoming the lords and masters of much of Central Mexico lie to the west and north of present-day Mexico City. But the centuries-long lure that prompted wave after wave of migrants, among the
last of whom were the Aztecs, to move south was the Central Valley. Technically, the Central Valley is not a valley at all but an oval basin surrounded
by mountains on three sides and high terrain to the north. The basin is
roughly 70 miles (120 kilometers) from north to south and 40 miles (70
kilometers) from east to west.[1]

When the Aztecs arrived, this closed drainage basin contained three
large lakes at slightly different elevations and of varying degrees of salin-
ity. Lake Texcoco lay in the center and received water from Lake Xaltocan in the north and Lake Xochimilco in the south. Accordingly, Lake
Texcoco, as "the ultimate destination of all drainage, was extremely
saline." Xochimilco was about nine feet (three meters) higher than Texcoco and contained the freshest water, especially along its southern shore,
which contained numerous springs. This permitted the growth of floating vegetation "so thick one could walk on it," as well as crops that were
later planted on artificial islands known as *chinampas*.[2] However, during
heavy seasonal rains and runoff these lakes became one continuous body
of water but still at slightly varying levels. Abundant fish and game from
nearby forests meant that hunters and gatherers did not have to travel far
to find food.

With certainty, homo sapiens have lived in the basin for at least fifteen thousand years. To the north of present-day Mexico City, the largest city in the world at the end of the twentieth century, the unearthed bones of an extinct mammoth display the unmistakable marks of stone implements used for butchering. Carbon-dating has determined that this animal died more than fifteen millennia ago. Human remains found in the Central Valley, so-called Tepexpan Man (actually a woman), date from about ten thousand to twelve thousand years ago.[3]

About ten thousand years ago, hunting and gathering was still the only mode of life in the Central Valley, but that was true for almost all other areas of the Americas. However, the end of the last Ice Age, combined with increasing population and the extinction of such megafauna as giant turtles, mammoths, and mastodons, provided impetus for primitive agricultural experiments. The potential for productive lakeside crops, generally adequate precipitation, and a usually frost-free climate made the basin one of the most desirable locales in all of Mexico.[4]

The emergence of an agriculture-based society in the Central Valley was driven by necessity. Preparing land for sowing, cultivating, and harvesting of crops proved much harder than reaping the fruits of a benevolent nature by gathering nuts and wild fruits and periodically killing plentiful game. But the shortage of meat made farming a much more dependable source of food. From a native plant called teosinte, which resembles corn (maize), came the lifeblood of sedentary living and urbanization. By about five thousand years ago, inhabitants along the shores of lakes with fresh water and at lower elevations in the surrounding mountains began to cultivate corn.

As Richard MacNeish has observed, agriculture was the "decisive step [that] freed people from the quest for food and released energy for other pursuits."[5] Only in agriculture-based societies can such specializations as stone carving and masonry, carpentry, pottery making, and metalworking develop. Food supplies beyond the dietary needs of those producing them also permit the rise of religious leaders, who gain prominence through their knowledge of time and seasonal changes—so essential to crop-dependent people—as well as through their role as intermediaries with the gods. And, of course, wealth and the opportunities for education produced a class of nobles from whom would come political and military leaders.

A truly great city in the Central Valley with the "roots and basic cultural molds that would later be diffused throughout the central zone of Mexico appear to be found in Teotihuacan," located about fifteen miles

Figure 1.1. Pyramid of the Moon and Avenue of the Dead, Teotihuacan. (Photo by author.)

(twenty-five kilometers) northeast of the megalopolis that is present-day Mexico City. Teotihuacan's architecture, its pyramids with their special orientation, and its plazas and palaces all helped provide a model for later urban centers in the region. Those structures and others built by an unidentified people reflect sophisticated knowledge and the use of surveying equipment. Millions of tourists have flocked there to view the great pyramids of the Sun and the Moon. They marvel at the Avenue of the Dead and the so-called Ciudadela (Citadel) with its frieze consisting of alternating stone heads of Tlaloc, the goggle-eyed rain god, and Quetzalcoatl, the feathered serpent. No less can be said about Teotihuacan's murals, "sculptures, superb ceramics, and obsidian work." It can also be argued that urbanization itself in the Valley of Mexico began in Teotihuacan.[6] The City of the Gods, another name for San Juan Teotihuacan, reached its cultural climax around 450–500, although it would be occupied during a decline that continued over the next 250 years.

A complex set of deities appears to have been venerated at Teotihuacan. In addition to Quetzalcoatl and Tlaloc, figures of Chalchiuhtlicue, Tlaloc's faithful companion, and Huehuehteotl, the old god of fire, have been found at the City of the Gods.[7] Since the true structure of the belief

Figure 1.2. Frieze of Tlaloc (left) and Quetzalcoatl (right), Temple of Quetzalcoatl, Teotihuacan. (Photo by author.)

system at Teotihuacan in ancient times is as yet unclear, the interrelatedness of these deities and their relative importance is uncertain.

Teotihuacan's murals, which León-Portilla has described as "ancient codices placed on walls," support the high position scholars give to the god Ehecatl Quetzalcoatl. Like many pre-Columbian gods, Ehecatl Quetzalcoatl had multiple forms—"the creator god [of man and earth], the morning star, the wind god, a culture hero, the emblem of the priesthood." The plumed serpent, along with other deities, gave solace and "legitimation of power and authority" in an uncertain world that would witness the rise and fall of great urban centers that antedated by many centuries the arrival of Europeans in Mexico.[8]

Finally, in addition to Teotihuacan's architecture and murals, thousands of clay-figurine representations of the city's most important religious and political leaders stand as mute evidence of what had been and what was to come. To Nahuatl-speaking people, Teotihuacan represented "the most ancient root of their religious thought, of their art, and, of the principal institutions of the subsequent cultures of Anahuac (central Mexico to the water's edge)."[9]

Despite its earlier brilliance as an urban center that may have contained more than two hundred thousand inhabitants at its peak, for reasons unknown, Teotihuacan was in full decline during the years 650–750. Around the end of this period, its ceremonial buildings were burned, and the site became a ghost of its former self.[10]

About two centuries later, a small village about forty-five miles (seventy-two kilometers) north-northeast of present-day Mexico City began to attract a few settlers and grow in importance. It was a slow process that led to the founding of Tollan (present-day Tula, Hidalgo).[11] Little by little a new ceremonial center emerged, and the City of the Gods' influence on religious institutions and the worship of Quetzalcoatl seems apparent.[12]

Soon added to the mix of people at Tollan were warlike nomads (Chichimecs) from the north. Their importance is borne out by the sculpting of gigantic stone warriors, some of which may be seen on the remains of a pyramid at Tula. These plainsmen and those already living at Tula came to be called Toltecs.[13] It is essential to note that for the future Aztecs, Tollan (the "Place of Rushes") "was a symbol of sacred space and Quetzalcoatl was a symbol of sacred authority." Quetzalcoatl was likewise "the standard for the vital relationship between kingship and divinity," or, as Camilla Townsend observes, "his name became a priestly title . . . whose role it was to connect those on earth with those beyond."[14]

Figure 1.3. Stone Warriors, Tula, Hidalgo. (Photo by author.)

What seems apparent in the rising importance of Tollan are the multiple influences of the people who had occupied Teotihuacan and their descendants, for it is unlikely that the Toltecs on their own could have achieved so much so quickly without patterning themselves after those who had resided at the City of the Gods. To be *toltecayotl* (Nahuatl for the quality of being Toltec) meant significant accomplishments in art, architecture, painting, and sculpture in Central Mexico during the years 950–1150, or, as Gordon Brotherson notes, "indeed the very notion of skill."[15] The Toltecs were also great potters, creating multiple designs in clay.

By the middle years of the twelfth century, the southern end of the Central Valley, wherein lay the freshest water, older cities—some dating from the Teotihuacan period or even earlier—had become permanent fixtures on the landscape. These urban centers included Azcapotzalco, Culhuacan, Chalco, Texcoco, and Xochimilco, and by the thirteenth century, these city-states with varying degrees of power and influence claimed control over the valley.[16]

In the process, arable land in the basin became scarce, and latecomer nomads from the north found no desirable places to settle. Among the last to arrive were the Aztecs, who spoke the same language as the older residents. Aside from that advantage, however, these interlopers brought little with them other than "their indomitable force of will, by which they transformed themselves in less than three centuries into the supreme masters of ancient Mexico."[17]

The mythic origin of the Aztecs has become a passionate and politically charged topic among Latino activists. It has also occupied the attention of chroniclers and scholars since the sixteenth century. As I mention in the Introduction, among the early and most important of the missionary/ethnographers in New Spain was the remarkable Dominican Father Diego Durán. Durán was born in Seville and arrived in Mexico at an early age—not so early, in his words, as to acquire his "milk teeth" in Texcoco, where his family settled, but "I got my second ones there."[18] As a young man he undertook the study of Nahuatl and thoroughly mastered the language of the Aztecs. Because of his command of their native tongue, Durán gained the confidence of "informants who told him the stories, histories, myths, and anecdotes of their ancestors."[19]

The Aztecs' story begins with their origin on an island called Aztlan in Lake Mexcaltitlan. The location of this island and lake is much in question but appears to have been situated north and west of Tula, and Aztlan may well be more of a concept than an actual site. Durán's informants recounted that seven tribes—each prompted by a god—came forth from seven caves (collectively called Chicomoztoc). The Aztecs were the last to leave Aztlan, perhaps around 1111.[20] Again, because their origins were similar to those of tribes already settled in the Central Valley, the Aztecs spoke Nahuatl, so communication was not a problem for them. A well-accepted and perhaps more appropriate name for the Aztecs is Mexica ("they of Mexico"), for, to be precise, many cultures in the Central Valley can rightly be called Aztecs, that is, "people of Aztlan."[21]

In their journey from Aztlan to Tula, the Aztecs divided themselves into seven clans and carried an image of Huitzilopochtli ("Hummingbird from the Left") concealed in an ark of reeds. The idol was so sacred and so revered that no one dared look at it, much less touch it. When the Aztecs reached more-favorable locales, they stopped for as many as twenty years, during which they constructed ball courts and temples to house their idol. They also planted such crops as beans, amaranth, and chiles.[22]

On other occasions, the wayfarers left before crops reached maturity and therefore suffered many hardships, during which they apparently, by necessity, abandoned elders who could not keep pace. Often "going hungry, thirsty and almost naked," their spirits were lifted by the prospects of better days. Dreams sent to Aztec priests by Huitzilopochtli promised that his chosen people would someday become kings, lords, and rulers of countless vassals. And in that bright future, the Aztecs would come to enjoy great riches and fine clothing. In the meantime, however, they frequently supplemented what at best was haphazard agriculture by hunting deer, rabbits, birds, and snakes.[23]

Given that the Aztecs had a priesthood, knew and used the ritual calendar of pre-Spanish Mexico with its fifty-two-year cycle, practiced agriculture, and spoke Nahuatl, they were never as far from civilized life as were the nomadic Chichimecs from the north, who dressed in skins and sought shelter in caves. Accordingly, the Aztecs "definitely come within the pale of Middle American civilization, though possibly situated at the farthest extreme of its cultural spectrum."[24]

It took about fifty years for the Aztecs to reach Tula. By then, the city was in full decline. Its principal inhabitants were unimpressive bands of Otomi and more primitive Chichimecs. The Aztecs lingered at Tula long enough to get a sense of it as a once-great center of Toltec culture and to make a few minor improvements around the city. They also established a fictitious bond with the Toltecs and later projected themselves as heirs of that civilization. Equally important, a new personification of Huitzilopochtli sprang up.[25] This fully armed avatar of the god was of virgin birth from Coatlicue, the monstrous snake-skirted woman whose monolith stands in Mexico City's Museum of Anthropology and History.

Huitzilopochtli took on warrior god aspects, and under his influence the Aztecs became increasingly combative. As "masters of violence" they showed a tremendous proclivity for warfare and in short order came to love the clash of arms so much that their own death became essentially meaningless. In their later quest for dominance in the Central Valley, the Aztecs' willingness to bear arms and serve as mercenary allies would stand them in good stead.[26]

After enjoying a few years of repose, the Aztecs received a severe tongue-lashing from Huitzilopochtli, their divine guardian or tutelary numen. How dare they come to enjoy peace and comfort and forsake their martial mission! When they departed Tula, the Aztecs destroyed what few improvements they had made and left the city in ruins. Much later, Tula would serve as the principal inheritance of Moctezuma II's son Pedro. At this earlier time, however, the Aztecs followed the leadership of Huitzilopochtli, who said, "I will serve as your guide; I will show you the way." Lake Texcoco in the Central Valley would be their next stop. The exact year of their arrival is unknown, but it was likely around 1250.[27]

From the very beginning of their presence around the lakes, the Aztecs were seen as unwelcome squatters. The newcomers were expelled from one settlement after another over several decades, until at last they settled at Chapultepec, the famed "Grasshopper Hill," near the end of the 1200s. Chapultepec also provided nothing more than a brief respite, because the much more powerful people of Azcapotzalco claimed the site and forced the Aztecs to vacate it. Next came a temporary refuge on the south side of Lake Texcoco, a site claimed by Culhuacan. The settlers, still relatively few in number, begged the local king (Coxcotli) to assign them a permanent residence, and he agreed to do so.[28]

The new locale was Tizapan, a barren and rocky region to the south of present-day Mexico City that was filled with poisonous vipers. Regarding the Aztecs as undesirable neighbors, Coxcotli hoped they would either starve or be killed by the snakes. Quite the opposite happened: "Instead of dying from the bites of vipers, the Mexica killed them and transformed them into their sustenance."[29]

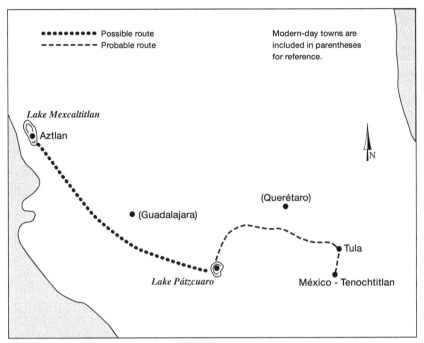

Figure 1.4. Migration Routes of the Aztecs. (Adapted from Davies, Aztecs, *9. Center for Media Production, University of North Texas.)*

The Aztecs, in addition to their penchant for waging war, were like their contemporaries in Renaissance Europe in another respect. They quickly saw the benefits of strategic marriages with the daughters of their more powerful and settled neighbors. With this strategy, they especially sought to shed their image as semibarbarous nomads and establish ties with the Culhuas, who could claim descent from the Toltecs. Thus they lived and plotted at Tizapan for about twenty-five years, during which time the Mexica strengthened their ties with Culhuacan by serving as its ally in a war against Xochimilco.[30]

In about 1323, at the behest of their ancient numen, the Aztecs nearly made a fatal mistake. They asked the lord of Culhuacan (Achitometl) to give them his virgin daughter so that they might pay her a "special honor" by making her a goddess. To his eternal regret, the aging Achitometl agreed. Unknown to him, the Mexica immediately sacrificed and flayed his daughter to honor their deity Xipe Totec. They then invited Achitometl to a darkened temple filled with incense. When his eyes had adjusted to the darkness and the smoke had cleared a bit, he saw an Aztec priest dancing in his daughter's skin.[31]

Understandably, the king of Culhuacan "howled for his warriors to avenge the deadly insult." They pursued the bewildered Mexica, who thought they had bestowed a great honor on the young virgin, and drove them into the waters of Lake Texcoco. There the Aztecs took refuge on one of several "squashy little islands" named Zoquitlan, which has been translated as "Mudville."[32]

Because Zoquitlan was a no-man's land bordering the territory of Azcapotzalco, Texcoco, and Culhuacan, none of the three powers asserted sovereignty over it, fearing that such action might prompt war with a powerful neighbor over an essentially worthless and swampy island.[33] This would later prove to be a bad mistake, especially on the part of Azcapotzalco.

Left undisturbed, the Aztecs soon observed the fulfillment of a prophecy made by Huitzilopochtli, reflected today in the motif of Mexico's flag and its coinage. Their fierce war god had told his people that the end of their long migration from Aztlan would be foretold by seeing an eagle with a snake in it beak perched on a nopal cactus. Having observed this omen on Zoquitlan, the Aztecs had found a permanent home. Here the Mexica began the construction of their great capital on the renamed island of México-Tenochtitlan in 1345.[34]

Around 1372, the Aztecs decided to choose a leader with ties to an external dynasty that would lend greater prestige to their island kingdom. Since their relations with Culhuacan had improved markedly after a disastrous start, and since the Culhuas were heirs of the Toltecs—whom the Mexica wished to emulate—the choice of an Aztec nobleman married to a princess of that city-state had much to recommend it. So it was that Acamapichtli became the first in a line of Aztec kings that would extend into the 1520s.[35] At the same time as Acamapichtli's accession, a son of Tezozomoc, the powerful Tepanec monarch, became the first ruler of the Tlatelolco dynasty.[36]

Acamapichtli and his followers soon faced a crisis with the powerful Tepanecs of Azcapotzalco. The Tepanecs decided to exert a questionable claim to the island of México-Tenochtitlan, primarily because they had the strength to do so and because they wished to squelch any increase in power by the Aztecs under their new monarch. Accordingly, the Tepanecs arrogantly insisted on tribute items spelled out in such excruciating detail

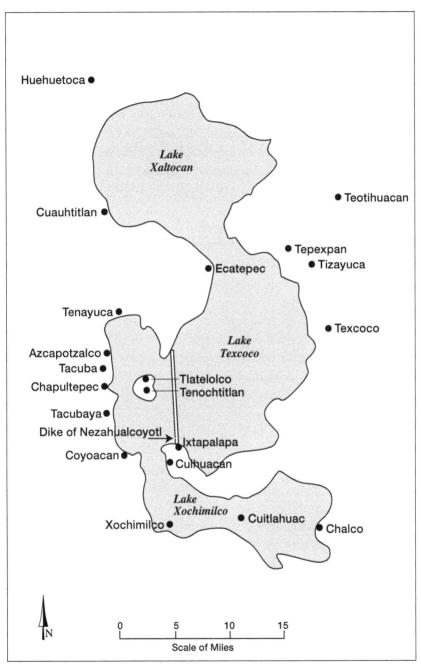

Huehuetoca ●

Lake Xaltocan

● Teotihuacan

Cuauhtitlan ●

● Tepexpan
● Tizayuca

●Ecatepec

Tenayuca ●

Lake Texcoco

● Texcoco

Azcapotzalco ●
Tacuba ●
Chapultepec ●
──Tlatelolco
──Tenochtitlan

Tacubaya ●
Dike of Nezahualcoyotl
●Ixtapalapa
Coyoacan ●
●Culhuacan

Lake Xochimilco

Xochimilco ●
● Cuitlahuac
● Chalco

↑N

0   5   10   15
Scale of Miles

Figure 1.5. Towns and Lakes of the Central Valley. (Center for Media Production, University of North Texas.)

that it seemed impossible for the Aztecs to provide them. For example, not only were the Mexica to supply ordinary items such as ears of corn, beans, tomatoes, chiles, and wild amaranth, they also were to bring a heron and a duck. Both fowl must be sitting on eggs, and at the precise moment of delivery to the Tepanecs, the chicks were to be pecking out of their shells. This, however, turned out not to be a problem. Huitzilopochtli's numen was equal to the task, and the Tepanecs had to acknowledge that their most outlandish demands had been satisfied.[37]

Aztec submission to the humiliating demands of the Tepanecs continued throughout the reign of Acamapichtli and that of his *tlatoque* successors, Huitzilihuitl and Chimalpopoca. Particularly onerous were the demands of Tezozomoc, the high lord of Azcapotzalco, made during the early years of his reign.[38] Still, despite the galling persecutions of the Tepanecs, the Aztecs continued to build their capital with calculated slowness. Should the city manifest too-rapid growth, it would surely alarm their more powerful enemy. And the Mexica knew full well the inevitable outcome of an all-out attack by Tepanec warriors—certain defeat, destruction of their city, and enslavement of all survivors.

Early on, the Aztecs began to create arable plots in the shallows of Lake Texcoco, which contained the freshest water. This involved making *chinampas*, a system of agriculture and land reclamation already in use by older basin cultures.[39] The enclosures were enormously labor intensive, and the snail's pace with which they were built failed at first to alert the watchful Tepanecs.

Chinampas started with the cutting and weaving of mud-soaked reeds that poked through the surface of Lake Texcoco. Lashed together to form crude rafts of vegetation, these artificial islands (erroneously called floating gardens) were maneuvered into location and then covered with mud brought in by canoe or by silt scooped up from the lake's bottom. Vegetable, corn, and amaranth seeds were then planted in rich, saturated soil that had been elevated a few inches above lake level. This form of agriculture required no irrigation and, barring floods—unfortunately, a recurring hazard in the basin—or drought, the populace of México-Tenochtitlan had a dependable food supply, often from two harvests each year. This is especially important, because the Aztec capital could support a large population.[40]

The Aztecs in this manner continued to build gardens and fields that lay adjacent to their ever-expanding city. Separating the *chinampas* at regular intervals were sluggish canals that permitted poled canoes to course amid the crops. The water in Lake Texcoco was always too saline to be potable, and the constant disturbance of the lake's silt-laden bottom made it exceedingly turbid for other domestic uses. Consequently, all fresh water had to be transported by canoe from Chapultepec into the city, where it was dispensed at the public market.[41]

Any interruption of the supply of potable water would place the Aztecs in dire straits. The springs at Chapultepec poured forth thousands of gallons of pure water each day, but that source belonged to Azcapotzalco. This fact alone does much to explain the Mexica's near-total subservience to their hated Tepanec masters.[42] That stranglehold had to be broken if the Aztecs were to achieve the greatness promised by Huitzilopochtli.

As Tezozomoc aged and entered the final years of his rule as *tlatoani* of Azcapotzalco, he became less demanding of the Mexica—for example, they did not have to deliver any more miraculously timed hatchings of heron and duck eggs. But his death in 1426 "completely changed all this." Tezozomoc's fierce son Maxtlatzin, became the new Tepanec ruler, and he despised the Aztecs. To demonstrate his awesome power, Maxtlatzin apparently arranged the assassination of Chimalpopoca within his own city of Tenochtitlan. Stunned and frightened by the powerful Tepanecs, the Mexica then elected their fourth king, Itzcoatl, the son of Acamapichtli.[43]

Itzcoatl, the new *tlatoani* of Tenochtitlan, received conflicting advice from his most trusted advisers. Should he or should he not humble himself before the great Maxtlatzin? Were the Aztecs now strong enough to wage a war that would liberate them from Tepanec vassalage and in doing so secure a dependable source of water for their city? As the debate continued, Tlacaelel Cihuacoatl ("Snake Woman"), destined to become perhaps the most influential Mexica leader in the fifteenth century, entered the arena. This nephew of Itzcoatl, then only twenty-nine years of age and full of fight, counseled war with Azcapotzalco, and he eventually carried the day. Finding a willing ally in the equally persecuted Texcocans, the Aztecs launched the first war with the Tepanecs in 1427. This date also marks the year when the Aztecs became an imperial power.[44]

The battles that followed were fierce. They began on an elevated causeway that linked Tenochtitlan with dry land. Down this corridor marched the Tepanec army, confident of victory. Legend holds that the

Tepanecs' humpbacked numen of war, Coltic, clashed with the Mexica's counterpart, Huitzilopochtli. Burr Brundage has properly labeled this battle "an Aztec Armageddon." Blood flowed into the canals, and the Aztecs fought as they "had never fought before." The dead and wounded on both sides sank into the muddy bottom of Lake Texcoco, but in the end, warriors of the great Huitzilopochtli forced Coltic and his followers to flee.[45]

Next, the Aztecs launched an all-out siege of Azcapotzalco, one of the great urban centers in the basin, which Tezozomoc had made into an imperial city. For four months the Mexica and their Texcocan allies fought desperate battles with Tepanec warriors. When the city finally fell to Mexica forces led by Tlacaelel, a horrible slaughter ensued. The pent-up rage of the Aztecs vented itself. "King Itzcoatl ordered the soldiers who had remained with him to devastate the city, burn the houses, and spare neither young nor old, men or women."[46]

Tacuba (or Tlacopan), which had remained neutral throughout this phase of war with the Tepanecs, became the most important city on the west side of Lake Texcoco. In slightly more than one hundred years it would become the patrimony of Moctezuma II's principal heir, known to the Spaniards as doña Isabel. Following the destruction of Azcapotzalco, Tacuba joined Tenochtitlan and Texcoco in a triple alliance (in 1428), which would last for slightly less than a century.

During successful wars with the Tepanecs, which established Aztec ascendancy, four great leaders took center stage. Two of them are familiar names—King Itzcoatl and young Tlacaelel. The latter is often regarded as the bona fide military genius of his time. Another brother of Tlacaelel was Moctezuma Ilhuicamina. Last but hardly least was brilliant Nezahualcoyotl of Texcoco. This future "poet king" was the wisest of the wise and an unparalleled engineer.

At the conclusion of the Tepanec wars, the three Mexica leaders all held titles of office. Itzcoatl, of course, was king of the Aztecs; Tlacaelel became lord of the House of Darts; Moctezuma Ilhuicamina, general of the Mexica armies.[47] But none would be as important as Tlacaelel, who became chief counsel of Itzcoatl and continued as the power behind the Aztec throne. He would perhaps occupy that role for approximately five more decades.[48]

As a result of the Tepanec wars, Tenochtitlan controlled land on the shores of Lake Texcoco. Not only did this give the Aztecs access to the great freshwater springs on Chapultepec's heights, but the conflict also brought hundreds of defeated and enslaved Tepanecs under Aztec control. The Mexica used this slave labor to link their city to surrounding lacustrine sites by building additional elevated causeways. Construction involved moving by hand thousands of tons of rock and dirt, which served as fill. Eventually, these corridors, all of which contained a number of gaps covered by removable bridges, ran to the south, west, and north of the capital. The bridges permitted canoe traffic to circle the lake by passing under their spans, and their movability gave security to the city should it be besieged by outside forces. But given where the Aztecs were headed over the next ninety years, the prospect of a native power greater than theirs must have seemed highly improbable.

Peace in the early 1430s, in the aftermath of some five years of war with the Tepanecs, permitted Tlacaelel to institute a number of reforms. But first he had to "modify" Aztec history.[49] Tlacaelel would change the history of his people by declaring that Huitzilopochtli needed a great temple built in his honor. In gratitude, Huitzilopochtli would then assure the success of Aztec expansion at the expense of other people living in the basin and, in the process, remake their histories, too.

Huitzilopochtli was perhaps the most important deity in the Aztec pantheon, although his sanctuary atop the Great Pyramid in Tenochtitlan would later be shared by a similar structure devoted to Tlaloc, the rain god. Like other important Mexica gods, Huitzilopochtli had many forms: he was "a sorcerer, an omen of evil; a madman, a deceiver, a creator of war, a war-lord, an instigator of war."[50]

Almost half of the designations for Huitzilopochtli relate to war, and in that context he would become exceedingly important. With Tlacaelel in command, the Aztecs conquered the people who controlled Xochimilco, Cuitlahuac, and Chalco, all located near the southern end of Lake Texcoco. This completed, the Mexica seized and burned the codices and picture manuscripts of the defeated. They then did the same with similar sources of their own. Now "history" could be reformulated in such a manner as to deny their seminomadic origins. In the process, the Aztecs claimed ties with the ancient Toltecs and even with the powerful Purepechas (Tarascans) of present-day Michoacán, who were not Nahua in origin. Part and parcel of this approach was to elevate their numen, Huitzilopochtli, and his mother, Coatlicue, to a level "with the creator deities of the Toltec period."[51] Thus the Aztecs adopted a vision of Tollan as the wellspring of high culture, political organization, and refined arts. Or, to again use the words of Gordon Brotherson, a Mesoamerican "image in time."[52] This projection intensified throughout the fifteenth century and reached its climax under the reign of Moctezuma II in the early sixteenth century.

Tlacaelel also drew on ancient Nahua beliefs to give still another vitally important role to Huitzilopochtli's numen. According to the Aztecs' cosmogony, the world had gone through four cycles, each ending in cataclysm. They, however, lived in the fifth era, the new Sun "of movement," which was destined to end in calamity, as had the previous Suns of Earth, Wind, Fire, and Water. Huitzilopochtli, now identified with the sun itself, must be fed the "the precious liquid" (blood) that kept humans alive so that the great orb would have the energy to make its daily journey across the sky. And as long as Huitzilopochtli received a continuous supply of blood from sacrificial victims, the Mexica's world would never end. So, how would the Aztecs ensure this dependable supply of food for their war/sun god?[53]

The obvious answer is that they would launch successful conquests of other peoples in Central Mexico. Young men would then be marched into Tenochtitlan and sacrificed. Above all, an absolutely dependable source of human hearts and blood had to be found. Given the success of Aztec imperialism, what if the Mexica should run out of enemies and not be able to acquire the requisite number of sacrificial victims, or what if their wars had to be fought in such distant regions that capturing and marching prisoners back to Tenochtitlan was not feasible? Still another consideration was the quality or acceptability of certain tribes' blood as an appropriate offering to Huitzilopochtli. Preferred victims came from five city-states that contained quality people, rather than crude barbarians like the Huastecs. The choice of these nearby cities as a source of largely Nahuatl-speaking victims may have been a matter of convenience.[54]

Moctezuma Ilhuicamina (Moctezuma I), Itzcoatl's successor, relied heavily on his brother and principal adviser, Tlacaelel, and the latter thought it important that a great king have his house and court in order. Joining the new Aztec king were a host of appointees—agents, stewards, headwaiters, doormen, pages, and lackeys. Also needed were officers of the treasury charged with keeping track of tribute from subject people. Functionaries likewise included a multitude of religious ministers, in such profusion that there was one for each five commoners.[55]

Tlacaelel also insisted on enlarging the great pyramid. To honor the god of war properly, the Aztecs under Moctezuma Ilhuicamina undertook conquests of nearby dominions and later of those more distant.[56] In each case, the offerings to Huitzilopochtli and other deities increased commensurate with the expanding scale of the Great Temple (Templo Mayor).

The logistics of acquiring sacrificial victims in remote lands and then marching them back to Tenochtitlan must have proved especially troublesome. Accordingly, the resurgence of flower wars (*xochiyaotl*), many years after the death of Itzcoatl in 1440, became commonplace. The *guerra florida* took place between the Aztecs and specific opponents, among which were the inhabitants of Tlaxcala, Huejotzingo, and Cholula. These engagements may be compared to a tournament in that they took place at arranged times and on specified grounds. Such contrived combat between forces roughly equal in size was conducted in theory on a "give-and-take basis." In short, the Mexica recognized that they would lose warriors, who would be sacrificed on the altars of their opponents, while they themselves would likewise obtain an acceptable number of victims.

In practice, however, this must have been difficult to orchestrate. Grown men clashing with weapons almost certainly presented a problem, because "violence, once unleashed, is notoriously difficult to control." Almost certainly, some of these sham battles must have turned into mortal combat, especially as the demands for sacrificial offerings increased.[57]

Following the first ten years of Moctezuma Ilhuicamina's reign, a disaster of biblical proportions began in the first years of the 1450s. Four years of famine, presaged by a plague of locusts in 1446 and a devastating flood in 1449, prompted Moctezuma Ilhuicamina to seek the help of Nezahualcoyotl of Texcoco, his old ally in the Tepanec wars. Under the direction of the Texcocan sage, workers constructed a bulwark against future inundations. A dike, which also served to separate sweet water from the saline waters of Lake Texcoco, stretched for 5.4 miles (9 kilometers) across Lake Texcoco. Ironically, its completion was followed by four years of very poor harvests, occasioned by drought and crop-killing frosts.[58]

Nezahualcoyotl also turned his attention to supplying potable water to Tenochtitlan. He supervised the construction of two parallel aqueducts of wood and stone that ran three miles (five kilometers) from Chapultepec's underground springs into the heart of the Aztec capital. Each aqueduct, elevated so as not to interrupt boat traffic on the lake, was approximately six feet (two meters) in diameter, although only one was used at a time. This arrangement permitted repairs and cleaning of the unused channel, ensuring that Tenochtitlan had an uninterrupted flow of that other "precious liquid"—water.[59]

During the great famine that spanned the years 1450–1454, Aztec conquests of outlying areas were generally placed on hold. However, campaigns over the next fourteen years of Moctezuma's reign reached into the northern Gulf Coast—the modern-day states of Puebla and Tlaxcala—as well as Oaxaca in the south. Thus, when this powerful king died in 1468, the Aztecs had conquered areas once controlled by Huastecs in the north and by Mixtecs in the south.[60]

Counting 1468, it was still fifty-two years before Spanish forces led by Cortés would land. In the calendar system used by the Aztecs, the equivalent of a century was a fifty-two-year cycle, arrived at by meshing the "gears" of two disks—one containing 365 teeth (the solar calendar) and one containing 260 teeth (the ritual calendar), each representing a day. A given day on the first calendar coincided with a given day on the second calendar only once in fifty-two years, and then the cycle (called a bundle, or binding, of years) repeated. The years of the solar calendar had four names (Rabbit, Reed, Flint, and House), which were preceded in each cycle by numbers one through thirteen.[61]

With the death of Moctezuma Ilhuicamina, the title of *tlatoani* was perhaps offered to Tlacaelel. If so, he declined the honor, remarking that, "after all, the previous kings did nothing without my opinion and counsel, on all matters, civil or criminal. . . . Thus, do not worry, because I will point out to you who should be your king and lord."[62]

Tlacaelel's choice as the new king of the Aztecs was Axayacatl, Itzcoatl's grandson. In 1469, the year of Axayacatl's accession, a son of the new king named Xocoyotzin (the future Moctezuma II) was about two years of age. In the first years of Axayacatl's reign, violence erupted between Tenochtitlan and Tlatelolco in 1473. The Tlatelolcas were also Mexica, as well as kinsmen of the Aztecs. They occupied a city just north of México-Tenochtitlan, and they had always been subjects of the rulers of Tenochtitlan.[63]

Trouble started between the two cities when some mischievous sons of noblemen in Tenochtitlan encountered maidens in the Tlatelolco market who were the daughters of Tlatelolca lords. Flirting and joking by the young males received similar responses from the young virgins, who allowed the former to accompany them toward their homes. En route the maidens were set upon and violated. The young women's male relatives vowed revenge, and matters escalated in the next few days, when a newly dug canal for canoe traffic into Tlatelolco was presumably vandalized by Tenochcas. And at this juncture the Tlatelolcas declared themselves independent.[64]

Both Tlatelolcas and Tenochcas began arming themselves to settle real and imaginary issues. For example, in past military campaigns warriors of the two cities had fought side by side, but the Tlatelolcas believed that their men had not received the credit due them in victories boasted of by the Aztecs.

The initial clash of arms was horribly destructive of life on both sides, but the Tenochcas had the upper hand in a battle fought within their city. Then, inspired by a fiery speech delivered by Tlacaelel, they prepared for all-out invasion of Tlatelolco. The old warrior reminded his legions that "the enemy lies right behind our houses. You will not have to climb mountains or go down cliffs. You will not have to march through valleys." Victory would require little more effort than shooing flies off their bodies. The leaders of Tlatelolco were equally militant and overconfident by declaring that Tenochtitlan "will become the dung heap and place of excrement for Tlatelolcas."[65]

The final clash of arms went decisively against the Tlatelolcas. As the tide of battle turned against them, warriors took to their heels rather than fight. Desperate to halt the Aztec juggernaut, Tlatelolco's leaders resorted to a diversionary tactic: They ordered a large number of women to disrobe completely and form a squadron in front of the Tenochca attackers. Some of the naked women slapped their stomachs in a suggestive manner, while others squirted milk from their breasts. It was all to no avail. The women were captured, and the leaders of Tlatelolco died fighting atop an altar to Huitzilopochtli.[66]

Thinking their armies invincible, Axayacatl and Tlacaelel carried out an ill-advised invasion of the powerful Purepechan kingdom to the west and northwest of Tenochtitlan. The Purepechas, armed with copper weapons, resoundingly defeated the Aztecs, at this juncture their only loss in real warfare against other native forces.[67]

This, however, was nothing more than a bump in the road of Mexica imperialism. Tlacaelel appears to have died in the late 1470s, but his passing certainly did not spell the end of Aztec imperialism, and human sacrifice on an unprecedented scale lay in the near future.

Shortly after the death of Tlacaelel and Axayacatl (1481), Tizoc became the new king, but he proved to be of a different mettle from his predecessors in that he had little taste for warfare. It seems that "members of Tizoc's court, angered by his weakness and lack of desire to enlarge and glorify the Aztec nation, hastened his death with something they gave him to eat. He died in the year 1486, still a young man."[68]

What Tizoc lacked in martial spirit was more than compensated in Ahuitzotl, the third of three brothers to succeed Itzcoatl. Chosen in the year of Tizoc's death, Ahuitzotl ordered the largest expansion ever of the great pyramid in Tenochtitlan. To obtain an appropriate number of sacrificial victims, the Aztecs marched their armies "to the far corners of Mesoamerica." Their conquests stretched as far as the Isthmus of Tehuantepec, to Soconusco, and into Guatemala. Then came long marches for captives who would surrender their hearts and blood to commemorate the completion of work in 1487 on the Great Temple, which now towered more than one hundred feet (about thirty-one meters) from its base.[69]

Intended victims ascended steps leading to the top of the pyramid, where one at a time each was handed over to four priests, each of whom seized a limb and flopped the unfortunate on his back. He was then bent backward over a large convex stone, the *techcatl*. With pressure on his limbs, the victim's back was severely bent. A fifth priest then plunged a razor-sharp flint knife into the taut belly just below the rib cage, ripped out the heart, held it skyward as an offering, and then threw it into a sacred receptacle, where it was burned. "The body, spilling blood, was then flung off the stone and went tumbling and bumping down the steep slope [of the pyramid] to come to rest on the flat space near the base called . . . 'the blood mat.'"[70]

The ritual slaughter was immense and continued for four days. With machinelike efficiency, Aztec priests dispatched an undetermined number of victims—estimates range into tens of thousands. One can scarcely imagine the tons of human hearts and rivers of blood resulting from this religion-inspired massacre.[71]

It should be noted, however, that the Aztecs did not invent human sacrifice, even within the confines of Mesoamerican culture. What sets them apart in that milieu is the scale and "inflationary process" of their immolation of people. If at one time ten sacrifices seemed sufficient to propitiate a god, it was not long until that number escalated to a thousand. This may be explained in part by the Aztecs' controlling such a densely populated, large empire. A corollary argument—that such massive and horrific public executions served as an instrument of terror by which subject peoples were cowed into subservience—does not stand up well to analysis, because other cultures in Mesoamerica did not treat their prisoners any better. And the leaders or princes of those outlying communities did not themselves have to face being "altar fodder" in Tenochtitlan.[72]

A bizarre and "highly contentious theory" that the Aztecs practiced human sacrifice and cannibalism because they lacked animal protein has been advanced by Michael Harner and Marvin Harris. Since the consumption of human flesh was an exclusive privilege of the nobility, it hardly aided the dietary needs of common people. Furthermore, only the arms and legs of sacrificial victims were consumed—a clear indication that cannibalism involved more than the consumption of "human livestock" for sustenance. In short, Aztec "sacrifice, inseparable from religion, involved the killing of *certain* people on *certain* occasions and was in no sense an act of mass gourmandism."[73]

In my view, the most plausible explanation for large-scale human sacrifice in the Aztec empire is offered by Nigel Davies. Increasingly, scholars have questioned Huitzilopochtli's position in the Aztec pantheon—important, without question; preeminent, questionable. For example, it is well to remember that Tlaloc *and* Huitzilopochtli had altars atop the Great Temple. Furthermore, it can be argued that Huitzilopochtli was in contention for supremacy with either Tezcatlipoca or Quetzalcoatl, although the latter seems not to have been especially venerated at Tenochtitlan.[74] Leaving this question aside, as well as the names and overlapping functions of other Aztec deities, who shared a "very crowded pantheon," each god had its cult of followers. And "to preserve the cosmic order, the gods demanded ever vaster ceremonies . . . [and] the mania for religious ceremony knew no bounds, a process generated less by piety than by a compulsive will to power." Likewise, the deities' elite cults sought to differentiate themselves from lesser folk not just by engaging in ritual and ceremony but also by a "mania for lavish display, which thus tended to become an obsession."[75]

Aztec elites valued such goods as jade and quetzal feathers, made more exotic because they came from distant lands. So the Mexica's military arm was the key to exacting tribute items from afar and to acquiring sacrificial victims beyond those supplied by the flower wars. The lavish ceremonies carried out at the Great Temple served the state "in the same way that individuals may strive for wealth, not to eat more food or drink more wine but to display their success to others."[76] In gratitude, sacrifices were made to a multitude of deities, which pleased their cults of followers and served to sustain and increase these immolations.

Rapid expansion of the Aztec empire is associated with the reigns of Moctezuma I (1440–1468) and Ahuitzotl (1468–1502). Because the latter died at a relatively young age, scholars have widely attributed his death to an accident that befell him some two years earlier. Another engineering project, which brought sweet water from Coyoacan to Tenochtitlan, was to be the highlight of Ahuitzotl's internal improvements for the Aztec capital. When a holding dam burst in 1500, it produced such a volume of water that a flood enveloped Tenochtitlan, killing hundreds. Panicked by fear of drowning, Ahuitzotl supposedly fled his palace in such haste that he failed to duck beneath the stone lintel of a low doorway. Having never fully recovered from head injuries, he died of complications from a severe concussion.[77] However, Diego Durán offers a more plausible explanation for Ahuitzotl's death. The Dominican chronicler states that the emperor died of a malady contracted during his last military campaign: "It was a strange and terrible illness and the doctors could not understand it. . . . With the disease he withered up, began to lose his vigor, and when he died he was reduced to skin and bones."[78]

The new *tlatoani* of the Aztecs was thirty-four years old and took the name Moctezuma Xocoyotzin (Moctezuma the Younger), to distinguish him from his great grandfather, Moctezuma Ilhuicamina. The new emperor, also known as Moctezuma II, appears to have been a man of great talent but false modesty. And he was the last Aztec emperor to receive the full ceremony of coronation. His principal successors, Cuitlahuac and Cuauhtemoc, were engaged in defending Tenochtitlan against the Spanish and did not have the luxury of formal induction into office.[79]

This second Moctezuma was the sixth emperor since the Mexica freed themselves from Tepanec subjugation and the ninth since the line began near the end of the 1300s. He was a seasoned warrior and a pro-

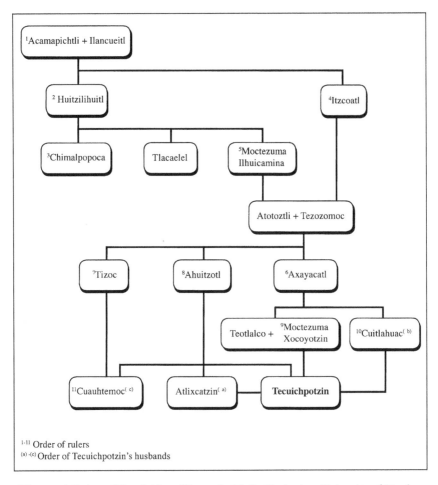

Figure 1.6. Rulers of Tenochtitlan. (Center for Media Production, University of North Texas.)

foundly religious person who was given to meditation and private study. Sources generally agree that on the occasion of his choice by electors as *tlatoani* of Tenochtitlan, he had to be informed of the honor in the temple of Huitzilopochtli, where he had gone to meditate.[80]

Once in office, Moctezuma II shed his pretensions of modesty and took steps to put his stamp on internal and external affairs. He dismissed the bureaucrats who had served Ahuitzotl and replaced them with servants and officials of his own choosing. He did so because those appointed by his uncle "were of low rank or children of commoners." As such, they were viewed as unworthy to serve a high-ranking individual like him.[81] Sons of the highest nobility in Tenochtitlan, Texcoco, and Tacuba, all products of the elite centers of learning (*calmecac*), became members of his personal staff. These *pipiltin* (nobles) were further educated in the precepts of their new mentor.

Initially, Moctezuma II was far less bellicose than was Ahuitzotl. As León-Portilla has conjectured, Xocoyotzin's scholarly bent drove him to consult the surviving ancient codices to guide his actions, rather than to follow automatically the aggressive policies of his immediate predecessor.[82]

At some point in the early 1500s, Moctezuma II married Princess Teotlalco, who became his principal wife. Of particular interest here is a daughter named Tecuichpotzin, likely born in 1509. In the years prior to the birth of his beloved daughter, Moctezuma II displayed an arrogance unparalleled in the annals of Aztec kings, and "his status now verged on the divine."[83]

Since Moctezuma placed himself on a footing that approximated that of the creator gods, any offense—real or imagined—to his person was tantamount to blasphemy or treason, and punishment was likely to be death. Many years after his death, Diego Durán questioned an Indian informant about the facial features of the emperor: "Father, I shall not lie to you or tell you things I do not know. I never saw his face." The Indian explained that had he dared lay eyes on Moctezuma, "he would have been killed in the same way that others who looked upon him were slain."[84]

Moctezuma II paid a high price for making himself a near man-god, probably patterned in the main after the tutelary numen Huitzilopochtli. How could he explain failures or adverse circumstances when he presented himself as a quasi all-powerful deity? Most tyrants know the answer. *They* are never at fault; others must shoulder the blame. In the near future, things were about to go badly for Xocoyotzin.

By the time of Tecuichpotzin's birth, Spaniards had conquered and partially settled Española, Puerto Rico, and Jamaica. Their expeditions also touched the shores of present-day Colombia and Panama by 1509, and within two years, Diego de Velázquez would initiate the conquest of Cuba. Given the far-reaching extent of Aztec imperial contacts, it is perhaps likely that rumors of a different kind of human being reached the fringes of the Aztec world.[85]

Prior to the arrival of Spaniards in New Spain, Moctezuma opened a campaign against Tlaxcala that went badly. The Aztecs suffered through indecisive battles and, worse, defeats. In one engagement, the Mexica lost a majority of their forces, including their leaders, while taking only sixty prisoners. By 1518 the outnumbered Tlaxcalans stood unconquered, because they "had fought all the harder . . . having more to lose than their opponents." Significantly, when Cortés arrived in the following year, "he found the Tlaxcalans roused but not routed."[86]

Nevertheless, the Aztec armies did score victories in other areas, including a campaign into Chichimec territory by way of the Huastec region. The Mexica also occupied parts of present-day Tabasco/Campeche, a possible foothold for expansion into Yucatán. Furthermore, by 1519 the powerful Cholulans had become an ally of the Aztecs. As Ross Hassig has noted, "How far the Aztecs might have expanded had the Spanish conquest not cut their rule short we cannot say. But there is little evidence that . . . [they] had already achieved their height and were on the wane."[87]

The two Spanish sea expeditions that foretold Cortés's landing on the coast of present-day Veracruz were led by Francisco Hernández de Córdoba, to Yucatán in 1517, and by Juan de Grijalva, along the coast of Veracruz in 1518. When news of the first sighting of a Spanish ship, described by a peasant as a "round hill or house" moving about on water, reached Moctezuma, far from lapsing into lethargy and depression, he "actually behaved like the experienced twenty-year sovereign he was." From this point on, the emperor had the sea watched from several locations.[88]

Two years passed, and the floating houses appeared yet again. The ships of Fernando Cortés and his men appeared off the coast of present-day Veracruz. They brought with them "huge deer," which they had tamed and learned to ride; they had "magical sticks" that resounded like thunder and spit lightning; and they had ferocious dogs that obeyed their masters.[89]

The decision about how to respond to this unsettling news lay with Moctezuma II. His course of action was far more certain and constant than is generally portrayed. He would watch the intruders very carefully and gather information about them, and he was not without hope. Perhaps if he offered sumptuous gifts, the unwelcome guests would be satisfied and go away; perhaps the powerful Tlaxcalans, whose empire lay between the coast and Tenochtitlan, would defeat them; or perhaps they could be invited into the capital, where they would be cut off from the coast. What did not occur to Moctezuma was that these bearded strangers would have a falling out among themselves, or that Fernando Cortés would have to deal with powerful enemies in his own world.

Two

The Survival and Accommodation of Isabel Moctezuma, 1519–1532

THE CONQUEST OF THE AZTEC EMPIRE by Fernando Cortés, his Spanish soldiers, and their Indian allies sealed the fate of Moctezuma II and profoundly influenced the lives of his children. Their future would depend heavily on the conqueror's entreaties at the court of Charles I (later Emperor Charles V of the Holy Roman Empire), on Cortés's shrewdness, and on his understanding of Spanish legal precedents and procedures. That failing, the children of the emperor might have fared much worse than they did.

By Easter Sunday, 1519, Cortés had learned that a powerful emperor named Moctezuma Xocoyotzin lived in the interior of a land Spaniards would call New Spain. Somehow, he had to induce that great ruler to acknowledge an even greater power—that of his sovereign king in Spain.[1]

Cortés, from his position on the central coast of Veracruz, remained in close contact with Moctezuma's emissaries for just less than a month. During that time, the Aztec agents gathered information on the strangers and bestowed gifts, including gold objects, on them. Two things became clear: Moctezuma wanted the Spaniards to remain on the coast, and he did not want them to come to Tenochtitlan. When the Aztecs discerned that the emperor's wishes would not be honored, they broke off contact on May 12.[2]

After founding Villa Rica de la Vera Cruz, Cortés marched to Cempoala, where he learned that the Totonacs, who were tributaries of the Aztecs, were displeased with their powerful overlords. As Cortés soon perceived, other indigenous cities harbored similar complaints against the Aztecs and expressed a willingness to join the Spaniards as allies. These and other alliances with indigenous people in New Spain would crucially alter "the power balance for the Spaniards."[3]

There is no doubt that the Spaniards were technologically superior to all New World natives. They had gunpowder, harquebuses, and cannons; steel swords, lances, crossbows, and armor; horses and mastiffs; and ships that could resupply them.[4] Furthermore, a host of European diseases, especially smallpox, aided and abetted the Spaniards' advantages by killing thousands of Indians.[5] But even with the odds on Cortés's side, "there was no possibility that . . . [he] could conquer the Aztec empire." His soldiers "were so few that they could be overwhelmed and destroyed by sheer numbers." Success would depend on dividing Indians and pitting one group against another.[6]

Before leaving the coast, around August 8, and marching toward the highlands en route to Tenochtitlan, Cortés took a bold course of action that committed his army to success or likely annihilation. He stripped his ships of removable parts such as rigging, anchors, tackle, and guns, and scuttled them. Such action no doubt raised questions about his sanity among the fainthearted.[7]

Cortés, at times in contact with Moctezuma's agents, gained a clearer understanding of the emperor and the Aztecs through his co-interpreters, doña Marina (also known as Malintzin or Malinche) and Jerónimo de Aguilar. Doña Marina, a linguistically accomplished Mexica from a village near Coatzacoalcos, had lived for a time in Yucatán, where she learned Maya. Aguilar, a victim of shipwreck on Cozumel, knew both Spanish and Maya.[8] This team served as interlocutors between Cortés and Moctezuma's emissaries, who were magicians, wizards, and sorcerers, as well as wise men and seasoned warriors. The Aztecs also supplied Cortés and his army with a great variety of food items while learning more about them and their intentions. On one occasion, to determine the nature of the interlopers, they gave the Spaniards tortillas soaked in blood and observed that the intended recipients were revolted and nauseated by the offerings.[9]

Moctezuma was well aware that the Spaniards must traverse the kingdom of the powerful Tlaxcalans, whom the Aztecs had often fought but had not decisively defeated. The Tlaxcalans were the first formidable opponents that Cortés encountered in New Spain, and his ability to subdue them and, more important, recruit them as allies was much in doubt. The vastly outnumbered Spaniards fought at least two day battles and a night engagement with the Tlaxcalans before the natives sought peace, which came none too soon. Ross Hassig presents shocking numbers about the weakness of Cortés's army at this point. It contained about 250 Spaniards (many of whom were wounded), 10 horses (all injured), around 200 noncombatant porters, and fewer than 100 Indian allies. Nothing more dramatically underscores the importance of the impending, unwavering alliance of Cortés's army with the Tlaxcalans.[10]

After spending about a month among his powerful allies, Cortés chose to continue toward Tenochtitlan by way of Cholula. It will be remembered that the Cholulans had recently become allies of the Aztecs and that they were enemies of the Tlaxcalans. Their city was one of the great religious centers of pre-Spanish Mexico, with scores of temples and one of the strongest cults of Quetzalcoatl. Cholula also had the "largest pyramidal structure in the world," which housed the temple of Tlaloc.[11] What occurred after Cortés's army arrived there is a source of great controversy.

Cortés claimed that, through intelligence gathered by doña Marina, he learned of Moctezuma's intent to ambush his army outside the city, or he may have decided to solidify his ties with the Tlaxcalans by slaughtering their Cholulan enemies. Still another possibility is the conqueror's desire to secure his lines of communication with the coast by not leaving a place as powerful as Cholula intact at his rear. Whatever his motivations, in the words of Diego Durán, "it was a sorry affair." Cortés turned on the Cholulans who had brought food for his soldiers and fodder for his horses. Insisting that Cholula's chieftains had come in disguise and in great numbers with the intent of harming him, the Spanish commander "had them massacred, sparing no one."[12] The conqueror's critics are many regarding his conduct at Cholula, and to this day many Mexicans regard the affair as one of the blackest marks on his career.

Nonetheless, the horrible slaughter at Cholula seems to have been a major turning point for Moctezuma II. He offered no opposition as Cortés's army continued its march toward Tenochtitlan. Ross Hassig offers a plausible explanation for Moctezuma's passive admission of a foreign army into his capital. First, given the small number of Spaniards Cortés commanded (around three hundred), Moctezuma probably misperceived their strength and superior weapons, believing that he had little to fear. Second, the Spaniards had professed peaceful intentions toward the Aztecs and were not viewed as an attacking army. And third, Cortés was fortunate to have marched toward Tenochtitlan near the end of the harvest, when commoners, who formed most of the Aztec army, were engaged in gathering crops.[13]

Cortés's army and its Indian allies entered Tenochtitlan on November 8, 1519. Upon meeting Moctezuma on the southern causeway, Cortés dismounted his war-horse and sought to embrace the fifty-two-year-old emperor. Mexica nobles, insisting that no one touch the royal body, rushed forward to restrain the conqueror. Cortés would later remark that Moctezuma "was so feared by all, both present and absent, that there could be no ruler in the world more so."[14]

Nonetheless, shortly after being quartered in the city, the Spaniards seized Moctezuma and held him prisoner. Unfortunately for him, the Aztecs viewed their emperor's failure to resist as a sign of weakness, and he would never again regain full authority. But in defense of Moctezuma's submission to captivity, it is possible that he was biding his time and hoping to weaken the Spaniards by undermining their alliance with Tlaxcala.[15]

J. H. Elliott maintains that, despite the awesome power of the Aztecs and the perils of a completed conquest that lay ahead, in many respects Cortés "had more to fear from some of this own countrymen." That assessment has great merit, and it relates directly to the conqueror's "highly equivocal position, both in relation to his immediate superiors and to the Spanish crown."[16]

Those "immediate superiors" were Diego de Velázquez, who, although governor of Cuba, was only a deputy of Diego Columbus, hereditary successor to the great Admiral of the Ocean Seas. Velázquez, an ambitious man anxious to win honors in his own right, had sponsored the sea expeditions of Hernández de Córdoba (1517) and Grijalva (1518). In a deliberate move to circumvent the authority of the younger Columbus, the Grijalva undertaking had gained the approval of the three Hieronymite friars who were serving as governors of Española (Santo Domingo) and temporary replacements for Diego Columbus, then in Spain. Second, Velázquez dispatched two agents to the Spanish court. Gonzalo de Guzmán and Benito Martín sought the title of *adelantado* of Yucatán for their sponsor, as well as the right to conquer and colonize Grijalva's new discoveries.[17]

A third expedition, commanded by Cortés in 1519, was to expand

Figure 2.1. Great Pyramid of Tlaloc, Cholula. (Photo by author.)

Velázquez's claims to the Yucatán region. Cortés's original instructions denied him the right to colonize new lands, because the governor of Cuba did not then have authorization to do that. Better known are Velázquez's last-minute attempts to remove the headstrong Cortés, the failure of that effort, and the conqueror's determination to strike out on his own. Accordingly, Cortés set out from Cuba as a conquistador without proper authority. He was certainly viewed as such by Velázquez.

Recognizing that he was on shaky legal ground, Cortés took steps to shore up his position in Spain and New Spain. From the Mexican coast, he dispatched Alonso Hernández de Puertocarrero and Francisco de Montejo across the Atlantic on July 26, 1519. With them went bundles of letters and gold. Among the papers was Cortés's so-called First Letter to King Charles.[18] By that time, the conqueror had already taken steps in New Spain to remove the dangerous label of "traitor" that hung about his

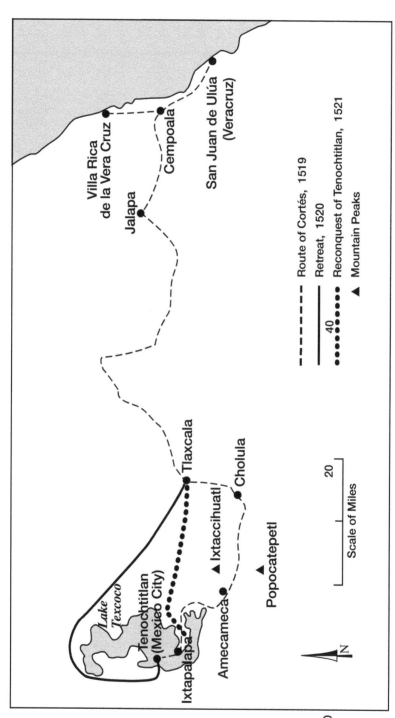

Figure 2.2. Routes of Fernando Cortés, 1519–1521. (Center for Media Production, University of North Texas.)

Villa Rica
de la Vera Cruz

Cempoala

San Juan de Ulúa
(Veracruz)

Jalapa

Tlaxcala

Cholula

Ixtaccihuatl

Popocatepetl

Lake
Texcoco

Tenochtitlan
(Mexico City)

Ixtapalapa

Amecameca

Route of Cortés, 1519

Retreat, 1520

Reconquest of Tenochtitlan, 1521

Mountain Peaks

40

20

Scale of Miles

N

neck like a millstone. To do this, he had to rely on a knowledge of Castilian law and practice, which he had apparently acquired in his youth.

The late France V. Scholes spent the better part of his adult life studying the career of Fernando Cortés but admitted that he could write everything he knew about Cortés's early years in three or four pages. Scholes believed that Cortés, born in Medellín (Extremadura) in 1484, lived as a young man in Salamanca for about two years, during which he worked as a scribe for his uncle, Francisco Núñez, who was a notary. The future conqueror probably used this time to study Latin and read law. Cortés relied on that knowledge, as well as his familiarity with the great compilation of Castilian codes known as the *Siete Partidas*, and then put that information to good use at the first Spanish settlement in New Spain. He also knew Castilian customs and depended on the advice of close friends, especially Gonzalo de Sandoval and Pedro de Alvarado.[19]

This background and experience led Cortés to regard lightly his defiance of Velázquez. He would act as the direct agent of the king, who was the ultimate source of justice, and in New Spain he would serve the best interests of his monarch, who was sovereign of Castile. He also knew that his king had been entrusted by the pope to spread the Roman Catholic faith among the pagans. Therefore, Cortés was directly subordinate to Charles I, and no other. And by virtue of a papal donation in 1493, all natives of New Spain were vassals of the crown of Castile.[20] But there was more.

Once on the soil of New Spain, Cortés could claim, in accord with the *Siete Partidas*, that even the laws of Castile could be set aside by the insistence of all good men of the land. Moreover, the conqueror gave himself a measure of legality by urging the formation of a new community of Spaniards, Villa Rica de la Vera Cruz—all with the intent of again upholding the best interests of the king. Members of the new municipality then appointed officials, including Cortés as *alcalde mayor*. The city's founders also drafted what has become widely regarded as Cortés's "First Letter," which accompanied Montejo and Puertocarrero to Spain.[21]

Before the Cortés emissaries left the coast of New Spain, word arrived that the crown had appointed Velázquez *adelantado* of Yucatán on November 13, 1518.[22] Clearly, Montejo and Puertocarrero had much work to do in Spain if the conqueror was to shed the mantle of renegade conquistador. That goal seemed a long shot, since Juan Rodríguez de Fonseca, chief counsel of the crown for the Americas, held Cortés in low regard. In fact, Fonseca had been instrumental in obtaining the title of *adelantado* for Velázquez.

Montejo and Puertocarrero disembarked at Seville, only to face Velázquez adherents, who persuaded officials of the Casa de Contratación (House of Trade) to confiscate their personal funds and the gifts of gold and beautiful quetzal feathers intended for the king. Stripped of visible evidence of Moctezuma's treasures, the two men, in the company of Cortés's father, set out for Barcelona, where they knew Charles to be in residence. But they arrived too late. The king was on his way to Burgos en route to Flanders and beyond, where he would be crowned Holy Roman Emperor. The trio finally overtook Charles's entourage near Valladolid in early March 1520.[23]

In the meantime, word of the sumptuous nature of the items impounded at Seville had reached Charles. He ordered the treasure sent north immediately, and it reached him at La Coruña about two weeks before he was to sail for the Low Countries on May 20. At the port city, the king again heard last-minute appeals from the three men on behalf of Cortés and themselves. Charles was impressed. On May 10 the future emperor issued a royal decree that freed the confiscated monies of Montejo and Puertocarrero in Seville.[24]

When Charles I departed Spain, he left a country in turmoil. A complex uprising known as the Revolt of the Comuneros (May 1520–April 1521), driven in large measure by the unpopularity of the foreign-born, non-Spanish-speaking monarch and the rapacity of his Burgundian advisers and Flemish officials, plunged Spain into civil war.[25] In this atmosphere, how could an accused rebel hope for royal validation?

Fonseca's hand, however, was not as strong as before. He had suffered some erosion of authority as part of Charles's unpopular sojourn in Spain (1517–1520). But Fonseca still held what he thought to be a trump card. He knew that Velázquez, armed with the title of *adelantado* of Yucatán, planned to challenge Cortés by sending a huge army into New Spain. That force, commanded by Pánfilo de Narváez, which outnumbered the adherents of the conqueror by more than three to one, would settle the score with Cortés once and for all. Unfortunately for Fonseca and Velázquez, the red-bearded Narváez was a less-than-competent captain.

Narváez landed his sizable army on the coast of New Spain in April 1520 and established his headquarters at Cempoala. At that juncture, Cortés occupied the Aztec capital and held Moctezuma II captive. The

Figure 2.3. Monument to Fernando Cortés, Medellín, Spain. (Photo by author.)

conqueror was seemingly in a weak position—both legally and militarily. If Narváez held a direct commission from the king, then Cortés had no choice but to honor it. On the other hand, if Narváez did not have such a mandate, Cortés intended to claim authority over the land in the name of Charles I. In any case, the conqueror suggested a meeting to work out a compromise. Narváez rejected that approach, believing his superior numbers gave him the whip hand. The issue would have to be settled by clash of arms.[26]

Cortés divided his army in Tenochtitlan. He left about 80 men under the command of Pedro de Alvarado, while more than 250 followed the conqueror on a forced march back to Villa Rica de la Vera Cruz. There his ranks swelled with the addition of 120 adherents who had founded another town farther down the coast.[27]

Under cover of darkness, Cortés's much smaller but more experienced army quickly routed Narváez's forces. In fighting on the steps of Cempoala's pyramid, Narváez wielded a great two-handed broadsword, but in the darkness he did little damage with it. One of Cortés's soldiers managed to thrust a pike inside the deadly arc of the broadsword. It struck don Pánfilo in the face and plucked out his right eye. This took the fight out of Narváez, and the rest of his army quickly surrendered. The battle was not costly, claiming perhaps fifteen of Narváez's men and two of Cortés's.[28]

A victory celebration at Cempoala had hardly ended when word of disturbing happenings in Tenochtitlan arrived via a Tlaxcalan runner. The news could not have been much worse. Pedro de Alvarado, perhaps operating on false information and fearing for the safety of his small command, had ordered an attack on Mexica nobles during one of their most important festivals (Toxcatl). The flower of Mexica aristocracy, including many relatives of Moctezuma, died in a slaughter during which "the blood of the brave warriors ran like water."[29] In the aftermath, a general uprising swept the city, pinning Alvarado's army within the confines of the palace once occupied by Moctezuma's father, Axayacatl.

Cortés had to return immediately to the Aztec capital. Once again he force marched his men, this time toward Tenochtitlan. Upon reaching Lake Texcoco, Cortés's army circled its northern perimeter to reconnoiter. Entry into the city came by way of the western and shortest causeway. Passage was unopposed, and within the city not a single Mexica could be seen. The only greeting was an ominous silence.[30]

Alvarado and his men were of course delighted by the arrival of so many fellow soldiers and Cortés himself. They were short of food and water, for the great market in the city was closed. Moctezuma likewise welcomed the conqueror with open arms, but his greeting was not reciprocated. The full brunt of Cortés's white-hot anger fell solely on the emperor, who lapsed into despair. Several of don Fernando's lieutenants asked him to soften his stance, to which he replied, "Should I be moderate to a dog who had secret relations with Narváez and does not even give us anything to eat?"[31]

It is important to grasp the nature of Cortés's anger. His master plan of presenting intact a great Mexican empire to King Charles was in jeopardy. This circumstance also threatened the status of Moctezuma II and his offspring.

Central to the future of Moctezuma's children was Cortés's argument, set forth in his Second Letter, that their father was a great lord who ruled over a vast empire. Shortly after his peaceful entry into Tenochtitlan, the conqueror decided for his safety and that of his men not to leave Moctezuma "in complete liberty," although at first he was confined by nothing more than palace arrest. Also, with the emperor in Cortés's power, the people Moctezuma controlled might more easily submit to the recognition and service of an even greater lord or sovereign— Charles V, whom Cortés then knew to have acquired the office of Holy Roman Emperor. Indeed, the Second Letter begins with the words, "Most High and Powerful and Catholic Prince, Most Invincible Emperor and Our Sovereign."[32]

In custody, the Aztec emperor served Cortés's purposes quite well. The conqueror informed lesser chieftains that it was Charles V's wish that they continue to honor Moctezuma. By doing so, they would recognize that Charles wished the Aztec king to remain in power; at the same time, Moctezuma would acknowledge the sovereignty of an even greater emperor in a distant land. Because Moctezuma was allowed to enjoy the company of his family, Cortés came to know the emperor's daughters. Three of them would later receive the Christian names of Isabel, María, and Mariana.[33]

Cortés thought it important to note that once Moctezuma had submitted to house arrest, the Aztec ruler gave his full cooperation to the Spaniards. Although the truth of Cortés's claims is suspect, he insisted that he treated Moctezuma so well that the emperor refused to leave even when repeatedly offered the opportunity to return to his own house. On each occasion, the captive ruler is said to have replied that "he did not wish to go, for he lacked nothing, just as if he were in his own home."[34] The important point is that the conqueror needed to establish that Moctezuma had become a willing agent of Spanish control over his empire.

Following the horrible slaughter inflicted on the Mexica nobility during the feast of Toxcatl, the infuriated populace stormed Axayacatl's palace. They might well have succeeded in capturing it and killing Alvarado's men, except for their lack of leadership and the alleged entreaties of Moctezuma and his aides. The emperor is said to have tried to calm the populace and did his best to call off the battle. Likewise, the Mexica governor of Tlatelolco implored the attackers to let the "battle be abandoned." This seems to have had a calming effect, but in the long run it further weakened Moctezuma's credibility with his subjects.[35]

With the second arrival of Cortés's army in Tenochtitlan, the total number of Spanish soldiers within the city was about fourteen hundred. The conqueror's forces had been strengthened by the addition of new equipment, young men, and fresh horses, all acquired from the Narváez expedition. But this was not enough to overcome a perilous situation, because a serious mistake by Cortés would soon cut off all outside food and water.[36]

With many of their nobles murdered by the swords of Alvarado's men, the Mexica, accustomed as they were to the centrality of Moctezuma's authority, continued to drift without a recognized leader. Cortés, in an attempt to secure provisions for his soldiers, prevailed on Moctezuma to order the reopening of the great market. The emperor replied that he was powerless to do so. Instead, a member of his retinue should be called on to accomplish that. Cortés then permitted Moctezuma to choose this person, who turned out to be the emperor's brother, Cuitlahuac.[37]

Cortés did not know that Cuitlahuac was a defiant warlord who had apparently counseled all-out resistance to the Spaniards when they first set foot on the shores of New Spain. As soon as he walked out of Axayacatl's palace, Cuitlahuac threw himself into the job of organizing resistance. All of the portable bridges that spanned gaps in the major causeways leading into and out of Tenochtitlan were either removed or destroyed. Cortés's worst nightmare was realized—he was trapped within the city.[38]

During the last few days of June 1520, there were constant battles, many of them street fighting between Spaniards and Mexica. In desperation, Cortés placed Moctezuma in irons and induced the governor of Tlatelolco to appear on the palace terrace and address an angry crowd of Mexica. According to Sahagún, the high official, speaking for Moctezuma, who was also on the terrace, shouted, "We are not the equals of [the Spaniards]! Let [the battle] be abandoned! . . . let there be a cessation [of war]. They put him [Moctezuma] in irons, they have placed irons on his feet." The Mexica, "much inflamed with rage," replied by denouncing Moctezuma as a rogue and by showering the terrace with arrows, but the Spaniards protected the Indian governor and the emperor with their shields.[39]

Under circumstances that may never be clearly understood, Moctezuma appears to have died on the morning of June 30.[40] Among his final requests was that Cortés become the guardian of his daughters, especially Tecuichpotzin, whom he regarded as his principal heir. What is certain is that the Spaniards planned to flee Tenochtitlan at midnight July 1.[41]

They began the retreat on schedule in mist or light rain. At first all went well, but a Mexica woman spotted the silent column and sounded an alarm. Her cry—"Mexicans! Come all of you! Already they go forth! Your foes already go forth secretly!"—echoed through the city, and the male population took to their canoes.[42] Cortés's "secret weapon" was a portable bridge made of planks that could span breaks in the causeway, and there was some hope that the bridge could be used more than once. But in the words of Bernal Díaz, "as fortune is perverse at such times, one mischance followed another, and as it was raining, two of the horses slipped and fell into the lake. When I and others of Cortés' Company saw that, we got safely to the other side of the bridge, and so many warriors charged on us, that despite all our good fighting, no further use could be made of the bridge, so that the passage or water opening was soon filled up with dead horses, Indian men and women, servants, baggage, and boxes."[43]

In all, perhaps six hundred of Cortés's soldiers and many more Tlaxcalan allies died or were captured during what Spaniards would call their "Noche Triste." All of those taken alive were later sacrificed. Among the Indian fatalities were Moctezuma's son Chimalpopoca, and his sister, known to the Spaniards as "doña Ana."[44] Three of his daughters somehow survived. It is uncertain whether they remained behind in the palace or were rescued by their countrymen during the early hours of July 1, 1520. If we are to believe Cortés that he honored Moctezuma's dying request and accepted the guardianship of these young women, it may well have been the latter.

Cortés and his depleted army managed to fight their way out of the Central Valley and retreat to the mountain kingdom of Tlaxcala. At no time did the conqueror lose his resolve to reconquer Tenochtitlan, but that lay in the future.

• • •

Let us now examine the role played by Moctezuma's principal daughter, Tecuichpotzin, who remained in Tenochtitlan until the fall of the capital in August 1521. As mentioned in Chapter 1, the Mexica were intent on establishing cultural ties with the ancient Toltecs. To do so they recruited Acamapichtli of Culhuacan as their first king. Susan Gillespie notes that Acamapichtli may or may not have been a full Culhua prince but his wife (or mother) was assuredly Culhua. So the strongest ties of the Mexica with the Culhuas were through a woman who "gave the fledgling dynasty its nobility." Gillespie notes that as the mother of Acamapichtli, this woman was a goddess named Atotoztli; as his wife, Ilancueitl—in short, "for certain conceptual purposes"—the same woman.[45]

The second woman of prime importance in Aztec leadership was the daughter of their fifth king, Moctezuma I. Her name was Atotoztli, the same as the creator of half of the Tenochtitlan dynasty. Following the death of her father, Atotoztli may well have served briefly as interim ruler.[46] Thus, when Moctezuma II died on or around June 30, 1520, there was a precedent for a daughter taking his place as Tenochtitlan's monarch.[47]

Pedro Carrasco states that when Cortés first arrived in Mexico, Tecuichpotzin had married Atlixcatzin, the son of Ahuitzotl. This husband, the most likely successor of Moctezuma II, had died by 1520. Since Tecuichpotzin had ties to both Ahuitzotl and Moctezuma, this probably gave her "the right to be the main wife of her father's successors," and it does much to explain her subsequent marriages to Cuitlahuac and Cuauhtemoc (see Figure 1.6).[48]

A full explanation of the Aztecs' complex concept of legitimacy for the offspring of an emperor lies beyond the scope of this work. In any event, succession to the throne of Tenochtitlan was more often brother to brother or uncle to nephew than father to son or daughter. More important to this study is the Spanish view of what constituted legitimacy and its application to three children fathered by Moctezuma and a fourth by Cortés.[49]

The multiple marriages of Tecuichpotzin, by then known as doña Isabel, to Spaniards will be dealt with a bit later. But to address further the question of her ascendancy, it is necessary to forward to 1544. In that year, Juan Cano, Isabel's third Spanish husband, agreed to an interview on Española with Gonzalo Fernández de Oviedo, official historian of the Indies. In the exchange, Cano—probably using information related by his wife—described in some detail the important difference between the marriage of an Aztec king to a principal wife and liaisons with a host of lesser wives and concubines. In the case of the former, certain formalities had to be observed in a public ceremony. Parents of the betrothed couple first agreed to a formal contract of marriage, followed by a nuptial banquet and dance. As the couple retired to the privacy of the wedding chamber, their parents tied the skirt of the bride to a cotton blanket that covered the groom. The marriage was consummated over the next three days, during which a female servant provided food and other necessities to the royal pair. Throughout that period, there were constant dances and feasts outside the royal bedroom but those festivities ceased when the couple emerged from postnuptial confinement. Without these formal ceremonies and observances, high Mexica nobility were not united with a primary wife, nor were their children regarded as principal heirs.[50]

It may be assumed that Cuitlahuac and Tecuichpotzin never observed the ceremony of tied blanket and skirt during the brief time that the emperor ruled. However, Cano maintained that Cuauhtemoc and Tecuichpotzin had wed in this manner and that Cuauhtemoc ruthlessly consolidated his power by imprisoning and later killing Axayacatl, his bride's brother and the only surviving son of Moctezuma and Teotlalco.[51] For reasons relating to his wife's inheritance, it naturally served Cano's interests to claim that she was Moctezuma's sole legitimate heir, but that was also the prevailing attitude among other Spaniards in the aftermath of the conquest.

Tecuichpotzin remained with Cuauhtemoc for approximately one year before their relationship changed with the successful siege and recapture of Tenochtitlan by Cortés and his captains. The campaign, completed on August 13, 1521, involved unrelenting attacks along the major causeways and from thirteen shallow-draft vessels (brigantines) on the lake. As the ruined capital fell in the final assault, Cuauhtemoc and his young wife made a desperate attempt to escape across the waters of Lake Texcoco in a large canoe. Pursued and overtaken by the fastest brigantine, Cuauhtemoc surrendered with these words: "I . . . am your prisoner and I ask no favor other than that you treat my queen, my wife, and her ladies-in-waiting with the respect they deserve due to their sex and condition." Taking Tecuichpotzin's hand, the Aztec emperor then stepped aboard the Spanish vessel. His capitulation ended the escape efforts of other Mexica, who chose to share the fate of their leader.[52]

Tecuichpotzin, soon christened Isabel, lived another thirty years, but Cuauhtemoc's days were numbered. He was separated from his young wife in 1524, subjected to horrible torture as Spaniards sought the location of treasure they believed lay buried somewhere in the rubble of Tenochtitlan, and then forced to accompany Cortés on what proved to be a fatal march to Honduras.

• • •

The future of the victorious conqueror remained ominous because of events in Spain and the New World. Fonseca was still intent on trimming Cortés's sails, and Charles V had not yet determined Cortés's status. It was Fonseca, however, who was first to act. When news of Narváez's defeat reached him, the chief counselor for the Indies successfully prevailed upon Adrian of Utrecht, regent during Charles's absence in Germany, to intervene in New Spain. To this end, Adrian commissioned Cristóbal de Tapia, a royal inspector in Española.[53]

Tapia, armed with the authority to arrest Cortés, return him to Spain, and take over the government of New Spain, arrived at San Juan de Ulúa in early December 1521, about four months after the fall of Tenochtitlan. The inspector then proceeded up the coast to Villa Rica, where he presented his credentials to officials of that municipality. Those functionaries believed the royal agent's papers to be in order.[54] Once again Cortés faced a serious challenge, but he was equal to the occasion.

From contacts in Española, Cortés had learned of Tapia's commission before the inspector ever reached New Spain. The conqueror quickly organized a municipal government in Tenochtitlan, just as he had done two years earlier at Villa Rica de la Vera Cruz. He also moved to set up governmental machinery in two additional "towns" along the coast, which for the most part existed in name only. All of these municipalities of course claimed authority in the name of the king. Therefore, the collective government of New Spain lay with Cortés and four Spanish towns, which made Tapia's job much more difficult.[55]

Ever the clever manipulator, Cortés indicated to Tapia that he would be happy to travel to the coast to meet with him, but the officials of the four municipalities had urged him not to do so. If Cortés left the Central Valley, the Mexica might perceive division among the Spaniards and see the inspector as another "Narváez," thereby prompting them to revolt. So, instead, each town would send its *procurador* (representative) to confer with Tapia.

The meeting between the *procuradores* and Tapia most likely resulted in the use of a legal ploy that is all too familiar to students of colonial Latin American history. The representatives first determined that the inspector's papers were in order. They then read them, kissed them, and placed them over their heads—signifying their obeisance to a royal decree. But one or more of them, as the representative of his city, probably uttered the magical words, "Obedezco pero no cumplo" (I obey but I do not comply).[56]

The *procuradores* politely but firmly announced that circumstances in New Spain compelled them to make a direct appeal to the king rather than surrender power to the royal agent. They, as seasoned conquistadors, also argued that the Mexica would never accept the authority of an unknown official such as Tapia. They, on the other hand, had earned their status as experienced veterans by dint of battle. It appears that don Cristóbal did not press the issue; rather, he accepted a bribe and returned to Española, where he awaited results of the *procuradores'* direct petition to the king.[57]

While the status of Fernando Cortés hung in the balance at the Spanish court, the conqueror faced still another challenge in Pánuco, a Huastec province that lay inland from the modern-day port of Tampico. Cortés was aware that Francisco de Garay, the governor of Jamaica, had sought through his own agents at court a patent to colonize along a river explored by Alonso Álvarez de Pineda in 1519–1520. Garay's efforts bore fruit on June 4, 1521—about two months before the fall of Tenochtitlan.

When this much-delayed news reached Cortés, he argued that any appearance of an outside force in New Spain would encourage and embolden the natives. They would hope, just as Moctezuma had in 1520, when Narváez arrived on the scene, to play one Spanish element against the other. So in late December 1522, almost exactly a year after the Cristóbal de Tapia crisis had passed, Cortés led a sizable army of conquistadors and Indian allies into the Huasteca. Bitter fighting followed in the wake of an overland invasion along the valley of the Río Moctezuma, but

10

1112

the results were inevitable. Huastec resistance was crushed. Before withdrawing from the region, the conqueror founded a *villa* named Santiesteban del Puerto near the mouth of the Río Pánuco. Still another settlement with its own officials and government joined other municipalities in New Spain. It is also important to note that by March 1, 1523, Cortés had begun awarding *encomiendas* to Spanish colonists in Pánuco.[58]

On July 25 of the same year, Garay arrived at the Río de las Palmas, modern-day Río Soto la Marina. He captained a sizable expedition made up of six hundred men, more than one hundred horses, and eleven ships. The bulk of Garay's army disembarked at the mouth of the river and marched about 90 miles (150 kilometers) south to the new Spanish settlement on the Río Pánuco. Once there, Garay learned of a crown directive dated April 24, 1523, that expressly forbade his interfering in the government of the "said Fernando Cortés."[59] Garay bowed to the royal order, surrendered his command, and traveled to Mexico City, where, as a houseguest of Cortés, he died suddenly in late December 1523. At that juncture, the conqueror had not only weathered another challenge on the soil of New Spain but was about to reach the apex of his remarkable career.

Cortés's good fortune had rested, as before, on entreaties made in his behalf at the court of Charles V. The newly crowned emperor of the Holy Roman Empire returned to Spain on July 16, 1522. He had left a country in the throes of the Revolt of the Comuneros; he returned to a land at peace. In April of the previous year, Charles's partisans had won the final battle at Villalar and sealed the fate of the rebels.[60] Charles now had the opportunity to establish his credentials as the resident monarch Spaniards so ardently desired, and he remained in the country for the next seven years.

Charles spent the summer of 1522 reorganizing various councils and committees. It seems likely that the young emperor appointed and dismissed officials in large measure because of their record and that of their families during the recent revolt. However, Fonseca, whose brother had commanded forces loyal to Charles, did not himself fare well. Cortés's old enemy seems to have lost influence for different reasons. Hugh Thomas speculates that Fonseca's star began to fade quickly once Charles learned that the aging cleric had withheld information from him about Cortés.[61]

The emperor's efforts at reorganization included steps to set up a new institution of paramount importance to Spanish colonial America, the Royal Council of the Indies. Charles also appointed a special committee charged with the responsibility of advising him on what to do about the long-standing dispute between Velázquez and Cortés. Significantly, Fonseca was not a member of that group.

After considerable deliberation that involved testimony in behalf of both men, as well as the study of pertinent documents and letters, the committee rendered a decision favorable to Cortés. Charles essentially rubber-stamped that view. On October 11, 1522, the emperor bestowed impressive titles and powers on Cortés. He became *repartidor* (distributor of Indians as vassals) and, most important of all, *capitán general* (supreme military commander) and *gobernador* (civil governor) of New Spain. Plus, Charles expressly ordered Velázquez to stay out of Cortés's government in New Spain, just as he commanded Garay in the following year.[62]

Important as this was for Cortés, it was one thing for Charles V to make a decision in Spain and quite another for the news to reach New Spain. The latter, even in that day and age, took "unconscionably long." It was not until September 13, 1523, that Rodrigo de Paz and Francisco de las Casas, both relatives of the conqueror, arrived in Mexico bearing the king's good tidings. Cortés claimed that he was so grateful to the emperor that he could have kissed his feet a hundred thousand times. Among his followers, the news touched off "much happiness and many celebrations" in Mexico City. As icing on the cake, the messengers also delivered the emperor's decree of the previous April, which, as noted earlier, defused the dangerous situation in Pánuco by thwarting Garay's ambitions there.[63]

Cortés's official acceptance as governor, captain general, and distributor of Indians in New Spain served primarily to validate what had already become his de facto powers. Among the chief beneficiaries of his powers as *repartidor* would be Cortés himself, his close friends, and Moctezuma's children.

During the years Cortés spent on Española and Cuba, he had observed firsthand the devastating impact of *encomienda* on Indians of the Caribbean islands. He was determined to avert a similar disaster in New Spain, yet he had to face the crucial question of establishing an economic relationship between victorious conquistadors and defeated natives. Cortés also recognized that Indians in New Spain had achieved a higher order of civilization than their counterparts in the West Indies. Indeed, he saw the former as having "much greater intelligence" and sufficient ability to conduct themselves as citizens in a civilized country.[64]

Despite serious reservations, Cortés claimed that he had yielded to pressure from his soldier-companions. Having risked everything to conquer a great empire for their king, how could these brave men be expected to accept nothing more by way of reward than fifty or sixty pesos in gold? So, without a semblance of legality, the conqueror issued his first grants of *encomienda* in April 1522. And, as mentioned earlier, he repeated that same practice in Pánuco during the spring of 1523. Cortés kept for himself the revenues from some of the most populous and lucrative towns in that province, just as he had done in New Spain proper.[65] By 1524 Cortés had distributed much of the Indian population of Central Mexico. These grants went to himself, to his old comrades-in-arms, and, later, to the Christianized daughters of Moctezuma II.[66]

Cortés seemed to have accomplished all he might have hoped for by early 1524. He was rich and vested in office as governor and captain general of New Spain. In that same year death had claimed two of his most potent enemies—Fonseca in Spain and Velázquez in Cuba. As it turned out, this was a watershed year for the conqueror. Things would never again be quite as good for him.

As often happens in history and indeed in life itself, at the very time Cortés reached the apogee of power and influence in his remarkable career, forces were already at work to undermine his achievements. They began with the appointment in October 1522 of four royal treasury officials who were to "assist" the conqueror in governing New Spain. These royal bureaucrats were harbingers of a process repeated over and over again in Spain's postconquest governance of America. They had no following in the New World, as did Cortés; they owed their office solely to the king; and they served the royal objective of "divide and rule." But perhaps most important, this new breed of officials reflected crown concerns that the necessary qualities of a successful conquistador—boldness, independence of thought and action, initiative, and at times charismatic leadership—were the same attributes that would bear watching in the postconquest era. After all, recalcitrant nobles had dared oppose the king on his own terrain during the Revolt of the Comuneros, and down the not-too-distant road lay additional challenges to royal authority in Peru and in New Spain itself.[67]

So, who were these new appointees and what were their responsibilities? Alonso de Estrada held the title of treasurer; Gonzalo de Salazar, as *factor* (overseer of royal properties); Rodrigo de Albornoz, as accountant; and Pedro Almíndez de Chirino, as *veedor* (inspector-overseer charged with securing the king's share of precious metals).[68] The four officials were to "watch Cortés" and likewise "watch each other." Although there is not one shred of reliable evidence that Cortés was ever less than loyal to his king, this did not stop rumors to the contrary or the allegations of his enemies.

In 1524 Cortés learned that Cristóbal de Olid, once one of his most trusted captains, had repudiated the conqueror's leadership and right of governance in Honduras. Cortés's reaction was threefold. He dispatched Francisco de las Casas by sea, with orders to arrest and execute Olid as a rebel; he placed the government of New Spain in the hands of the treasury officials; and he organized an overland march from Mexico City to Honduras, which was intended as backup for Las Casas.

Accompanying the conqueror on an incredibly difficult trek to Central America was a host of individuals who included Spanish soldiers, Indian allies, doña Marina, and Franciscan priests. The cavalcade also contained Cuauhtemoc of Tenochtitlan, Coanacochtzin of Texcoco, and Tetlepanquetzaltzin of Tacuba—all incumbent *tlatoque* of the Aztec Triple Alliance cities, or major *altepetl*. En route, Cortés charged these chieftains in a legal proceeding as conspirators who were trying to mobilize native resistance against his army. Found guilty, they were executed in 1525.[69] With their deaths, the most prominent Indian royals in Central Mexico became Cuauhtemoc's widow, doña Isabel, and her half-siblings, doña Mariana and don Pedro Moctezuma.

Cortés's two-year absence from Mexico City (1524–1526) produced chaos in the government. Initially, two treasury officials identified themselves with a pro-Cortés faction and two with an anti-Cortés faction. The former, Estrada and Albornoz, maintained things for a time much as the conqueror himself might have wished. They, however, soon lost power to Salazar and Chirino. The *factor* and *veedor* then ruled with a mailed fist for more than a year. They persecuted the conqueror's adherents, including torturing and then executing Cortés's young cousin Rodrigo de Paz; they revoked *encomiendas* assigned by Cortés and reassigned them to his detractors. During that time, word spread that Cortés and his followers had perished on the march to Honduras. This prompted Salazar and Chirino to divest him of several rich *encomienda* towns, including Tacuba.[70]

Then a different word arrived in Mexico City. The conqueror was alive. He had safely reached Honduras, and on his arrival there he found that Las Casas had already overthrown Cristóbal de Olid and executed him. This news produced a countercoup in Mexico City, during which

Cortés's supporters removed Salazar and Chirino from power and supplanted them with Estrada and Albornoz. The latter imprisoned the former in huge wooden cages, where they became the object of public ridicule and abuse.[71] Estrada and Albornoz also reversed Salazar and Chirino's *encomienda* grants.

Needless to say, this two-year interregnum produced a veritable "blizzard" of protests by disgruntled settlers in New Spain, during which objections were sent across the Atlantic to the Council of the Indies and Charles V. To royal officials it must have seemed that the colony was on the verge of anarchy and civil war. Anxious to remedy the situation, the crown appointed Licentiate Luis Ponce de León and ordered him to go immediately to New Spain. There he was to remove Cortés from power and exercise supreme governmental authority while he conducted Cortés's *residencia*. Selected in November 1525 as a tandem appointment with Ponce was Nuño de Guzmán, who was to govern a separate jurisdiction in the province of Pánuco.[72]

Cortés returned to New Spain in May 1526. It is said that he was so emaciated by the grueling Honduran march that old friends on the coast hardly recognized him, but his reentry into the capital touched off a great celebration among his original soldier-colonists. The conqueror resumed his authority as governor and captain general but his tenure was cut short a few weeks later with the arrival of Luis Ponce. Don Luis announced his commission, and Cortés bowed to the royal mandate. But in short order Ponce was racked with fever and delirium. He died only days after reaching the capital but not before transferring authority to the hands of the aged Marcos de Aguilar.

Aguilar was hardly the man to take charge, for his health soon necessitated that he suckle a wet nurse. Somehow he lived until the first months of 1527, and on his deathbed appointed Alonso de Estrada, an old ally of Cortés, as his successor. Joining Estrada as co-governor was Gonzalo de Sandoval, perhaps the conqueror's most steadfast friend. Most important for this study, however, Cortés continued to exercise distributor powers over Indian affairs, and in this capacity he shaped the future of three descendants of Moctezuma II.[73] By executing Cuauhtemoc of Tenochtitlan and Tetlepanquetzaltzin of Tacuba in 1525, Cortés had widowed doña Isabel for the third time and created a void in the leadership of Tacuba. He addressed this matter on June 27, 1526, about one month after his return to New Spain and just prior to the arrival of Ponce de

León in Mexico City. Cortés reclaimed Tacuba from Chirino and granted it to Isabel Moctezuma as part of her dowry in an arranged marriage. The *encomienda* was a rich entitlement that included Tacuba and its multiple *sujetos* (subject towns), consisting of 1,240 tributary units. Significantly, the "Señora de Tacuba" received the grant in the name of the king, given to her and her successors "para siempre jamás" (for all time).[74] Cortés, in justifying the Tacuba *encomienda* grant of 1526, remarked that the emperor's daughter had reached an age that required her to marry an honorable Spanish gentleman, one who had served both the king and him. Cortés himself would choose doña Isabel's husband.

In the document of conveyance, Cortés takes pains to establish Moctezuma II's unwavering friendship for Spaniards. This historical "revisionism" was necessary in order to win approval from the king for such a generous grant to the emperor's daughter. Missing, of course, is Cortés's earlier assertion that Moctezuma had planned a massive ambush after the Spanish army passed through Cholula, as well as a later claim that the emperor had been in secret contact with Pánfilo de Narváez. Instead, the conqueror fixes blame for the insurrection that forced his retreat from Tenochtitlan on dissension within the Spanish forces, occasioned by the coming of Narváez's army. This and this alone prompted the uprising led by the emperor's brother Cuitlahuac.[75]

Cortés's choice of a worthy husband for Isabel Moctezuma was Alonso de Grado. The first reference to Grado's presence in the New World apparently dates from late 1514, when he received an *encomienda* on Española. He is listed the following year as an *encomendero* from Alcántara, Spain, living in the village of La Concepción.[76] Between 1515 and 1519, Grado relocated to Cuba, and from there sailed as a member of Cortés's expedition to New Spain.

Grado accompanied Cortés on the march inland toward Tenochtitlan, but Bernal Díaz regarded him as a soldier lacking valor. For example, when it became apparent that the Tlaxcalans were a formidable opponent, Grado counseled retreat to Villa Rica de la Vera Cruz in the hope of gaining reinforcements from Cuba. However, soon after occupying Tenochtitlan, Cortés sent Grado back to the coast as *alguacil mayor* (chief constable) of Villa Rica de la Vera Cruz. In that capacity, Grado established a sorry record of exploiting peaceful natives and demanding payments from them in foodstuffs, jewels, and pretty Indian women.[77]

In early 1520 Grado quarreled with Gonzalo de Sandoval at Villa

Rica. Sandoval then stripped Grado of office, in large measure because of the trouble he had stirred up by speaking favorably about Velázquez and seditiously about Cortés, and sent him to Tenochtitlan as a prisoner. En route to the capital, a hot-tempered and unforgiving Pedro de Alvarado met Grado about two leagues from the city. The prisoner completed the trip on foot, with his hands tied and a rope around his neck. When Grado reached Tenochtitlan, Cortés's partisans placed him in wooden stocks that smelled of garlic or onions and showered him with insults for "mucho tiempo" (a long time). During that time, Alvarado insisted that Cortés dared not leave Tenochtitlan for even a day or two, because when he returned he would find Grado hanged as a *bellaco* (rogue).[78]

Fortunately for Grado, Cortés apprised himself of facts in the matter and then dismissed all charges against the former *contador* (accountant) and *alguacil mayor*. The conqueror also disagreed with the harsh treatment that his lieutenants had inflicted on Grado, whom he regarded as a loyal friend. Later, Cortés would reward Grado with Isabel Moctezuma as his bride and appoint him *visitador de indios* (inspector of affairs relating to Indians). The couple wed on June 27, 1526, and on the following day the *cabildo* (municipal council) of Mexico City endorsed Grado's appointment.[79]

Thrice widowed, Isabel Moctezuma was still only about seventeen years of age on the occasion of her first Christian marriage. If we may believe Bernal Díaz, doña Isabel was an attractive woman. He twice describes her as "very beautiful" and as "a very pretty woman for an Indian [para ser india]."[80] Her marriage to Alonso de Grado, however, lasted only about a year. By 1527 he had died of undetermined causes, and she was a widow once again.

In May of that same year, a much-delayed Nuño de Guzmán arrived at Santiesteban del Puerto to assume the governorship of Pánuco. As mentioned, Guzmán had received a joint appointment with Ponce de León in November 1525. From his instructions and those of Ponce de León, it is clear than the crown had not totally brushed aside the flood of complaints against Cortés. To ensure that the conqueror and his adherents were brought to heel, Guzmán was to assist Ponce in every respect, just as the licentiate was to support Guzmán in Pánuco.[81]

Ponce and Guzmán arrived at Española in late spring 1526. There Guzmán fell victim to a serious illness, probably malaria, and was bedfast for months. By the time he recovered and reached Pánuco, in May 1527, the licentiate had been dead for approximately a year, and Cortés and his confederates still held sway in Mexico City and Santiesteban del Puerto. Over the next year, as Guzmán put his stamp on the government in Pánuco, relations between that province and New Spain proper remained tense.[82]

During that same time, Cortés, whom Amada López de Meneses has described as "having conquered no fewer women than towns," moved Grado's widow under his own roof. There doña Isabel soon became pregnant.[83] As his amorous intentions drifted elsewhere, Cortés sought a new husband for the Aztec princess and settled on Pedro Gallego de Andrade. Gallego, a native of Burguillos del Cerro, Spain, had arrived in Mexico as a member of the Narváez expedition. Like hundreds of others who came with the incompetent Narváez, he quickly switched his allegiance to Cortés. After the reconquest of Tenochtitlan in 1521, Gallego served under Cortés in the conquest of Pánuco, as well as in other campaigns. Some five or six months after her fourth marriage, to Gallego, doña Isabel gave birth to the conqueror's illegitimate daughter, named Leonor Cortés Moctezuma. The child was removed from the Gallego household and placed under the care of Licentiate Juan Gutiérrez de Altamirano, a cousin of Cortés by marriage and subsequent administrator of the conqueror's vast estates in New Spain.[84]

By 1528 time was running out for Cortés in New Spain. In the previous year, the crown had appointed the first Audiencia of New Spain, consisting of four *oidores* (judges) and a president, Nuño de Guzmán, who also retained his title as governor of Pánuco. The Audiencia's charge was to remove Cortés from power, assume the governorship of New Spain, and conduct Cortés's *residencia*. Recognizing that public opinion was against him, the conqueror left Mexico in March and returned to Spain in mid-May.[85]

Despite changes in government, during the next two years the fortunes of Moctezuma II's principal daughter remained secure. In 1530 doña Isabel bore a son, named Juan de Andrade (Gallego) Moctezuma, to Pedro Gallego. The celebration of Juan's birth in Tacuba was a gala affair marked by fiestas and banquets with honored guests in attendance. Juan de Zumárraga, first bishop of New Spain, administered the sacrament of baptism. For Pedro Gallego it was a proud moment. His aristocratic Indian wife had given him a son; the revenues of Tacuba and his own *encomienda* made him a wealthy man; he had ingratiated himself with the new governors in Mexico City; he moved in the highest social circles;

and the bishop himself had sprinkled holy water on his first son. But Gallego's good fortune was short-lived. Within two months he was dead—like Grado, of undetermined causes—and at twenty-one doña Isabel had been widowed for a fifth time. None of her husbands had survived for more than a few years, her second, the militant Cuitlahuac, for only eighty days.[86]

Despite doña Isabel's catastrophic marital record, there was no shortage of Spaniards willing to accept her hand in marriage. As Elinor C. Burkett notes in the case of sixteenth-century Peru, "Spaniards quickly realized that through marriage to . . . [the daughters of Indian royals], their children would gain positions of leadership in indigenous society for themselves and thus, by extension for the Spanish."[87] In the spring of 1532, after having been deprived of Tacuba for a time by the first Audiencia, doña Isabel married for a sixth time. This union, with Juan Cano de Saavedra, would prosper for nearly two decades and produce five more children for Isabel Moctezuma.[88]

Three

Isabel Moctezuma

S PANIARDS REGARDED ISABEL MOCTEZUMA as the principal
heir of the late emperor, Moctezuma II. In recognition of her status, doña Isabel received the lucrative revenues of one of the cities that
had formed the Triple Alliance of the imperial Aztecs. As mentioned earlier, Cortés bestowed this grant on June 27, 1526, shortly after returning
from the Honduran expedition. In awarding Tacuba and its *sujetos* to doña
Isabel by grant of *encomienda*, Cortés made her one of the most unusual
encomenderas in New Spain: Isabel, as well as her half-siblings, Mariana and
Pedro, received the services of other Indians. In this respect, they were
probably unique in sixteenth-century New Spain.[1] The daughters were
assuredly exceptional in that their *encomiendas*, granted in the name of the
king, were given as dowry and security (*en dote y arras*) and as perpetual
grants (*para siempre jamás*).[2] Given the pattern of privately held *encomiendas* escheating to the crown over the course of the century of conquest,
this latter proviso proved to be of paramount importance. These special
concessions to Indian elites also signal Spain's recognition of them as natural monarchs with inherent rights.

Spaniards were predominantly city dwellers. The dangers of frontier
life during the centuries-long Reconquest reinforced this pattern of
seeking safety in numbers. Their first political unit in New Spain was the
hastily organized municipality of Villa Rica de la Vera Cruz, so, in the
aftermath of the conquest of the Aztec empire, it seemed reasonable to
govern through "exploitable clusters of people." As Bartolomé de las
Casas observed, "One does not require witnesses from heaven to demon-

strate that . . . [the natives] were political peoples, with towns, inhabited places of large size, *villas*, cities, and communities."[3]

What developed in New Spain, then, was a mixing of Spanish urban concepts with what Spaniards *perceived* as greater and lesser indigenous municipalities. For example, they used the designation of "*ciudad*" (city) sparingly. Obviously, Tenochtitlan received it, and in the sixteenth century so did Tacuba, Texcoco, and Xochilmilco. Second in importance were groupings of people in "*villas*," which included only Coyoacan and Tacubaya in the Valley of Mexico. All other places in the valley, regardless of size, fell into the category of "*pueblo*" (town). But of greater importance in understanding the true worth of Isabel's *encomienda* are "*cabeza*" or "*cabecera*" and "*sujeto*."[4]

"*Cabeza*" was the preferred term in Spain to designate the capital, or head town, of a district. The most important *cabezas* were also *ciudades*, and within their regions often included one or more *villas*. But *villas* could likewise be the *cabeza* of one or more *pueblos*. Ranked at the bottom of Spanish urban entities were tiny clusters of people in places called "*aldeas*" and "*lugares*."[5]

In New Spain, however, Spaniards used the term "*cabecera*" for the most important municipality of a region; its subject communities carried the designation of *sujetos*. Because of the *cabecera*'s size, contiguous subdivisions within it were called *barrios*, or districts. Noncontiguous and smaller Indian dwellings were known as "*estancias*," rather than by the Spanish "*aldeas*" or "*lugares*."[6]

Since the imperial Aztecs demanded tribute from their subject provinces, great wealth flowed into Tenochtitlan on a regular basis. Some fifty collectors (*calpixque*) operated in the Central Valley alone. As long as Moctezuma II was alive, this system continued to operate, much to the benefit of Fernando Cortés while he held the emperor captive. Native picture manuscripts, the most important being the "Matrícula de tributos," spell out this manner of tribute collection in brilliant detail. Naturally, disruption caused by the conquest and destruction of Tenochtitlan put an end to the native pattern of centralized collection.[7] Replacing it was a decentralized system known to Spaniards as "*encomienda*," and it is clear that the assignment of these grants reflected intelligence gathered in part from the "Matrícula." Cortés reserved the most lucrative towns for himself, his favored partisans, and Moctezuma's daughters.[8]

Isabel Moctezuma received tribute from 120 households (tributary

units) in Tacuba proper. The remainder of her 1,120 households were situated in satellite groupings of people. Typically, tribute assessments were
due every eighty days or quarterly, and in the later years of the sixteenth
century the customary assessment was one silver peso and one-half *fanega*
(about eight-tenths of a bushel) of corn for each unit.[9] Because natives
and, indeed, many Spaniards did not operate in an economy based on
money, tribute was most commonly paid in kind. Items included a variety of foods, such as turkeys, chickens, quail, eggs, fish, fruit, cacao beans,
chile peppers, *elotes* (ears of green corn), and tortillas. Nonfood items
were often blankets, firewood, gold, and silver.[10] Teocalhueyacan was an
original *sujeto* of Tacuba, but Cortés awarded it and its *estancias* to Alonso
de Estrada and his wife. It remained a separate *cabecera*, despite protests
from Isabel and Juan Cano and the Indians of Tacuba.[11]

Ample evidence makes it clear that "the early demands made by
Cortés and the encomendero class, as well as by royal officers and members of the first audiencia, strained to full the native capacity to pay." The
classic case involves levies exacted on the Indian communities of Huejotzingo and others by President Nuño de Guzmán and two *oidores* of the
first Audiencia of New Spain.[12]

After serving approximately a year and half as resident governor of
Pánuco (May 1527–December 1528), Guzmán left the province to assume
his new office in Mexico City. There he joined *oidores* Diego Delgadillo
and Juan Ortiz de Matienzo, who had survived the rigors of a trip across
the Atlantic Ocean that claimed the lives of two fellow appointees shortly
after they reached New Spain. Significantly, Guzmán retained the governorship of Pánuco while heading the new governmental agency in the
capital.[13]

The rule—perhaps "misrule" is a better term—of the first Audiencia is
arguably the most dismal period in sixteenth-century New Spain. Among
its responsibilities, the Audiencia was to conduct the lengthy *residencia* of
Cortés, then absent in Spain. But the conduct of Guzmán and the two
judges was truly scandalous. They revoked *encomiendas* granted by the conqueror, including that of Isabel Moctezuma; accelerated the enslavement
of Indians; and engaged in unseemly quarrels with Franciscan padres,
especially Bishop Juan de Zumárraga, who held the title "Protector of
Indians." Aside from their misconduct in office, Delgadillo and Matienzo
kept a large number of harems of Indian women for their sexual pleasure,
which naturally drew the heated condemnation of the clergy.

Underlying their shameful conduct was Delgadillo and Matienzo's knowledge that the first Audiencia was a temporary agency, and that a new Audiencia would soon arrive to replace it. Accordingly, the *oidores* operated as though tomorrow might not find them in office. Guzmán was especially frustrated by the meager resources he found in Pánuco and was anxious to prove his mettle as a successful conquistador. In the summer of 1529, he began plans for a new campaign west and northwest of Mexico City. Not least in his thinking was his intent to be absent from the capital during impending *residencia* proceedings against the first Audiencia.

Guzmán's venture required some six months of preparation. In all, it included three hundred to four hundred Spaniards and five thousand to eight thousand Indian auxiliaries. To equip his soldiers and native allies, Guzmán levied exorbitant tribute on Indian towns such as Huejotzingo, which had to supply warriors' equipment and other items.[14] A few days before Christmas 1529, Guzmán departed Mexico City with one of the largest and best-equipped expeditions ever assembled in New Spain.

In that same year and again the following year, the judges of the first Audiencia collected tribute items from Huejotzingo that seem beyond avarice. These included a total of 8,400 turkeys, 7,200 quail, 58,400 eggs, and 7,160 loads of corn. And this assessment did not include food items for the *calpixqui* (tribute collector). That extortion is typified by payments of 1,170 turkeys, 23,200 eggs, 300,000 tortillas, and 53,500 cacao beans. Still additional demands were made on an *estancia* for the collector and his interpreter, Antonio Velázquez.[15]

It appears that Isabel Moctezuma lost the revenues of Tacuba for the better part of a year. When Delgadillo and Matienzo finally faced *residencia* proceedings at the hands of the second Audiencia of New Spain, among the witnesses who testified against them was none other than the Señora de Tacuba.[16] At the conclusion of their *residencia*, the two *oidores* were found guilty of multiple offenses and returned to Spain, where they died in prison.

In the meantime, Fernando Cortés had fared exceedingly well in Spain, and therein lay the path of redemption for the dispossessed Aztec princess. It will be remembered that the conqueror, seeking vindication for his services to Charles V, left Vera Cruz for Spain in March 1528. Accompanying him were selected veterans of the conquest, as well as a number of prominent Indian nobles of New Spain. The conqueror also brought visible proof of New World riches, such as gold, silver, precious gems, and items of Indian manufacture.[17]

From the south of Spain, the conqueror traveled to Toledo for an audience with Charles V, the twenty-eight-year-old Holy Roman Emperor. Bernal Díaz in his classic account of the conquest of New Spain often credits Cortés with the ability to speak in "honeyed words," and the conqueror's powers of oratory were about to serve him well. Cortés's face-to-face meeting with the most powerful monarch in western Europe took place before his *residencia* in New Spain had even begun. But he was far from awed by circumstances. He spoke at length and forcefully about his signal accomplishments in the New World, and he backed the worth of his deeds with evidence—beautiful feather mosaics, native treasures, and native nobles themselves.[18]

Although Cortés did not immediately receive honors, they were forthcoming the following year. On July 6, 1529, he received twenty-two *encomienda* towns, mostly in the Oaxaca Valley of southern New Spain, and the services of Indian vassals not to exceed twenty-three thousand in number. Like the earlier grants that Cortés had made to Isabel and Mariana Moctezuma, Charles awarded these towns to the conqueror and his successors in perpetuity.[19] This concession alone, which in due time came to encompass approximately fifty thousand vassals, secured Cortés's place among Spain's *ricos hombres* (wealthy men). Although he would later expend significant sums of money on a flurry of lawsuits in New Spain and fruitless Pacific Coast explorations, his last will and testament provided generous bequests to both legitimate and illegitimate heirs.

On July 6 Charles V also granted the title of Marqués del Valle de Oaxaca to Fernando Cortés. Out of consideration for his leadership, especially in the discovery and conquest of New Spain, and for his loyal service to God and the crown, Cortés and his descendants entered the Spanish peerage. Over time, the name Cortés gave way to that of Marqués del Valle.[20] The emperor, however, did not restore the title of governor, a bitter disappointment for the conqueror. He had won that honor in 1523 but lost it with the arrival of Ponce de León as his *residencia* judge in 1526. By 1529 the first Audiencia had been in place for about a year, soon to be followed by the second.

Cortés, armed with the new title of Marqués del Valle de Oaxaca and the potential riches it entailed, returned to Vera Cruz on July 15, 1530. His dispossessed and oppressed partisans, who had suffered under the tyranny of the first Audiencia, hailed him as a savior, much as they had four years earlier on his return from Honduras. But the conqueror could do little other than await the arrival of the judges of the second Audiencia and their assumption of power in Mexico City.[21]

Cortés mistakenly believed that the four *oidores* would arrive in New Spain about the same time as he did. When he left Spain, he knew of their forthcoming selection, but the actual appointments did not come until three days before he reached Vera Cruz. Chosen on July 12 were Juan de Salmerón, Alonso Maldonado, Francisco de Ceynos, and Vasco de Quiroga. The newly chosen president of the second Audiencia, Bishop Sebastián Ramírez de Fuenleal, was then in Santo Domingo.[22]

The four judges sailed from Spain on September 16, 1530, but delays kept them from assuming their office in Mexico City until January 12, 1531. At that time, they were able to restore the *encomienda* of Isabel Moctezuma, because Charles V, prior to leaving Spain in 1529 to confront Turkish forces advancing on his empire along the Danube River, had confirmed the conqueror's grants of perpetual *encomienda* to Isabel and Mariana Moctezuma. During Charles's absence from Spain, his wife, the Empress Isabel of Portugal, handled affairs of state. On June 9, 1530, she ordered the restoration of Tacuba to Isabel and her husband.[23] The restored revenues from Tacuba and its *sujetos* gave Isabel Moctezuma a comfortable income, but she would soon, through a series of petitions, beseech the crown for an expanded inheritance.

In postconquest New Spain, Isabel Moctezuma enjoyed the highest status accorded an indigenous woman. Nevertheless, the sudden uprooting from her family, her culture, and her patrimony in 1521, as well as permanent separation from Cuauhtemoc by 1524, subjected her to what Serge Gruzinski has called "the lasting shock wave of conquest." Doña Isabel, of course, fared much better than Indian women of lesser birth, but her position as an Aztec princess also meant people held higher expectations of her. To adapt and survive in the "totally unprecedented context" of a dominant European society, it was necessary for her to undergo rapid Hispanization and learn from the Spanish consorts who were thrust upon her.[24]

Tacuba and its *sujetos* (as enumerated by Cortés) had accompanied doña Isabel through her three marriages to Spaniards. Her child by Gallego, Juan de Andrade (Gallego) Moctezuma, was her eldest son, and he became part of the Cano household. Over the next several years he was joined by five half-siblings: Pedro Cano de Moctezuma, Gonzalo Cano de Moctezuma, Juan Cano de Moctezuma, Isabel Cano, and Catalina Cano. Isabel Moctezuma's sons by Cano, listed here from eldest to youngest, would all marry and have children, as did Juan de Andrade Moctezuma. Both daughters, however, became nuns. The lives of these six children, as well as that of Isabel's illegitimate daughter, Leonor Cortés Moctezuma, will be detailed later.[25]

Unfortunately, we know little about the life of Isabel Moctezuma, which ended in late 1550, when she was about forty-one years of age. As the wife of Juan Cano and *encomendera* of Tacuba, Isabel Moctezuma demonstrated her conversion to Christianity by giving generously to charitable causes in the 1530s and the 1540s. While other wealthy Indians provided money to build the impressive Capilla de San José, attached to the Franciscan monastery in Mexico City, she gave *limosnas* (alms) to the Augustinian order. Incredibly, she "gave so prodigally in the post-conquest period that the Augustinian beneficiaries felt obliged to ask her to desist."[26]

Throughout the rest of her life, many Spaniards viewed Isabel Moctezuma as the single most important example of *mestizaje* (mixing of Spanish and Indian ancestry). Cortés was especially intent upon having her serve in this capacity. Her marrying within the laws of the Catholic Church would likely set an example that would be followed by hundreds of Indian women anxious to emulate the daughter of the great Aztec emperor. In this manner, Indian women would be exposed to the customs and mores of European society, and therein lay the surest path to *mestizaje* in New Spain. Above all, Cortés wanted doña Isabel to become a model of Christian marriage and demonstrate the important difference between base passion, as exemplified by the actions of Delgadillo and Matienzo, and marital ties.[27] But in truth, the exploitation of Indian women by the *oidores* of the first Audiencia differed only in degree and the prominence of their office from that by many other Spanish conquistadors and settlers in New Spain.

It is well to remember that Spaniards did not intend to exterminate the Indians of the Americas or completely dispossess them of their lands. Rather, the goal was to bring them under the control of orderly Spanish government and inculcate the economic, religious, and cultural orientation of Spain itself.[28] Needless to say, that goal was far from met with the fall of Tenochtitlan in 1521. Indian insurrections outside the Central Valley and problems with Indian cultures, both sedentary and nonsedentary, on the northern frontier of New Spain delayed assimilation for centuries.

Starting with first contact in 1492, a variety of factors furthered the mixture of Spanish and Indian blood ties. Spanish men almost exclusively made up the early expeditions that crossed the Atlantic. This was entirely reasonable, because Spaniards viewed unexplored regions in distant lands as too dangerous to allow the emigration of women and children. Accordingly, the scarcity if not total absence of European women meant

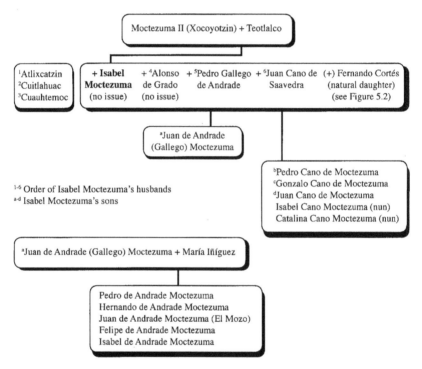

Dr. Alejandro González Acosta, mentioned in the Introduction, identifies María del Carmen Enríquez de Luna y del Mazo of Granada, Spain, as the current Countess of Miravalle and 15th in the line of descendants from Isabel Moctezuma.

For family claimants to mercedes in the seventeenth century, see Chapter 6, note 16.

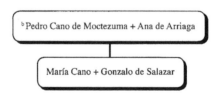

Figure 3.1. (This page and next) *Genealogy of Isabel Moctezuma (Tecuichpotzin). (Center for Media Production, University of North Texas.)*

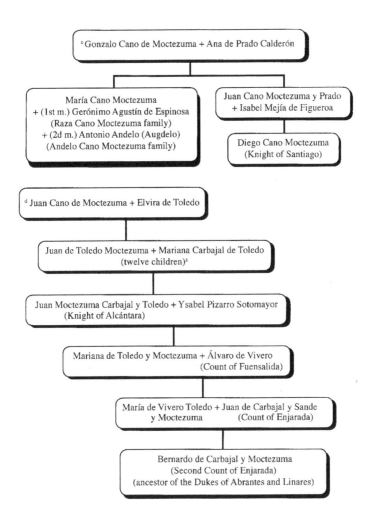

[c] Gonzalo Cano de Moctezuma + Ana de Prado Calderón

María Cano Moctezuma
+ (1st m.) Gerónimo Agustín de Espinosa
(Raza Cano Moctezuma family)
+ (2d m.) Antonio Andelo (Augdelo)
(Andelo Cano Moctezuma family)

Juan Cano Moctezuma y Prado
+ Isabel Mejía de Figueroa

Diego Cano Moctezuma
(Knight of Santiago)

[d] Juan Cano de Moctezuma + Elvira de Toledo

Juan de Toledo Moctezuma + Mariana Carbajal de Toledo
(twelve children)[z]

Juan Moctezuma Carbajal y Toledo + Ysabel Pizarro Sotomayor
(Knight of Alcántara)

Mariana de Toledo y Moctezuma + Álvaro de Vivero
(Count of Fuensalida)

María de Vivero Toledo + Juan de Carbajal y Sande
y Moctezuma   (Count of Enjarada)

Bernardo de Carbajal y Moctezuma
(Second Count of Enjarada)
(ancestor of the Dukes of Abrantes and Linares)

[z] For names of the other children, few of whom had heirs, see AGI, México 764, Tabla VII.

a "natural and explainable" biological phenomenon that produced "el mestizaje."[29] This was especially true for Spaniards, because they did not share the aversion to pagan and nonvirgin women that would characterize the attitudes of early English settlers at Jamestown. As Martin H. Quitt has remarked in a brilliant article, "Like the Indians, the English were ethnocentric; unlike them, they were deeply xenophobic. English leaders wanted to convert the Indians to Christianity, but they did not intend spiritual equality to bring social intimacy." Quitt further points out that "the settlers' standard of sexual morality made marriage out of the question. Englishmen preferred to marry virgins."[30]

In contrast, Spanish conquistadors and settlers in the Indies were not inhibited by such moral or social restraints, and most of them saw Indian women as desirable sexual partners. They, as one historian has remarked, "felt the physical appearance of Indians, in certain respects, to be heterogeneous, but for the most part not esthetically repugnant. In general, their stature and appearance, such as their countenances, made an agreeable impression on the Europeans." Christopher Columbus had underscored that sentiment by remarking on the physical attractiveness of Indian men and women, with their handsome faces and beautiful, large eyes.[31]

Spaniards also embraced Catholicism, an inclusive and convert-seeking religion that was and is mostly color-blind. They likewise had more familiarity with darker-skinned peoples, given their Iberian experience with Muslims and Africans. This is not to suggest, however, that getting to know someone better invariably leads to more tolerance. Rather, the ravishing of Muslim women by Spanish soldiers during the Reconquest was often reprised, depending on circumstances, with Indian women in New Spain.

Not all Spanish captains demanded the same discipline of their followers. For example, Cortés severely reprimanded those who robbed peaceful Indians of their goods or seized their women. This included his close friend and valued lieutenant Pedro de Alvarado, who committed such transgressions on the island of Cozumel. On the other hand, Spanish soldiers under the command of Francisco de Garay in Pánuco ran amok, collecting women in groups of fifteen or twenty. In the words of Bernal Díaz, "They went about robbing towns, seizing women by force, stealing blankets and turkeys as though they were in the lands of Moors, taking everything they found."[32]

Under more orderly and legalistic circumstances, no small number of Indian women and young females fell under the control of Spanish conquistadors in New Spain. Indians who accepted Spain's "right" to rule them under terms of the Requirement (1512) were protected by law as free vassals, but those who resisted a "just war of conquest" or remained bellicose, including noncombatant women and children, could be imprisoned and enslaved. Following La Noche Triste (June 30–July 1, 1520), Cortés ordered that all Indians who had pledged obedience to the king but had subsequently joined the Aztecs in rebellion or had been guilty of killing Spaniards be enslaved. Specifically, he charged natives with killing more than 860 Spaniards and Indian allies, as well as sixty horses.[33]

In short, there were ample means, including the vehicle of slavery, for Spaniards to acquire Indian women as sexual consorts. Moctezuma himself had offered Cortés the daughters of prominent *caciques* as appropriate to the retinue of a great captain. And if observers elsewhere in the Indies accurately describe the situation in New Spain, then no Christian there was content with four Indian women if he could have eight, and those with eight were not as satisfied as those with sixteen, and so on. "Indeed, it was a poor man who had fewer than five or six women, while the majority of those [in better circumstances] had fifteen to twenty to thirty to forty." The only limitations were the conscience of the community and the collective sentiments of Spaniards, or concern over igniting the disapproval and resistance of other natives.[34]

There is no question that Juan Cano saw Isabel Moctezuma as the finest role model of desirable *mestizaje*. As mentioned earlier, while passing through Española on his way from Spain to Mexico, Cano agreed to an interview with Fernández de Oviedo. In their exchange, he commented on his wife: "Although born in our Spain [Mexico], there is no person who is better educated or indoctrinated in the Faith. . . . And it is no small benefit to or advantage of the tranquillity and contentment of the natives of this land, because she is the gentlewoman of all things and a friend of Christians, and because of respect and her example, quiet and repose are implanted in the souls of the Mexicans."[35]

By this juncture, about twelve years after Cano's marriage to Isabel Moctezuma, the couple had tried with limited success to increase the value of the Tacuba inheritance. Indeed, Cano had spent more than two years in Spain (1542–1544), during which time he not only visited relatives and looked after properties in Cáceres but he also made personal entreaties at court. Central to his and Isabel's petitions was their contention that Tacuba in the pre-Spanish period had held more *sujetos* than those specified in Cortés's grant of 1526. Evidence clearly supports that assertion. Cortés himself acknowledged as much when he later admitted that additional Tacuba *sujetos* were then claimed by other *encomenderos*. The conqueror stated that he had refrained from awarding these *pueblos* to the Aztec princess, pending the king's decision about who the rightful owners were.[36]

Trying to identify these disputed *pueblos* is an exasperating task for a modern researcher. Not the least of the problem lies in variant spellings and changes in orthography made by copyists. In some cases the names of small municipalities in the postconquest era changed completely over a relatively short period of time. The *pueblos* specifically mentioned by Cortés and included as *sujetos* of Tacuba are Yetepec, Huizquilucan, Chimalpan, Chapulmaloyan, Azcapotzaltongo, Xilotzingo, Ocoyoacac, Catepec, Telasco, Guatuzco, Coatepec, and Tlazala. Despite Ocoyoacac's inclusion in the Cortés grant of *encomienda*, Isabel did not receive it when the crown restored Tacuba to her, and it would take seven years of litigation to regain it.[37]

Although Isabel Moctezuma did not significantly increase the scope of her Tacuba inheritance during the 1530s and the 1540s, she slowly acquired appurtenances more befitting a Hispanicized Aztec princess. By her own admission, when she married Cano she had no material possessions. She lacked a single piece of furniture and had no jewels, nor did she have any money. All she brought into her marriage were "Indians and pueblos," meaning tributary units. As for Cano, Isabel claimed that when they wed he owned a number of cattle and a sum of money, but she did not know the exact amount of either at the time she executed her will.[38]

With dependable income from Tacuba and its *sujetos*, however, as well as contributions from Cano's independent holdings, by 1550 Isabel Moctezuma had accumulated a sizable estate. Her improved status after twenty years of marriage to Juan Cano is evident in her will. She and her husband jointly owned an unspecified number of male and female Indians as slaves; all were to be set free at her death. Indicative of her thorough conversion to Catholicism, the Aztec princess ordered that the first one-fifth of her entire estate be set aside and used by her executors to pay for masses and contributions to pious works in behalf of her soul. She likewise commanded the three executors to liquidate all her outstanding debts, such as the unpaid salaries of servants and other matters relating to the discharge of her conscience.[39]

Because Isabel Moctezuma left no written comments during her forty-plus years of life, we can only speculate about her personality. Having spent the first decade of her life in the royal household, followed by marriages to Atlixcatzin, Cuitlahuac, and Cuauhtemoc, it would seem that Isabel possessed many, if not all, of the qualities of a good Aztec noblewomen, as recorded by Sahagún: she was "revered, esteemed, respected . . . a protector—one who loves, who guards people. . . . The good noblewoman is venerable, respectable, illustrious, famed . . . one who belittles no one, who treats others with tenderness."[40]

The material possessions that Isabel enumerates in her will help flesh out more of her personality and lend insight into her acceptance of Hispanization. The order in which Isabel lists those items is likewise revealing. Her most prized possession was fine jewelry. Unfortunately, she says nothing specific about it other than that it existed in some quantity. She next speaks of her bed accessories, of both local and Castilian manufacture. She had acquired tapestries and rugs, as well as cushions, embossed leathers, and pillows. The last things enumerated are hand cloths, handmade crafts, and personal clothing. The dying woman specifically requested that these personal items be given to her daughters, and she expressed her strong intent that none be sold at public auction. Apart from these enumerated possessions, Juan Cano could sell all other pieces of property, but one-third of the proceeds must also go to her daughters.[41]

The exact ages of the daughters in 1550 is unknown, but they were likely in their early to mid-teens. By then, both had no doubt demonstrated a preference for a religious rather than a secular calling. Their compassionate mother realized that she should specifically provide for her daughters' future, because entry into a desirable convent would require a substantial fee. In this regard, Isabel Moctezuma fulfilled a central role of women in New Spain by transmitting the essence of religion to her children. She also aided the Catholic Church in its mission by making religion an integral part of her maternal responsibilities.[42]

More important to the financial well-being of her sons was the manner in which Isabel Moctezuma disposed of her *encomienda* holdings. This was destined to become a thorny legal thicket fraught with irreparably broken family relationships and seemingly endless lawsuits that pitted family against the crown, father against son, brother against brother, and niece against uncle. The bitter litigation spanned two continents and several decades, in large part because Tacuba and its *sujetos* were a prize worth having. As mentioned earlier, Tacuba was a perpetual holding. Accordingly, it fell outside the restrictive laws that curtailed privately held *encomiendas* in the sixteenth century. By 1550, when Isabel Moctezuma executed her will, Tacuba had advanced from the ninth-largest *encomienda* in the Valley of Mexico to the largest. The eight larger *encomiendas* awarded to Spanish *encomenderos* had escheated to the crown.[43]

Isabel Moctezuma considered her eldest son, born during her brief marriage to Pedro Gallego de Andrade, her principal heir. One can only speculate that this created considerable tension within the Cano household as Juan de Andrade (Gallego) Moctezuma grew up among three half-brothers, two half-sisters, and a stepfather. Despite what must have been determined opposition from his stepfather, Andrade received the lion's share of the Tacuba inheritance.[44] He and his successors received in perpetuity Tacuba proper and all of its *sujetos* save four. The excluded towns, along with their subject communities, were Ocoyoacac, Chapulmaloyan, Coatepec, and Tepexoyuca. As mentioned, Cortés included the first of these four municipalities in his grant of 1526, but it was soon divested from Tacuba and reassigned to Antonio de Villagómez—most likely by the *oidores* of the first Audiencia.[45] Its complete recovery by Isabel Moctezuma in 1540 represents a successful petition to restore this original *sujeto* to its rightful *encomendera*, but this had not been easy.

Villagómez died around 1533, and at that time both Juan Cano and the *fiscal* (legal expert and prosecutor), Antonio Ruiz de Medina, claimed Ocoyoacac. The *fiscal* seized the *sujeto* for the crown, and Isabel's husband filed suit against him. Initial victory, as well as subsequent judgments, went to Cano. The viceroy and Audiencia of New Spain awarded the disputed town to him on October 27, 1536. The *fiscal* then asked the same body to review the case, which it agreed to do. Not surprisingly, on March 24, 1537, the Audiencia upheld its original decision. Twice rebuffed, Ruiz sent the case on appeal to the Royal Council of the Indies, which received it on June 20, 1538. The *fiscal's* main contention was that Ocoyoacac was not a part of the perpetual grant made by Cortés in 1526. Had it been so regarded, it could not have gone to Villagómez. Nevertheless, on November 23, 1540, the council endorsed the decision of the viceroy and Audiencia of New Spain. Juan Cano and Isabel Moctezuma received clear rights to the disputed *sujeto* and a judgment of fifteen hundred *doblas* in damages for lost revenue.[46] But doubts had been raised about the status of Ocoyoacac as a perpetual grant, and Isabel was at pains not to include it in the bequest to Juan de Andrade.

The aforementioned excluded *pueblos*, likewise granted in perpetuity, went to Gonzalo Cano and his heirs. As a final proviso, Isabel Moctezuma considered the possibility that both Juan de Andrade and Gonzalo Cano might die without legitimate heirs, in which case their inheritances would pass to her and Juan Cano's eldest son, Pedro.[47]

As a final bequest, Isabel Moctezuma ordered the executors of her

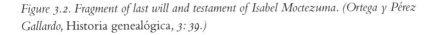

TESTAMENTO DE LA PRINCESA DOÑA ISABEL MOCTEZUMA,
HECHO EN 10 DE DICIEMBRE DE 1550.

En nombre de la Santísima Trinidad, Padre, Hijo y Espíritu Santo, tres personas y un solo Dios verdadero, que vive y reina por
siempre sin fin, y loor y gloria y alabanza de Nuestra Señora la Vir-
gen María, á quien tengo por mi Señora y abogada. Por ende sepan
cuantos esta carta de poder vieren, como yo, Doña Isabel de Moctezuma, mujer legítima que soy de Don Juan Cano, mi Señor y marido, vecino de esta gran Ciudad de Tenoxtitlán, México de esta Nueva España; estando enferma del cuerpo, del mal y enfermedad que
Dios Nuestro Señor ha sido servido de me dar, y en mi buen seso y
juicio y entendimiento natural, con licencia y facultad y expreso con-
sentimiento que demando al dicho Juan Cano, mi Señor y marido
que presente está, si de derecho conviene y es necesario, que para
que por mí misma pueda hacer y otorgar esta escritura de poder, según que en ella será contenido; y yo el dicho Juan Cano, que soy
presente, otorgo y conozco que doy y concedo la dicha licencia y facultad á vos la dicha Doña Isabel mi mujer, según que por vos me

Figure 3.2. Fragment of last will and testament of Isabel Moctezuma. (Ortega y Pérez Gallardo, Historia genealógica, *3: 39.)*

will to acknowledge that she had six legitimate heirs—Pedro Cano, Gonzalo Cano, Juan Cano, Isabel Cano, and Catalina Cano, as well as Juan de
Andrade. Aside from the one-third of revenues from the sale of her
unspecified property at public auction, which, as noted, Isabel reserved
for her two daughters, the remaining two-thirds was to be divided
equally among all her heirs. She insisted that her wishes in this regard be
honored so that none of her children would be shamed by poverty. She
concluded the specific provisions of her will by imploring the king of
Spain to confirm and approve the disposition of her estate as proper
remuneration for what was due her as the legitimate daughter and heir of
Moctezuma II. She further pointed out that the king's acceptance of her
request was proper recompense for what was due her father as a natural
monarch.[48]

Although not specified as a formal codicil, a supplement to Isabel
Moctezuma's will was added immediately after her death. Diego de Isla,
the royal scribe who penned the testament, noted that in conformity
with the departed's last wishes, overheard by her three executors, Juan
Cano was reimbursed six hundred *pesos de oro común* for burial expenses

and the cost of masses said for the soul of his deceased wife. Of those monies not yet distributed from the original one-fifth set aside to settle this aspect of Isabel Moctezuma's estate, one-fifth was to be paid to Leonor Cortés Moctezuma, the illegitimate daughter of the Aztec princess and Fernando Cortés. This may well have served as additional dowry for the pending marriage of doña Leonor to Juan de Tolosa, the discoverer of rich silver mines at Zacatecas.[49]

* * *

Because doñas Isabel and Catalina chose the veil over marriage and children, they figure only tangentially in the legal disputes over inheritance that embroiled their father and brothers. In 1540 Bishop Juan de Zumárraga founded the first nunnery in New Spain and the Americas—El Convento de la Concepción de la Madre de Dios. Originally set up "for the purpose of teaching Indian women," La Concepción never filled that role in its three-hundred-year history. Instead, like other convents, it became a center of spirituality that "emphasized seclusion and the salvation of the soul."[50]

Aspirants wishing to enter this religious house were to be older than thirteen years but not of an "advanced age." Initially, all novitiates had to be legitimate *peninsulares* (i.e., born in Spain) or *criollas* (born in the New World) in good health, be able to read and write and handle numbers, perform women's tasks, and contribute a dowry of four thousand pesos. Those who could not meet the literacy qualification could receive an entrance dispensation; however, they must wear the white veil of the novitiate rather than the black worn by fully qualified nuns. By 1553 doñas Isabel and Catalina were *monjas profesas* (professing nuns) in this convent. Since both were *mestizas*, acceptance into this prestigious nunnery indicates their favored status as granddaughters of Moctezuma II and daughters of the Señora de Tacuba.[51]

Having obtained the necessary entry fees into La Concepción from their parents, Isabel and Catalina would spend the rest of their lives in the serene atmosphere of conventual pursuits. In this respect, they must have felt grateful for being spared the legal maelstrom that engulfed their brothers and father.

For those who have experienced the bitterness and broken family ties that often come in the wake of disputed inheritances and contested wills, the aftermath of Isabel Moctezuma's death will come as no surprise. As Charles Gibson has observed, "of all the *encomiendas* of the Valley of Mexico, Tacuba has the most intricate history." Because of the lawsuits that swirled around this *encomienda*, truer words have seldom been penned. In looking at the complexities of legal maneuvers related to Tacuba, one is also reminded of Gibson's brilliant insight that Spanish American law served more as a commentary on events than a shaping of them.[52]

Except for a period of about one year, when judges of the first Audiencia took Tacuba from Isabel Moctezuma, it remained with her through three Christian marriages. Isabel's second Spanish husband, Pedro Gallego, claimed Tacuba for a brief time; Juan Cano claimed it for just less than twenty years. Despite the assertions of *encomienda* ownership by Isabel's husbands, however, it is clear that she was always the legal possessor of Tacuba, and that disposition of it lay entirely within her rights. But as doña Isabel approached the end of her life and the necessity of executing her last testament, she was undoubtedly pressured by Juan Cano to make bequests that he felt more equitably rewarded his biological sons.[53] That she did not do so reflects her independence and her rights as a woman within both the Nahua and the Castilian legal systems.

As Susan Kellogg notes, Mexica men and women in the early colonial period "held roughly equivalent inheritance rights in three distinct categories of property: houses, land, and movable items." Furthermore, these rights do not appear to have derived solely from Spanish laws that gave women the right to hold property in their own name.[54] Rather, in the late pre-Spanish era, Mexica women's "access to property—whether gained through dowry or inheritance—allowed them to function somewhat autonomously of their husbands. For example, the property that women brought into marriage was kept separate from that brought to the marriage by men." So there was a striking similarity between Castilian and Mexica laws regarding dotal and paraphernal property.[55] And there were no legal challenges to Isabel Moctezuma's rights as *encomendera* of Tacuba from either her husbands or her children during her lifetime.

During their marriage, Isabel Moctezuma and Juan Cano repeatedly used legal instruments to try to expand the Tacuba inheritance and protect what they possessed. In addition to the aforementioned lawsuits aimed at recovering all of Tacuba's *sujetos*, doña Isabel received a favorable judgment from the Empress Isabel in 1538. This suit involved an all-too-common complaint in sixteenth-century New Spain. Indians within the jurisdiction of the Tacuba *encomienda* had suffered much damage to their crops from livestock—specifically, turkeys, pigs, oxen, and horses—that strayed from nearby farms and milling operations owned by Spaniards. Among the owners responsible for this destruction were the Marqués del Valle de Oaxaca and others not identified by name. The empress sent orders to the president and judges of the second Audiencia of New Spain to settle these losses in the most convenient and just manner.[56]

At the time of Isabel Moctezuma's death, her Tacuba properties were initially awarded in strict accordance with her last testament.[57] Juan de Andrade (Gallego)Moctezuma received by far the largest portion of doña Isabel's holdings, but this did not satisfy him. He argued that *all* of the property, the *cabecera* and every one of its *sujetos*, belonged to him and to him alone. And the intrafamily lawsuits began.[58]

Andrade brought his suit before the Audiencia of New Spain in September 1551. Much of the testimony centered on his being a legitimate son of Isabel Moctezuma and Pedro Gallego de Andrade, and that Tacuba and its *sujetos* were held jointly by his parents. Andrade pointed out that when his father died he was a small child left in the care of his mother, who later married Juan Cano. During his youth, continued Andrade, the revenues from Tacuba went to his parents. Now, as an adult, he was married and had an income of only two thousand pesos per year. Since Juan Cano was one of the richest men in Spain, he did not need or deserve the revenues from Tacuba. The Audiencia of New Spain agreed with Andrade and ruled in his favor.[59]

Cano, not willing to accept the devastating judgment that denied inheritance to him and his three sons by Isabel Moctezuma, launched an immediate appeal. This resulted in a compromise that mandated a distribution of Tacuba in accordance with doña Isabel's will. That settlement, however, failed to satisfy either of the litigants, and both filed suits seeking to gain the entire *encomienda*. While that phase of the legal tangle was fought out in the courts, a third party stepped into the fray.[60]

It will be remembered that during the conquest of Mexico, Cortés allegedly agreed to look after the welfare of a second daughter of the Aztec emperor. Her given Christian name of Mariana is variously recorded as Marina, Mariana, or Leonor.[61] Like her half-sister Isabel, Mariana Moctezuma married more than once. Her first husband, whom she wed in 1527, was Juan Paz (or Páez),[62] who became the *encomendero* of Ecatepec. This important town formed Mariana's dowry, just as Tacuba served this purpose in Isabel's first marriage to Alonso de Grado. Like Grado, Paz died shortly after he was married, and the couple had no children. After a period of mourning, Mariana married Cristóbal de Valderrama and bore him a daughter, Leonor de Valderrama y Moctezuma. At maturity, doña Leonor married Diego Arias Sotelo. It was this Diego, the son-in-law of Mariana Moctezuma, who entered into the lawsuits over Tacuba.

Diego Sotelo, as he was commonly known, claimed that his mother-in-law was the true, legitimate heir of Moctezuma II. This entitled Mariana not only to Ecatepec but also to Tacuba. Sotelo's convoluted argument ran that Ecatepec had accompanied his mother-in-law throughout her two marriages, as indeed it had. Like Isabel Moctezuma's three husbands, Paz and Valderrama had claimed joint possession of the *encomienda* that came with marriage to an Aztec princess. According to Sotelo, had Tacuba been awarded to Mariana, as should have been the case back in 1527, then it would have devolved to him as the husband of Moctezuma's granddaughter. Suffice it to say that Diego Sotelo's claims to Tacuba were summarily rejected in court.[63]

Overall, however, there was nothing prompt about settling the dispute over Tacuba. Juan de Andrade's and Juan Cano's demands for Tacuba and its *sujetos* in totality were rejected by 1553. The compromise settlement mandated a six-part division of the *encomienda*—one-sixth going to each of Juan and Isabel Cano's children. But even this did not put an end to the legal battles. They continued for more than two decades. In May 1553, the daughters of Juan and Isabel Cano, then nuns in Mexico City, renounced their rights of inheritance to Tacuba. Isabel did so on May 2; her sister, Catalina, on May 4. Isabel stated that because she had entered religious life, she wished to bestow her one-sixth share of the *encomienda* on her father. She maintained that he had paid her entry fee into the convent of La Concepción, which helped support the prioress and nuns of that religious establishment. As recompense, Isabel wished to honor him and help sustain his house. Her share of Tacuba would also aid the marriages of her brothers. Two days later, Catalina also renounced her one-sixth share. That portion went to her brothers Pedro and Juan Cano and their heirs in equal parts.[64]

The eldest brother, Pedro Cano de Moctezuma, lived until the mid-1570s. His father's will named a brother (Pedro Cano) as executor of his estate but the chief beneficiary was son Pedro. When Juan Cano died in Seville in September 1572, Pedro for a brief time inherited the right to manage the family *mayorazgo* in Cáceres.[65] Pedro, however, did not live much longer than his father. With his death, Catalina's entire one-sixth passed to the surviving brother, Juan, who could dispose of it as his patrimony. To make her intent crystal clear, Catalina specified that her entire estate must remain in the family and with the descendants of Juan Cano, the elder, thereby excluding her half-brother, Juan de Andrade.[66] Accordingly, by the early 1570s, the *encomenderos* of Tacuba were Juan de Andrade and the two surviving sons of Isabel and Juan Cano.

As mentioned, Isabel Moctezuma expressed concern that Juan de Andrade and Gonzalo Cano might die without heirs. As it turned out, her fears proved groundless, because all four sons married and fathered offspring. Juan de Andrade married María de Iñíguez and the couple had five children (see Figure 3.1).[67] Pedro Cano, the eldest son of Isabel and Juan Cano, married Ana de Arriaga. The couple had only one daughter, María Cano, who married Gonzalo de Salazar. The next oldest son, Gonzalo Cano, married Ana de Prado Calderón.[68]

The third son of Isabel and Juan Cano, who carried his father's given name, was the most successful of all the male Canos. Relocating to Spain after the death of his mother, Juan Cano de Moctezuma married Elvira de Toledo in Cáceres on January 6, 1559. He would inherit the Cáceres *mayorazgo* after the death of his brother Pedro, and his progeny founded a great house that stands to this day in Cáceres.[69]

By the late 1570s, the only claimants to Tacuba were Gonzalo and Juan Cano de Moctezuma. Thus, Tacuba had gone from a six-part to a two-part inheritance. However, by this time, María Cano, the sole offspring of her deceased father (Pedro) and Ana de Arriaga, claimed the original one-sixth that was due her father. In addition, María petitioned for half of another one-sixth (one-twelfth) of the share renounced by Catalina. Gonzalo de Salazar, María's husband, filed a suit, primarily against Juan Cano de Moctezuma. But in an incredible exercise in litigiousness, Salazar insisted that his wife was also due one-third of one-sixth (one-eighteenth) of the part that Isabel left to her father.[70]

The original case resulted in a judgment that largely favored Juan Cano de Moctezuma. He received the entire one-sixth of Tacuba that had belonged to his brother Pedro. However, María Cano and her husband did not come away empty-handed. They received one-half of one-sixth (one-twelfth) from Catalina's donation, which had initially gone to Pedro, but got nothing from Catalina's sister's donation. Salazar and María Cano immediately appealed to the Audiencia of New Spain, which reversed the original court's decision, thereby divesting the couple of the one-twelfth portion and adjudicating it to Juan Cano de Moctezuma. The matter did not end there, however. The plaintiffs soon carried the case on appeal to the Council of the Indies.[71]

Attorney Sebastián de Santander represented Gonzalo de Salazar and María Cano. He asked that the decision by the Audiencia of New Spain be overturned and that the judgment of the court of first instance be upheld. Santander argued that Catalina's donation was to be divided equally between Juan and Pedro Cano, as well as among their heirs and successors. This was expressly stated in the renunciation. For the Audiencia to have ruled otherwise would have been a gross miscarriage of justice.[72]

Pedro de Castillo represented the interests of Juan Cano de Moctezuma before the council. He raised the argument that the donation and renunciation of Catalina's one-twelfth interest in Tacuba applied in the following manner: If one of the brothers died first, then the one-twelfth in his possession passed to the surviving brother—in this case, his client. Castillo maintained that only when Juan Cano de Moctezuma died could the inheritance be awarded to Pedro's successors.[73]

Both parties restated and submitted a flurry of arguments and briefs from February to November 1578. On November 22 the council handed down its final decision. It revoked the appellant judgment of the Audiencia and awarded Catalina Cano Moctezuma's one-twelfth portion to María Cano and Gonzalo de Salazar. Royal approval of this decision came on December 8, 1578.[74]

Some twenty-five years prior to the settlement of this litigation, Juan Cano de Moctezuma had followed his namesake father to Spain and settled into married life in Cáceres with Elvira de Toledo. With the beginning of his *mayorazgo* in Cáceres on February 22, 1577, this great-grandson of Moctezuma II and grandson of Isabel Moctezuma paved the way for his progeny, as children of the emperor, to achieve rank as counts and dukes. From Gonzalo, a brother of Juan Cano de Moctezuma who remained in New Spain, came the origins of the Cano Moctezuma, the Raza Cano Moctezuma, and the Andelo (Augdelo) Cano Moctezuma families.[75]

Not all descendants of Moctezuma II fared as well as Juan and Gonzalo Cano. As commonly happens when an estate is divided and subdivided over time, an individual share may become little more than a pittance, or, as happened to Pedro Cano's daughter, María, one could lose everything without the determination and resources to carry litigation across the Atlantic to the Council of the Indies, the highest court, in certain instances, regarding legal matters arising in the Spanish Indies. As a case in point for the first circumstance, by 1651 two members of the Andelo Cano Moctezuma family lived in Mexico City. Diego and Joseph were grandchildren of Gonzalo Cano and Ana de Prado Calderón. From their share of Tacuba and its *sujetos*, the brothers received only twenty pesos per year. They asked for a special stipend from the crown in recognition of their descent from *"los primeros conquistadores"* of New Spain, as well as from Moctezuma II. Diego and Joseph's request eventually brought a modest *merced* (grant) of fifty pesos. The same amount went to another brother. However, the crown made it clear that these grants were given to the three siblings as much, if not more, for their descent from former conquistadors Juan de Zaragosa and Miguel de Zaragosa as for their being distant relatives of the Aztec emperor.[76] Clearly, the value of claims of descent from Moctezuma II had decreased dramatically.

Beyond the intricacies of *encomienda* history, which thus far I have described in broad-brush treatment for only *one* of the three principal heirs of Moctezuma II, all descendants of the Aztec emperor sought additional and broader settlements with the Spanish crown. Their fundamental argument, eventually given some merit by Philip II in 1590, held that all concessions made to them by way of *encomienda* grants paled in comparison with their rightful patrimony as "natural lords" of New Spain and as descendants of the great Moctezuma II. That overall settlement with the children of the emperor and the rationale behind it will be detailed after looking at the *encomienda* grant made to doña Mariana and the inheritance of don Pedro.

Four

The Patrimony of Mariana and Pedro Moctezuma

S EVERAL OF MOCTEZUMA II'S DAUGHTERS—christened Isabel, Ana, María, and Mariana—were allegedly placed under the guardianship of Fernando Cortés by their father just prior to the Spaniard's chaotic retreat from Tenochtitlan on July 1, 1520. None of these young women reached Tacuba.[1] Ana lost her life on the western causeway, but the other three were reunited with their people. The fate of María Moctezuma is uncertain, although she evidently died between the fall of the Aztec capital on August 13, 1521, and the return of Cortés from the Honduran expedition in 1526. The conqueror refers to María's baptism, Christian naming, and acceptance of the Catholic faith after he regained the Aztec capital, but she does not figure into his grants of *encomienda* in the mid-1520s.[2]

On March 14, 1527, some nine months after Cortés granted Tacuba to Isabel Moctezuma, he bestowed Ecatepec on her half-sister Mariana.[3] Although not as rich as Tacuba, Ecatepec was nonetheless a prize worth having, especially since it was a perpetual grant. This important town occupied a strategic location on the western edge of the narrows that connected Lake Texcoco to Lake Xaltocan, and it had a long history in pre-Spanish Mexico (see Figure 1.5).

When the Tepenec War began (in 1427), Tenochtitlan and Tlatelolco were principal *tlatoque* sites. After the imperial Mexica defeated the Tepenecs, Ecatepec and Azcapotzalco were so designated as well. The first *tlatoani* of Ecatepec was Chimalpilli, a member of the ruling dynasty of Tenochtitlan. He assumed power in 1428, and subsequent *tlatoque* of

Ecatepec were related to the Aztec emperors: Tezozomoc, for example, was the son of Chimalpopoca; Matlaccohuatl was the father of Teotlalco, Moctezuma's principal wife and doña Isabel's mother.[4]

Given Ecatepec's worth and its long association with the Mexica rulers of Tenochtitlan, it is not surprising that Cortés gave special consideration to its status. He reinforced its rank as a *cabecera* by initially claiming it for himself and later awarding it to Mariana Moctezuma. Specifically mentioned as *sujetos* in the Cortés grant are Acalhuacan, Coatitlan, and Tizayuca (or Tecoyuca).[5]

Juan Paz, Mariana's first husband, was a conquistador. He had died by late August 1529, and about two years later, Mariana married Cristóbal de Valderrama. Don Cristóbal, also a conquistador, had served in Michoacán, Colima, and Zacatula.[6] Mariana and don Cristóbal had only one daughter, Leonor de Valderrama y Moctezuma.

Like her half-sister Isabel, Mariana Moctezuma claimed to be a principal daughter of the emperor, but evidence does not support her contention. Mariana's mother, Acatlan, was a favored consort of Moctezuma II, not a primary wife. Still, condition of birth was not a serious impediment to inheritance.[7]

Cristóbal de Valderrama lived for about six years after his marriage to Mariana. He died in November 1537, leaving his widow to care for their daughter. His executor was an hidalgo from Cáceres charged with being both guardian and tutor of young Leonor.[8] Mariana Moctezuma's daughter married Diego Arias Sotelo. However, don Diego's failed attempts in the early 1550s to secure the revenues from Tacuba for Leonor meant that the couple had to depend solely on tribute from Ecatepec and its *sujetos*. By then Mariana's Ecatepec inheritance had been substantially reduced by legal challenges.

Because Ecatepec was situated just north of Tenochtitlan, some of the *estancias* of the Aztec capital as well as those of Tlatelolco were near its *cabecera* jurisdiction. Cortés's inclusion of Acalhuacan, Coatitlan, and Tizayuca in the Ecatepec grant to Mariana drew immediate opposition from Indian officials of Tenochtitlan and Tlatelolco. They argued that those *estancias* should belong to Moctezuma's successors in office; that is, revenues from the disputed municipalities should go to the Indian *señores* (lords) and *principales* (members of the Indian upper class) of the two major cities.[9]

The Council of the Indies dealt with the claims of these native offi-

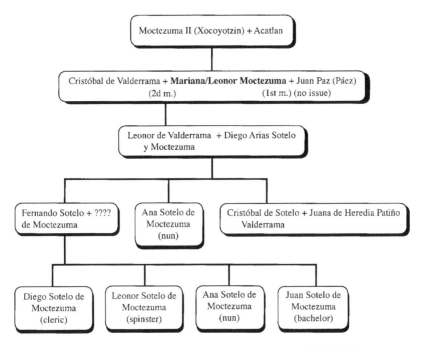

Figure 4.1. Genealogy of Mariana/Leonor Moctezuma. (Center for Media Production, University of North Texas.)

cials in a lawsuit that began in 1531 and lasted into the early 1560s. Tizayuca became a crown *encomienda* in 1531, thus eliminating it from the case. In 1553 Mariana Moctezuma's heirs scored a victory when the Audiencia of New Spain declared Acalhuacan to be a "true *sujeto*" of Ecatepec. The Indians of Tlatelolco immediately filed a formal protest, claiming that the town had traditionally paid tribute to Tlatelolco. The matter dragged on for the better part of a decade before the council finally denied the Indians' appeal in 1561.[10]

Other *estancias*, including Coatitlan, Tolpetlac, Ozumbilla, and Telalco, were also disputed possessions of Ecatepec and Tlatelolco. Cristóbal de Valderrama and Mariana Moctezuma contended that they were included in the 1527 grant, and they sought help from Cortés himself, who was then in New Spain. He did not help matters by testifying that he was uncertain about what he had granted and what he had not.[11]

Cortés's inability to define with precision his original grant prompted the Indians of Tlatelolco to adopt a different tack. They argued that the conqueror's failed memory was moot, because Ponce de León had arrived in New Spain in 1526 and removed him from power; thus by 1527 he had no legal standing. Ownership of the disputed *estancias* wound up before the Audiencia in 1536, which ruled in favor of don Cristóbal and doña Mariana. The high court in New Spain stated that these towns had belonged to Moctezuma; therefore it was appropriate to assign them to his daughter as her patrimony. But, of course, the matter did not end there. The Indians appealed to the Council of the Indies, which did not agree with the Audiencia's reasoning. The council in Spain ruled that the towns in question could not be inherited by Moctezuma's daughter, because they rightfully belonged to the Indians of Tlatelolco. The supreme court for the Indies further agreed with the plaintiffs by stating that Cortés lacked the king's authority to make such a grant, for such powers had expired with the arrival of Ponce de León.[12]

Rather than issue a firm order that divested these contested towns from Ecatepec, however, the council decided to leave the matter to the viceroy of New Spain, who had judicial authority in matters relating to Indians. In the final analysis, victory largely went to the upper-class natives of Tlatelolco. They were able to demand labor obligations from most of the *estancias*, but Ecatepec got to keep tribute payments from Coatitlan.[13]

In terms of its overall value in tributary units immediately after the Spanish conquest and the assignment of *encomiendas* in the Valley of Mexico, Ecatepec ranked eighteenth (Tacuba ranked ninth). Because it was a perpetual grant, it had become the ninth-most-valuable *encomienda* by the 1560s.[14] Thus, the Ecatepec-based descendants of Moctezuma II had fared reasonably well by this time, but this branch of the family failed to prosper in the long run.

When Mariana Moctezuma died, her son-in-law and her daughter succeeded her as second-life *encomenderos* of Ecatepec. Unfortunately, don Diego became a suspect in the Ávila-Cortés conspiracy that engulfed New Spain in the mid-1560s.[15]

In late August 1563, Visitor-General Jerónimo de Valderrama, a member of the Council of the Indies, reached Mexico City. Visitors-general were invariably vested with overarching authority that permitted them to look into all matters within a colony, and viceroys were expected to cooperate fully with them. Nevertheless, there was often a question about who had supreme authority at any given moment. Much to the irritation of Luis de Velasco, the second viceroy of New Spain, Valderrama was greeted with great pomp and celebration, which undermined relations between the two officials. And their lack of accord worsened over time. Slightly less than a year later, on July 31, 1564, Velasco died of an apparent heart attack. Then came unsettling news that the crown would not permit privately held *encomiendas* to extend beyond the life of the current holder, which made the political situation even more uncertain.[16]

Following Velasco's death, the *cabildo* of Mexico City passed a resolution and sent it to Philip II. The *regidores* (council members), most of whom were *encomenderos*, requested that the king not appoint another viceroy. Instead, high offices should go to the sons of the *primeros conquistadores* (first conquistadors). The *regidores* suggested that, for example, Martín Cortés, second Marqués del Valle de Oaxaca, be appointed captain general of New Spain.[17]

Members of the Audiencia initially failed to act decisively. Their irresolution emboldened several prominent sons of conquistadors, primary among them Alonso de Ávila and his brother, Gil González de Ávila. These *encomenderos* discussed among themselves the notion that Martín Cortés ought to assume even greater authority in the government of New Spain. Lacking, however, was any encouragement whatsoever from the second *marqués*, who possessed his father's strong sense of loyalty to the crown and stood to lose far too much by encouraging what he regarded as nothing more than "loose talk."[18]

The malcontents continued to grumble, hoping that young Cortés might grow more sympathetic to their cause. At one point, he urged the hotheads to await the arrival of the new viceroy, because Philip II had summarily rejected the *cabildo*'s request that his rights of appointment to the office end. Don Martín reasoned that should the king's choice as viceroy be ordered to claim for the crown all *encomiendas* at the death of the current holder, then the *encomenderos* could reassess their course of action.

Word then arrived from Spain that the Council of the Indies would not agree to the continuance of *encomienda* by extending the status of existing grants.[19] As the rhetoric of discontent swelled, and the Audiencia of New Spain formulated a plan.

First, the judges arrested Martín Cortés, charged him with treason, and later sequestered his estate.[20] They also apprehended the Ávila brothers and confined them in a common jail. Soon afterward, the judges incarcerated two other sons of Fernando Cortés, as well as *encomenderos* who had been activists, and still others who had sympathized with them. Among the activists arrested was Baltasar de Sotelo, the older brother of Diego Arias Sotelo.

Baltasar de Sotelo had served in Peru, where at one time he was associated with one of a number of postconquest rebellions. Crown authorities later exonerated him of complicity in the Cuzco revolt (1554) of Francisco Hernández Girón, who was beheaded for treason, however. After moving to New Spain, most likely in the late 1550s, Sotelo became a close associate and business partner of his younger brother, Diego Arias, the *encomendero* of Ecatepec.[21]

As the holder of a perpetual *encomienda*, Diego Arias was not directly threatened by the loss of his heirs' patrimony, but he was clearly sympathetic to those who were, and he was a *regidor* of the Mexico City *cabildo* when it sent its ill-advised petition to Philip II. But above all, Diego's reputation was tarred by kinship with his more outspoken and militant brother.

The Sotelos were attending to business matters in Michoacán when, on July 26, 1566, they were ordered to appear in Mexico City within twelve days under penalty of twenty thousand ducats for noncompliance. They spent the better part of the next two years, mostly from behind bars, defending themselves against charges of treason. Others suffered a swifter fate.[22]

After quick trials for the ringleaders, the executions began. Punishment came in the form of beheading on a public scaffold. The Ávila brothers were first, on August 3, 1566. Among those who also paid the supreme penalty was Baltasar de Sotelo. The *fiscal* proclaimed him a rebel on March 18, 1568, and soon after he was executed.[23] Exiled in that same year from New Spain but not deprived of the right to pass Ecatepec on to his heirs was his brother, Diego Arias Sotelo.[24] Mariana Moctezuma's heirs' right of continued possession of Ecatepec was an important victory, because the crown took punitive measures against a number of valley *encomenderos* in the wake of the Ávila-Cortés conspiracy.[25]

With the exile of Diego Arias Sotelo, his eldest son, Fernando Sotelo de Moctezuma, became the third-life *encomendero* of Ecatepec. His inheritance was immediately challenged by another son, Cristóbal de Sotelo Valderrama. Typically, the dispute dragged on for twenty years before the Audiencia of New Spain ruled in favor of Fernando in 1588. Cristóbal appealed the Audiencia's decision and won a partial victory in 1593. In that year the younger brother forced a three-part settlement whereby one-third of Ecatepec remained with Fernando, one-third went to the appellant, and one-third devolved to their sister, Ana Sotelo. Ana, a nun in the convent of Santa Clara in Mexico City, renounced her share in favor of Fernando, whereupon Fernando and Cristóbal became co-encomenderos of Ecatepec.[26]

Fernando's wife bore four children. Licentiate Diego Sotelo de Moctezuma became a cleric; Juan Sotelo de Moctezuma apparently never married; Leonor Sotelo de Moctezuma, also known as "la doncella" (the maid or virgin), obviously never wed; and Ana Sotelo de Moctezuma entered the convent of San Jerónimo.[27]

Cristóbal married Juana de Heredia Patiño but died intestate in 1607, whereupon his one-third share of Ecatepec remained with his wife. She immediately filed suit to claim half of the one-third share renounced by her husband's sister, Ana. The appellant essentially argued that since the Audiencia had ordered a three-part division of Ecatepec's revenues, it was not within Ana's legal rights to bestow her share entirely on one brother. The Audiencia, especially since it had issued a ruling on the matter some fourteen years earlier, found merit in Juana's contention but referred the case to the Council of the Indies. On December 18, 1608, the council awarded Juana de Heredia Patiño eleven thousand pesos, collectible in tribute payments for a one-sixth portion of rents that should have accrued to her from 1593 to 1608. Subsequent appeals by Fernando Sotelo de Moctezuma's sons reduced that amount to seven thousand pesos.[28]

Diego Sotelo de Moctezuma and Juan Sotelo de Moctezuma's father granted them permission to sell their share of Ecatepec to Fernando Bocanegra for 9,660 pesos in a document drawn up at Valladolid (New Spain) on June 19, 1618. The sale of Ecatepec rents occurred about two months later, on August 23, 1618.[29] Thus, near the end of the second decade of the seventeenth century, Ecatepec had passed completely out of the hands of the bloodline descendants of Mariana Moctezuma. The remaining portion of Ecatepec was sold in 1662 by Lorenzo Patiño de Vargas, Juana de Heredia Patiño's heir.[30]

• • •

After the conquest of Mexico, Pedro Moctezuma became the principal male heir of Moctezuma II. Pedro's descendants, unlike the heirs of his half-sister Mariana, were destined to hold onto their legacy and ultimately to triumph in spectacular fashion, although the road to the peerage and attainment of the highest office in New Spain was hardly smooth.

There is no doubt that Pedro Moctezuma had blood ties to the native rulers of Tula. As mentioned in Chapter 1, Tula lies about forty-five miles north-northeast of Mexico City on the outer rim of mountains that surround the Valley of Mexico. Perhaps because the Aztecs worked so diligently to relate themselves to the Toltecs, the rulers of Tenochtitlan during the fifteenth and sixteenth centuries were intent on developing close family ties with the Indian aristocracy of that ancient city.

Acamapichtli (1383–1396) and Ilancueitl had a grandson, Cuetlachtzin Teuctli, who went to Tula as its king. He married Xiloxochtzin, daughter of Cuitlaxihuitl, who had ruled as the "rey de [king of] Tullan." And "from this pair, all the nobility of Tullan descended."[31]

Still another Aztec emperor, Axayacatl (1469–1481), married Mizquixahuatzin, the daughter of the king of Tula (Aztauhyatzin), and their son ascended to the throne. Later, and more important to this study, Xocoyotzin (who would become Moctezuma II) married Miahuaxochitl, a princess in the ruling house of Tula. Their son Tlacahuepan, known to Spaniards as Pedro Moctezuma, thus had close ties to Tula. Of prime importance to Pedro's descendants is a municipality named Tultengo that lies adjacent to Tula.[32]

When Miahuaxochitl's father died in a flower war, Moctezuma II claimed hegemony over Tula because of his wife's prominent position in the province.[33] However, after the conquest of New Spain, which claimed the lives of many of the native nobility and the emperor's children, Moctezuma's principal heirs as recognized by Cortés and other Spaniards numbered only three—Isabel, Mariana, and Pedro.

Pedro's exact birth year is unknown, but he appears to have been born around the time of Moctezuma II's coronation (1503). Thus, he would have been about eighteen or nineteen years of age when the Aztec capital fell to Cortés and his Indian allies.

Pedro probably stayed in Tula during the siege that destroyed Tenochtitlan in 1521. In any event, he was in Tenochtitlan shortly after the conquest and supervised workers rebuilding one district of the city. By cooperating with the Spaniards, Pedro gained favorable treatment from Cortés when the latter began to allocate *encomiendas* in April 1522.

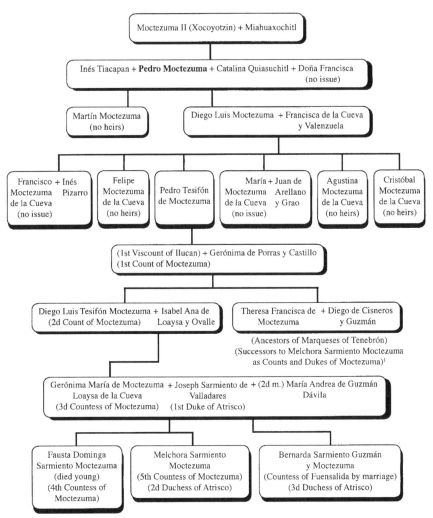

Figure 4.2. Genealogy of Pedro Moctezuma. (Center for Media Production, University of North Texas.)

Cortés bestowed rich *encomiendas* on Pedro de Alvarado (Xochimilco), Francisco de Montejo (Azcapotzalco), and himself (Coyoacan, Ecatepec, Chalco, and Otumba) and allowed Pedro to enjoy revenues from Tula.[34]

Pedro served the postconquest Spaniards as a kind of deputy emperor.[35] His doing so has not endeared him to many modern-day Mexicans, who are critical of him for his "collaborationist" conduct and quick acceptance of Christianity. The same criticism is often directed at his father, not, of course, for Moctezuma's acceptance of the Christian religion but for his cooperation with Cortés while the conqueror held him captive. In truth, however, no one can say with certainty what he or she might have done under similar circumstances. Perhaps one can better assess the price of Pedro's cooperation by looking at his and his heirs' successes and failures.

When Pedro Moctezuma received patrimonial rights in Tula, he adopted the position that his privileges included ownership of specific towns that had traditionally been held by his mother's family. At no time did he assert that he was entitled to all the municipalities within the province, and his rights in Tula remained essentially unchallenged until he accompanied Cortés on his first return to Spain in March 1528.[36]

In Pedro's absence from New Spain, Nuño de Guzmán and the judges of the first Audiencia began the sequestration of *encomiendas* held by Cortés partisans and reassigned them to themselves and their confederates. As mentioned earlier, Isabel Moctezuma lost the revenues of Tacuba for the better part of a year. By contrast, Pedro was not immediately divested of income from Tula but the power shift in Mexico City encouraged the surviving Indian nobility to seek broader rights through the vehicle of lawsuits.

Indian leaders in the Tula community first attempted to have Pedro removed from office as native governor. They argued that Franciscan missionaries in Tula had insisted on Pedro's appointment, primarily because of his quick acceptance of Christianity. Next, the *principales* argued that although Pedro's maternal grandfather and great-grandfather had been *tlatoque* of Tula, Moctezuma's wife had no rights of inheritance because she was illegitimate. The Indian nobility presented their pleas in a formal hearing before the president of the second Audiencia in the early 1530s. In response, Ramírez de Fuenleal canceled don Pedro's appointment as governor of Tula and exiled him from the province for "crimes and excesses." The *fiscal* also seized as crown property *estancias* claimed by Pedro.[37]

Figure 4.3. Coat of arms of Pedro Moctezuma. (Adapted from http://www.prodigy-web.net.mx/ryates/pag-ina9.htm. Center for Media Production, University of North Texas.)

Pedro Moctezuma took up residence in Mexico City and established a home in the *barrio* of San Sebastián near the church and convent of Santo Domingo. Perhaps he hoped that Antonio de Mendoza, who arrived as the first viceroy of New Spain in 1535, would reverse the Audiencia's ruling, but that did not happen.[38]

In the late 1530s, Pedro made a second trip to Spain and gained an audience with Emperor Charles V. This effort paid much better dividends. On October 15, 1539, the emperor approved a coat of arms (*privilegio de armas*) for Pedro in recognition of his status as the son of Moctezuma.[39] It is significant that Charles V, in recognition of Moctezuma's control over native kingdoms in New Spain, permitted Pedro to have thirty-two gold crowns in his *escudo* (coat of arms), a privilege denied the noble families of Spain since the days of the Catholic Monarchs. Thus, Charles V's concession represents clear recognition of noble status for native elites and their descendants in their own lands. This victory would later prove supremely important for some children of the Aztec emperor—a topic addressed in the final chapter.

While Pedro was absent in Spain, his mother continued to live in Tula. But the Spanish governor and Indian *principales* of the province seized control, "by force and violence," of all properties María Miahuaxochitl and her son claimed, leaving her without income. She sent news of her plight across the Atlantic, and Pedro used it to good advantage by informing royal officials that his inheritance had been forcibly taken.[40]

Charles V responded by sending a *cédula* (royal decree), dated September 20, 1540, to the Audiencia of New Spain. In it the emperor refers to Pedro as the son of Moctezuma II and specifically enumerates the *estancias* in Tula that rightfully belonged to him and his mother.[41] Charles V commanded the judges of the Audiencia to restore all towns and other properties taken from Pedro by Indians or Spaniards. The emperor also granted Pedro a single-payment *merced* of one thousand silver pesos, as well as an additional stipend of fifty pesos per year.[42]

Pedro Moctezuma, aware of the restitution of his patrimony, returned to New Spain. There he learned that on March 1, 1542, Viceroy Antonio Mendoza had instructed the treasury officials of New Spain to pay him one hundred silver pesos for one year. On July 7, Pedro appeared before the Audiencia. There he presented a petition asking the judges to restore the *estancias* enumerated by Charles V.[43] Pedro, of course, took exception to the contention of the Indian nobility of Tula that his mother was illegitimate. He also contended that his mother's ancestors had owned estates within the province of Tula for many generations, and that they were the ruling native nobility of that region.

Pedro asserted that no one had challenged his rights of inheritance in Tula until he went to Spain in 1528. He specifically asked for the restitution of his properties, as well as recompense for tribute payments while the towns were in the hands of Indian *principales* of Tula.[44] Perhaps Pedro had learned that the pace of judicial procedure in the Spanish system moved with glacial slowness, but surely he did not anticipate that fourteen years would pass before formal action was taken on his petition.

This inordinately long delay may be explained in large part by the arrival of the New Laws of the Indies (promulgated in 1542–1543) in New Spain in 1544. Although they covered vitally important issues relating to the treatment of Indians and colonial administration, their potentially ruinous restrictions on *encomienda* created an uproar. Specifically, they prohibited without exception the granting of any new *encomiendas*.

Worse, existing *encomienda* grants must be examined with the utmost scrutiny, and if it was determined that any *encomendero* or *encomendera* had mistreated Indians, they must immediately surrender their grant to the crown and forfeit any possibility of ever possessing it again. To ensure that there would be no conflict of interest in enforcing these unpopular measures, all royal officials and religious personnel must give up their *encomiendas* immediately. Finally, those *encomiendas* that passed muster and continued to exist were declared not inheritable by husbands, wives, children, or other heirs. In short, all privately held *encomiendas* would revert to the crown at the death of the current holder.[45]

Nowhere in the Spanish Indies were the New Laws enforced in their entirety. Opposition led, for example, to bloody civil wars in Peru and the death of a viceroy. Elsewhere, the wrath of colonists brought them to the brink of rebellion. And this was not a case of the crown relying solely on royal officials already stationed in the Indies to carry out the enforcement of enormously unpopular decrees. To ensure compliance, the crown sent out high officials in 1544 with sweeping powers. The *visitador-general* for New Spain was Francisco Tello de Sandoval, a member of the Council of the Indies.[46]

What likely kept New Spain from transforming into a colony bent on treasonous opposition to royal decrees was the wisdom of its first viceroy, Antonio de Mendoza. He used a procedure that is famous in Spanish colonial administration. After reading the New Laws and recovering from the shock, he uttered the magical words, "Obedezco pero no cumplo." The *cabildo* of Mexico City used the time this bought to good advantage by immediately sending a delegation of attorneys to Spain to present the grievances of New Spain's *encomenderos*. Eventually, the New Laws that applied to *encomienda* were revoked—much to the displeasure of such ardent defenders of the Indians as Bartolomé de las Casas. But, as mentioned earlier, allowing privately held *encomiendas* to stay in the hands of third-life holders prompted the Ávila-Cortés conspiracy of the 1560s. In the long run, however, *encomienda* did not receive a legal death sentence throughout the entire Spanish colonial period.

At times, Spanish administrators practiced the fine art of dissimulation. *Para disimular* meant to dissemble, or "wink" at, laws that looked good in print, laws that helped keep Las Casas and other defenders of Indian rights from badgering the crown, but also laws that were not enforced. Still, there was enough confusion and uncertainly over *encomienda* in the 1540s and the early 1550s to prevent any speedy resolution to Pedro Moctezuma's quest for restored revenues from Tula.[47]

It was March 22, 1556, before an assistant of the *alcalde mayor* of Tula received formal notice of Pedro Moctezuma's petition. The official, Diego de Almodóvar, ordered the Indians of Tula to respond to Pedro's request for restitution of his former estate. They presented testimony supported by a painting that showed the *tlatoque* of Tula from just prior to the conquest to when Pedro became governor, their point being that tribute payments from the *estancias* had been transferred from native recipients in the province to a son of Moctezuma II at the time of his governorship.[48]

• • •

The pictorial manuscript acknowledged that Ixtlilcuexhuaca was the son of Axayacatl, a brother of Moctezuma II. After Ixtlilcuexhuaca's death in a flower war (1506), his son succeeded him but soon died, leaving only a minor male heir, who passed away within three years. A *principal* named don Zacarias served as *tlatoani* until he was replaced by Pedro Moctezuma at the insistence of Franciscan missionaries.[49]

Once again the Indian nobility of Tula argued that Pedro's mother was illegitimate. Accordingly, neither she nor her son had rights of inheritance in the province. The *principales* also pointed to Ramírez de Fuenleal's decision in their favor, noting that the president of the Audiencia had permanently banished Pedro from the province for committing "crimes and excesses." They contended that from this decision forward all tribute had gone rightfully to the *tlatoque* of Tula.[50]

Pedro Moctezuma replied, as before, that his mother was entitled to full rights of inheritance, and he referred to earlier legal decisions that had upheld the patrimonial rights of his half-sisters, Isabel and Mariana. On October 25, 1557, the Spanish provincial official in Tula ordered the Indians to surrender the disputed *estancias* and make restitution to Pedro for accumulated tribute payments.[51]

This judgment came some twenty-five years after Pedro was stripped of his governorship and exiled from Tula, and an appeal by the divested *principales* to the Audiencia was as certain as night follows day. The preliminary ruling by the high court upheld the actions of the *teniente de alcalde mayor* (provincial official's lieutenant) in Tula. Not satisfied, the Indian nobility asked for a more thorough review of the case, and the judges agreed. The matter dragged on, and in 1560 Pedro asked Philip II for a grant of six hundred silver pesos per year in perpetuity, claiming that he had no adequate means of supporting his sizable family.[52]

With his first consort, Inés Tiacapan, daughter of the cacique of Tenayuca, Pedro fathered a son they named Martín Moctezuma Cortés.[53] His second union, with Catalina Quiasuchitl, described as a descendant of the kings of Mexico City and Tula, produced another son, Diego Luis Moctezuma. After Catalina died, Pedro married again, this time, an Indian woman known as doña Francisca, who bore no children. Thus, unlike his half-sisters, Isabel and Mariana, whose spouses were of different ethnicities, Pedro's wives were all indigenous.[54]

On December 14, 1560, a review decision signed by the viceroy and judges of the Audiencia confirmed the earlier ruling, but there were still delays in awarding Pedro tribute from the disputed *estancias* in Tula. Twice, in January 1561 and again in February of the same year, the Audiencia instructed the *teniente de alguacil mayor* to transfer the properties to Pedro Moctezuma, but it did not happen until a letter from Philip II arrived on May 5, 1561. The king commanded Gonzalo Cerezo, an official of the Audiencia, to go to Tula, conduct a survey, and award the properties in question to Pedro and his mother. This was accomplished by the end of June, some nineteen years after Pedro filed his petition. Cerezo stood in the main plaza of Tula with Pedro by his side and announced the transfer of the *estancias* from the *principales* to the successful litigant. Cerezo also warned all present that anyone who challenged the court and king's decision or dared disturb Pedro and his aged mother would suffer four years' exile from the province.[55]

Pedro and his mother enjoyed their victory for all of two months before they were again embroiled in a lawsuit over Tula properties. Two Indian brothers from the Tecontepeque *estancia* filed a *proceso* (lawsuit) against them on August 4, 1561. The suit alleged that Cerezo had improperly awarded towns that belonged to Tula proper, and the Audiencia agreed to hear evidence by sending an official to the province.[56]

Miguel de Luna, the Indian governor of Tula, agreed to testify on behalf of the brothers and summoned supporting witnesses (*testigos*). Those questioned were in agreement that Pedro, while governor, raised no objections when the Indians of those municipalities paid tribute to their *tlatoque*. It was only after Pedro's removal from Tula that he filed suit for revenues he had never before collected. Witnesses also stated that after Pedro had profited from the actions of Cerezo, he boasted of receiving more than originally requested. The *testigos* also complained about the numerous haughty Indians who had arrived from Mexico City with Pedro and his mother as servants and retainers. After hearing this testimony, the *fiscal* agreed to present the new evidence to the Audiencia.[57]

Pedro's attorneys countered that all deponents had been bribed to give false testimony. As proof, they summoned Indians who claimed that the governor of Tula and some of the *principales* had gathered all of the opposition witnesses at a house and plied them with food and drink to the point of drunkenness, as well as providing them with gifts of clothing and money. All had been coached in advance about how to answer each question. Finally, Pedro's lawyers contended that the witnesses were not who they purported to be, nor were they even residents of the towns in question.[58]

While the Audiencia studied this case yet again, Pedro's mother died. The exact date of her death is uncertain, but it likely occurred in the mid-1560s. Following the loss of his mother, Pedro, on March 25, 1566, asked Philip II for a yearly stipend of 1,000 silver pesos to support his children. He noted that his income from *estancias* not then contested amounted to only 721 pesos and 360 *fanegas* of maize.[59]

Pedro's final letter to the king is dated March 31, 1569. He again states that Moctezuma II was his father, and he contends that the Aztec emperor helped Fernando Cortés bring Mexico under the Spanish crown by urging his subjects to accept its authority. Furthermore, following the conquest, Moctezuma's descendants had readily accepted Christianity as the path to salvation and pledged themselves as willing subjects of his most Catholic majesty. Pedro reminds Philip II that great riches in gold, silver, and precious gems had flowed into Spanish coffers although Pedro himself was poor. The estates that he should have inherited from his mother, he continues, had been taken from him. As a consequence, he owed more than twelve thousand silver pesos, which he had borrowed to support his family. Now, he must humbly place himself in the hands of a benevolent monarch. He beseeches the royal heart to grant him three thousand pesos per year by way of a permanent inheritance. Pedro asserts that, with the king's largess, he can pay debts and provide for the needs of his family. In exchange, he will renounce all other rights as a natural ruler of Mexico.[60]

Fortunately for Pedro's heirs, Philip II decided to provide a measure of security for them. In a *cédula* dated March 23, 1567, the king states that

Moctezuma II granted hegemony to the Spanish crown. Accordingly, the emperor's children must be honored. Pedro and his heirs would receive a yearly stipend of three thousand silver pesos in perpetuity, payable in Indian tribute. That income, however, must be paid from then-vacant *encomiendas* or those that would become so shortly.

News of this *mayorazgo*, which prevented Pedro's heirs from selling or otherwise alienating this inheritance, failed to reach Mexico City until March 31, 1569. Philip also acknowledged María Miahuaxochitl as a legitimate wife of Moctezuma, with Tula as a part of her patrimony. The king's decision entitled the mother and her heirs to Tula's woods, waters, and tributary units. But between the drafting of this *cédula* and its arrival in Mexico City, Pedro dispatched his second son, Diego Luis, across the Atlantic to plead the family's case at court.[61]

Pedro Moctezuma was bedfast and near death in early September 1570. On the eighth of that month, he executed his last will and testament and added a codicil on the tenth. The dying man dictated his will in Nahuatl, and Francisco Osorio Rivadeo, interpreter for the Audiencia of New Spain, translated his words into Spanish. Of prime importance to Pedro was a special bequest to the monastery of Santo Domingo in Mexico City to cover the cost of his burial in its chapel and for masses said in behalf of his soul. He asks in his will that Francisco Morales Millán, a royal scribe from whom he had borrowed money to be reimbursed. He also decries the tribute taken from him by the Indians of Tula and mentions legal matters then pending before the Council of the Indies.[62]

In his will, Pedro Moctezuma proclaims Martín Cortés, his eldest son, born to Inés Tiacapan, to be the legitimate inheritor of any entailment in Tula and names Morales executor of his estate, noting that Martín does not understand Castilian law. All other children, including Diego Luis, are listed in the will as *hijos naturales*, meaning children born out of Christian wedlock. Pedro acknowledges in his will that he holds six *estancias* that are not then tied up in judicial proceedings. All contain sheep and goats, as well as crops of wheat and maize. Pedro awards these estates to his children by way of entailment, most likely on the advice of Morales, who had seen other Indians dispose of their lands, spend the money, and face abject poverty. Four of Pedro's children (see note 54, this chapter) received specific grants: Coculco went to don Bartolomé and doña María; Ilucan to don Lorenzo and doña Magdalena. Tultengo, a prized possession in Tula, was to be held in common by Pedro's heirs and could not be sold. Magdalena, the youngest of the children, was only thirteen years old and was placed in Morales's custody until she reached maturity.

Finally, Pedro makes provision for doña Francisca, his wife at the time of his death. She was to receive one hundred silver pesos and five *fanegas* of maize on a yearly basis for the rest of her life. Francisca could also occupy Pedro's large house in Mexico City for the remainder of her life.[63]

The codicil provided an extremely important provision. Should Martín die without heirs, which indeed happened, then Diego Luis as the eldest natural son would inherit any entailments. In short, this half-brother of Martín should then be considered as the legitimate heir of any entailed estate.[64]

On September 8, 1570, just two days before Pedro's death, the Audiencia awarded Tula *estancias* to him and his heirs. Possession came in the form of an entailed estate. Less than two years later, the Council of the Indies on August 16, 1572, confirmed Tula as an inheritance of the children of Pedro Moctezuma.[65]

Pedro Moctezuma spent nearly forty years trying to secure a patrimony for himself and his heirs, and he likely died without knowledge of Philip II's major concession. The obstacles that he encountered must have seemed insurmountable on many occasions. Each victory, such as receiving approval for a coat of arms and a yearly stipend from Charles V, was followed by seemingly endless lawsuits; exasperating delays that stretched over decades; initially favorable judgments, followed by formal appeals against them that tied up contested properties for still longer. And during all this litigation, tribute from properties finally judged to be his went elsewhere. One thing, however, remains obvious. The Indian nobility of New Spain, whether advantaged by being the children of Moctezuma II or by being *tlatoque* or *principales*, quickly learned to be just as litigious as the Spaniards who had conquered their land. It is a testament to Spanish law that it often served the interests of Indians, however imperfectly, on the scales of justice.

By now it should not be surprising that the legal battles over Tula were far from over. Owing in part to the somewhat irregular manner in which five of Pedro's six children were born, more time and money had to be spent on matters that would be decided by Spanish courts. Francisco Morales, as executor of Pedro's testament and financial adviser to the children, filed the will with the Audiencia, which heard testimony concerning its legality and provisions between October 5 and 16, 1571. Morales summoned a number of witnesses, who repeated the now-familiar claim that Pedro was indeed the son of Moctezuma II and his wife, María Miahuaxochitl. And the scribe himself affirmed that the document in question was positively the will executed by Pedro before his death. In opposition, the royal *fiscal* reiterated the claims of the Indians of Tula but to no immediate avail. Less than a year after Pedro's death, on August 16, 1572, the Audiencia gave its stamp of approval to the will and awarded the *mayorazgo* and right to collect rents to Martín Moctezuma Cortés. Annual tribute from *estancias* in Tula amounted to the significant sum of 3,444 silver pesos and 1,722 *fanegas* of maize.[66]

Not one to give up easily, the *fiscal* continued to plead the case before the Audiencia. The president and judges reaffirmed their original verdict on November 5, 1573, and again on April 3, 1576. By the time of the second ruling, however, it was clear that Martín had encountered resistance in collecting rents from some of his Tula properties. That circumstance was undoubtedly prompted in part by the *fiscal's* refusal to accept any ruling by the Audiencia as final, which stirred hope among Tula's Indians.[67]

The Audiencia sent one of its judges to Tula on June 19, 1576. The *oidor* reported that fifteen of Martín's *estancias* willingly paid tribute but six did not. The Council of the Indies still had not approved the provisions of Pedro's will, so the matter dragged on until June 19, 1579, when the council recognized Martín as the rightful possessor of the Tula *mayorazgo*.[68] By then, Martín Moctezuma Cortés had been dead for three years.

Martín died without heirs, but, as noted, a provision in Pedro's will addressed this eventuality and called for Diego Luis to inherit the entailed estate in Tula. But Diego Luis's illegitimacy served temporarily to block his inheritance. As mentioned, Pedro had dispatched this second son to Spain to plead the family's case in person before the king and the Council of the Indies. Diego Luis arrived in Spain in the late 1560s, and by the mid-1570s found himself in desperate financial straits. In 1576 he addressed a letter to Philip II in which he details his deplorable situation. Diego Luis notes in the letter that he has been in Spain for about eight years and found that the cold temperatures of central Spain adversely affected his health, forcing him to take up residence in Seville. Accordingly, it was not possible for him to spend time in Madrid, where he could petition the king in person. Worse, his impecuniousness had forced him to borrow money. Indeed, Diego Luis drafted this piteous missive to the king from the public jail of Seville, where he was incarcerated for unpaid debts.[69]

Forced to find a means of supporting himself in Seville, Diego Luis hoped to buy and sell decks of playing cards on a grand scale. To do this, in 1573 he had borrowed hundreds of thousands of *maravedís* to purchase 3,500 dozen packs of cards at 640 *maravedís* per dozen. He managed to get his cousin Juan de Andrade, also in Seville, to serve as guarantor of the loan. Unfortunately for the cousins, they not only owed the principal but also 600,000 *maravedís* to the king and Castile's treasurer general, Bernabé Álvarez de Loaysa, the crown representative in Seville. That sum was for 1,111 dozen packs of playing cards that did not bear revenue stamps containing the royal seal.[70]

Diego Luis and Juan de Andrade handed over the 3,500 dozen packs of cards to a peddler, because, owing to their detention, they had been unable to sell the merchandise. They, however, had languished in the Seville jail for more than two years. Diego Luis's failed business enterprise does much to explain his petition to Philip II for a *merced* that would cover his debts and buy his freedom.[71]

On June 5, 1576, the Council of the Indies ordered Diego Luis to appear before it and offer proof that he was the son of Pedro and grandson of Moctezuma. This prompted a second letter from Diego Luis to the king. Therein, he asks for a grant of two thousand ducats to pay his debts and buy passage to New Spain.[72]

Beginning on August 1 and continuing to October 26, witnesses testified before the council and asserted that Diego Luis was indeed the son of Pedro and grandson of the Aztec emperor. The deponents proclaimed Diego Luis to be a good Christian and pointed out that he was in Spain because his father had sent him there to plead the family's case for financial rewards. Near the end of testimony, news of Martín's death arrived in Spain, whereupon Diego Luis arranged passage across the Atlantic and laid claim to the *mayorazgo* in Tula.[73]

Diego Luis's rights of inheritance in Tula were of course challenged in the courts. On this occasion, the legal entanglements came from a cousin, a grandson of Isabel Moctezuma named Pedro de Andrade; from the cousin's wife, following Pedro's death; and from a woman who claimed to be Inés Tiacapan and the wife of Pedro Moctezuma. Diego Luis challenged the last, maintaining that his father thought the woman to be dead when he took up residence with doña Catalina. In any event, these lawsuits appear to have had little validity, but they caused lengthy delays in awarding the Tula *mayorazgo* to Diego Luis. To defend his interests, he crossed the Atlantic again and made a personal appeal before the Council of the Indies.[74]

On August 23, 1587, the council rejected the licitness of both lawsuits brought against Diego Luis—the one initiated by Pedro de Andrade and the second by the alleged former wife of Pedro Moctezuma. The council then awarded the Tula *mayorazgo* to Diego Luis, recognizing him as his father's son and heir. That decision, backed by a royal *cédula*, directed the Audiencia of New Spain to award the rents of twenty-one *estancias* to Diego Luis Moctezuma.[75]

The time it took to get the favorable judgment to New Spain and the Audiencia's choice of a receptor of rents for Tula meant that tribute payments from the *estancias* did not begin until February 10, 1589. The first payment, of some twenty thousand silver pesos, which included income from the Tula properties that had accrued since the death of Martín Moctezuma, was sent to Spain on February 5, 1590.[76]

Following his return to Spain, Diego Luis married Francisca de la Cueva y Valenzuela and settled in Guadix near Granada. The bride was a lady-in-waiting to the queen and a granddaughter of the powerful Duke of Alburquerque, a grandee of Spain.[77] It would appear that Diego Luis's Indian heritage was not an impediment to his marrying into the Spanish peerage, and the marriage presaged titles of nobility that would ultimately be awarded to this line of Moctezuma II's descendants.

It is unlikely, however, that Diego Luis received the lump sum of twenty thousand pesos, as 1590 closely followed Spain's loss of the Great Armada. Nevertheless, Philip II ordered a general settlement in 1590 that involved cash awards to many of the Aztec emperor's descendants. (I discuss the rationale for that landmark decision and specific aspects of it in the last chapter.)

In 1596, near the end of Philip II's life, he once again declared national bankruptcy. It had become common for the revenue-desperate crown to seize privately owned shipments of gold and silver bullion from the Indies and then issue *juros* (vouchers) in their stead.[78]

Five

Isabel Moctezuma's Descendants and the Northern Frontier of New Spain

THE ONLY CHILD OF ISABEL MOCTEZUMA born out of Christian wedlock was a daughter fathered by Fernando Cortés. Leonor Cortés Moctezuma drew her first breath in the household of Pedro Gallego de Andrade in 1528 (see Figure 3.1). Gallego was an Extremaduran who arrived in New Spain shortly after the fall of the Aztec capital. Accordingly, he was a *poblador* of Mexico City, rather than one of the first conquistadors. At the time of his marriage to then-pregnant Isabel Moctezuma, Pedro received one-half of an *encomienda* situated west of Pachuca.[1]

Soon after Leonor's birth, the infant was separated from her mother and placed in the home of Licentiate Juan Gutiérrez de Altamirano, a cousin of Cortés by marriage. For slightly more than two decades, doña Leonor lived as a ward of Altamirano until her marriage around 1550.[2]

As Leonor grew to maturity, events of the 1530s and the 1540s made it possible for her to acquire a husband deemed worthy of her lineage. These changes in the settlement of New Spain had begun under Cortés's governorship and accelerated with the ambitions of Nuño de Guzmán. They culminated with the successes of silver-hungry Spaniards.

Less than a year after the fall of the Aztec capital, Cortés turned his attention toward Michoacán, the homeland of Purepechas who had once defeated the powerful Aztecs. His motives for the campaign were the large size of the Purepechan kingdom and its rumored wealth. Chosen as commander was one of Cortés's most valued captains, Cristóbal de Olid. Few men in New Spain were then closer than Cortés and Olid. Their association had begun in Cuba and deepened during the crucial two years following the original expedition of 1519. Olid served as quartermaster of Cortés's army, shared the perils of La Noche Triste with his commander, and later served as head of one of the three divisions that assaulted Tenochtitlan over its major causeways.[3]

Olid organized his expedition in the early summer of 1522 and departed for Michoacán in July. Because of internal divisions among Purepechan leaders, the size of Olid's forces, and the paralyzing realization that these foreigners had defeated the Aztecs and destroyed their city made the Purepechan leaders believe opposition was futile. As a consequence, the conquest of Michoacán was largely bloodless. However, Spanish colonization of the region did not immediately follow in the wake of Olid's successes.

As mentioned in Chapter 2, the arrival of Francisco de Garay's large army in Pánuco in the summer of 1523 soon diverted Cortés's attention from the Purepechas. The region north of Veracruz had been conquered by Cortés earlier in the year, despite fierce opposition from Huastec Indians. The pacified province, however, erupted into rebellion as a result of unchecked criminality on the part of Garay's soldiers. This native insurrection forced Cortés to send Gonzalo de Sandoval into the Pánuco region to pacify it once again.

These events delayed a planned expedition to Honduras by Olid until January 1524. In violation of Cortés's orders, Olid stopped off in Cuba, where he defected to the archenemy, Diego de Velázquez. This breach of trust between old comrades in arms prompted Cortés's Honduran expedition of 1524–1526.

In Cortés's absence, New Spain entered the chaotic interim period of government by treasury officials. By then, Michoacán had been partially carved into *encomiendas*, and it was a focus of interest for those seeking gold, silver, and gems—either by mining them or by demanding that the native nobility hand them over. The king of the Purepechas, the Cazonci, was at that time the single most important native ruler in all of New Spain.[4]

The Cazonci had considerable authority in his kingdom, despite the presence of Spanish *encomenderos* and miners. But his very life depended on whether Spaniards saw him as having greater value as an agent or an opponent of their control of Michoacán. It took about six years to determine with certainty that the Tarascan king was "more an obstacle than a tool."[5]

During that time, Cortés returned from Honduras, and Ponce de León in Mexico City and Guzmán in Pánuco failed to unseat the conqueror and his adherents from power. The appointment of the first Audiencia of New Spain and its arrival in 1528 signaled to Cortés that the climate of opinion had shifted against him, whereupon he returned to Spain. The misrule of the Audiencia, with Guzmán as its president, lasted until 1531. At that time, Cortés arrived in Mexico City with the judges of the second Audiencia.

By the summer of 1530, Guzmán had recognized that the turn of events did not augur well for him. He decided to further his career by launching a bold new campaign into Michoacán and beyond. Although he was careful to justify the undertaking as one that would benefit the crown, there is little doubt that it served his personal ambition. He pointed to the proximity of the "tierra de guerra," from which barbarous northern tribes, collectively known as Chichimecs, raided the settled portions of New Spain near Mexico City. Guzmán claimed that the proposed *entrada* would secure and increase crown lands and bring the cross to pagan Indians. He also alluded to a persistent rumor that a land of Amazon women lay in the path of his campaign, which lent an air of excitement and expectation to the venture. But without doubt, Guzmán was unhappy with the certainty of being removed from power as president of the government of New Spain. Furthermore, if the inevitable *residencia* went against him, it would bring a premature end to goals as yet unrealized.[6]

For many years Spaniards would look to the north and northwest of Mexico City in the hope of discovering cities that would equal or excel the splendors of Tenochtitlan, and Guzmán was no exception. He had talked to an Indian who claimed to have visited rich cities in the north with his father, a trader who had operated between a region west of Pánuco and unexplored Pueblo country to the north. Don Nuño's informant described the journey northward as one of forty days across a desert between the seas.[7]

Between the summer of 1529 and December of the same year, Guzmán assembled a large and well-equipped force for a military campaign within New Spain. Shortly before Christmas, he led a force of three hundred to four hundred Spaniards and several thousand Indian auxiliaries toward Michoacán. Accompanying Guzmán as a hostage was the Cazonci.

During the second half of the 1520s, the Cazonci was at times free to move about in Michoacán, but on other occasions Spanish officials ordered him to Mexico City and placed him under confinement. Some four months prior to Guzmán's 1529–1530 campaign, the Indian king had to leave his homeland and stay in the capital. On the march through Michoacán, Guzmán intended to use the Cazonci as the key to untapped treasure, but things did not go as planned. In early February 1530, Guzmán brought the Purepechan king to trial on charges that he planned to ambush the Spaniards and their Indian allies in the environs of Lake Chapala. Judged guilty of planning to destroy Guzmán's army and other offenses, the Cazonci was executed at the conclusion of a judicial proceeding that included torture.[8]

On the northeastern shore of Lake Chapala, Guzmán ran into stiff native opposition, lending support to his contention that the Cazonci had organized resistance. Campaigns followed in the regions of Tonalá, Nochistlán, and Tepic. By late May 1530, Guzmán's forces had advanced to the north shore of the Río Grande de Santiago. There he announced that henceforth his expedition would carve out a "Spain" greater than Spain itself. In due time, Charles V's wife, the Empress Isabel, squelched that pretentious claim.[9]

Guzmán penetrated as far as the Río Acaponeta, where bad news reached him: his old enemy Fernando Cortés had returned to Vera Cruz with impressive titles. Then, worse than just bad tidings, the sudden rising of floodwaters hit the encamped army in the dead of night, and most of its supplies were either washed away or ruined. Massive sickness then struck Guzmán's Indian allies after the disastrous flood. Both Spaniards and Indians clamored to leave the expedition, but on Guzmán's orders, a few executions by hanging provided renewed incentives for others. Finally came the disappointment of finding that Cihuatlán, legendary home of the famed Amazons, turned out to be nothing more than an ordinary Indian village.[10]

At that time, Guzmán revealed the true intent of his relentless campaigning, which eventually reached as far as Culiacán near the Pacific. Somewhere to the north of Cihuatlán lay the fabled Seven Cities of Cíbola, which would make him and all of his soldiers incredibly rich. To ensure that the prize went to no one else, he thought it necessary to link the province he had conquered, now known as Nueva Galicia, with Pánuco. Buoyed by his appointment as governor and captain of the province, news of which reached him in mid-January 1532, Guzmán looked eastward to the Sierra Madre Occidental, one of the most formidable mountain barriers on the North American continent. Three attempts to find a path through the sierra ended in failure, but the fourth try brought success. In the spring of 1533, Guzmán founded the *villa* of Santiago de los Valles near his Pánuco jurisdiction, where he had held the title of governor for about six years. Thus, Guzmán completed his "Grand Design"—nothing less than controlling all access by land to the north country by dint of his governorship of two provinces that stretched from the Pacific Ocean to the Gulf of Mexico.[11]

His Grand Design, however, lasted only a few months. Guzmán had formidable enemies in Cortés and those who had lost their *encomiendas* during his presidency of the first Audiencia. After receiving numerous complaints, the crown detached Santiago de los Valles and Pánuco from his jurisdiction in 1533 and 1534, respectively. Don Nuño was removed as governor of Nueva Galicia with the arrival of his replacement in early 1537, whereupon he faced separate *residencia* proceedings for his two governorships.[12]

During Guzmán's six-year conquest and occupation of Nueva Galicia, he and his lieutenants founded a number of towns in northern Michoacán, southern Zacatecas, Jalisco, and central Sinaloa. The most important of these municipalities was Guadalajara, established in 1531 by Cristóbal de Oñate, then one of Guzmán's lieutenants. After being relocated a number of times, Guadalajara—named after don Nuño's birthplace in Spain—was settled at its present location in 1542. That year also marked the suppression of a two-year native uprising known as the Mixtón War.

The causes of this massive Indian revolt are not clearly understood. Explanations include Guzmán's vicious slave raids, which aroused opposition from a sedentary, agricultural people known as the Caxcanes. The Caxcanes may have seen the departure of Coronado's well-equipped army in April 1540 as a propitious time to strike the weakened forces of Lieutenant Governor Cristóbal de Oñate. Whatever the cause, the Mixtón War took its toll. It claimed the life of Pedro de Alvarado and it required that Viceroy Antonio de Mendoza take the field. Mendoza's army had to be reinforced by more than thirty thousand Aztec and Tlaxcalan allies to subdue the Caxcanes.

The Spaniards' victory brought a large measure of stability to the province of Nueva Galicia and paved the way for exploration into Cax-can territory to the northeast of Guadalajara. These *entradas* penetrated farther than anyone had dared venture before.[13]

• • •

Guzmán's successor as chief executive of Nueva Galicia was Diego Pérez de la Torre, but his administration was cut short when he died while attempting to suppress an Indian insurrection in 1538. His replacement as governor was none other than Francisco Vázquez de Coronado. With Coronado's departure for Pueblo country in April 1540, Captain Cristóbal de Oñate remained in charge of Nueva Galicia as its lieutenant governor.

By 1542, Spain had garnered considerable information about the north country. However, neither the Coronado expedition (which explored parts of New Mexico, Arizona, Texas, and Oklahoma and pene-trated as far as Wichita Indian villages along the Arkansas River in Kansas), nor the Hernando de Soto/Luis de Moscoso expedition (which traversed parts of ten present-day states in the United States from Florida to Texas), nor the sea expedition of Juan Rodríguez Cabrillo and Bar-tolomé Ferrelo (which reached as far as the Rogue River along the coast of Oregon) could report anything other than vast, unpromising territory to treasure-seeking Spaniards. These explorers and conquistadors found no booty in Florida, no riches in Texas, no wealthy Seven Cities of Cíbola in New Mexico, no Gran Quivira in Kansas, and no gold in California.[14] The best was yet to be discovered in the heartland of New Spain itself, and events in the mid- to late 1540s would lead to the rise of New Spain's silver aristocracy. One of the first wealthy men in northern Mexico would win the hand of Leonor Cortés Moctezuma, who would inherit her dowry from both Fernando Cortés and Isabel Moctezuma.

Four years after the last battle of the Mixtón War, a Spanish captain named Juan de Tolosa led a small number of soldiers and Indian auxil-iaries some 150 miles north-northeast from Guadalajara into the high country of the present-day state of Zacatecas. On September 8, 1546, he camped at the base of a hill that is still known as the Cerro de la Bufa. Tolosa convinced a few Zacateco Indians of his peaceful intentions and in exchange for trinkets, received gifts of a few stones. Samples of ore from La Bufa were collected, strapped to mules, and sent south to Nochistlán for an assay. The ore proved to be exceptionally high in silver content, giving rise to hopes of riches long dreamed of but unrealized since the fall of the Aztec capital. Mines had been worked in New Galicia as early as 1543, but the magnitude of the Zacatecas strike surpassed all earlier discoveries.[15]

Joining Tolosa at Zacatecas were three prominent veterans and prospectors: Captain Cristóbal de Oñate, acting governor of New Galicia before Coronado's appointment and during his absence in the field; Diego de Ibarra, an experienced soldier who had fought in the Mixtón War; and Baltasar Temiño de Bañuelos, who would assume a leadership role in future Indian wars. By early 1548, these men constituted the "Big Four" of the *villa* formally named Nuestra Señora de Zacatecas.[16]

Within two years, Zacatecas became a classic boomtown with sixty-one mine owners in residence. Tolosa, the original discoverer, lagged well behind Oñate in mining entrepreneurship. He owned only one stamp mill and smelter, while don Cristóbal had a total of thirteen mills and smelters, 101 slaves, and a residence containing a private chapel. Although Tolosa was obviously less successful than Oñate, he married well— Leonor Cortés Moctezuma.[17]

Doña Leonor was about twenty-two when she entered an arranged marriage with Tolosa. Her father had left her ten thousand ducats in his will when he died in 1547 at Castilleja de la Cuesta near Seville, and her mother provided an unknown amount when she died three years later in Mexico City.[18] She left the home of Juan Altamirano, where she had grown up, in the company of her half-brother Luis Cortés for the more than 350-mile trip to Zacatecas. Her marriage to Tolosa in the early 1550s united her with a somewhat older man.[19]

Unfortunately, we know very little about Tolosa's family and background. He was certainly Basque and possibly a native of the town of Tolosa in the present-day province of Guipúzcoa, although this "appears to be nothing more than mere speculation." J. Lloyd Mecham places Tolosa in New Spain at the time of the Mixtón War and credits him with being a veteran of that conflict. Despite the contention of some historians that neither a 1550 nor a 1594 *probanza* (court records) contains information to that effect, witness Juan de Amusco gave testimony that supports Mecham's assertion.[20]

Amusco stated that he knew Tolosa and saw him serve the king in the province of Nueva Galicia with arms and horses. Amusco specifically mentioned the uprising of natives that occurred during the governorship of Cristóbal de Oñate. The witness further added that at much risk and danger to himself Tolosa had fought against bellicose natives until the Indians were finally pacified.[21]

The most revealing information about Tolosa starts with his discovery of the Cerro de la Bufa in 1546. Most of it, however, comes from documentation recorded in 1594 at the behest of three children born to him and Leonor Cortés Moctezuma. In that year, Juan Cortés Tolosa Moctezuma, in his own name and that of his two sisters, began to compile information regarding the merits and services of their deceased father. The first of three *probanzas* of services began on April 13.[22]

Witnesses testifying in the third interrogatory, which started on May 17, were all old men claiming to be more than sixty years of age, in one case, more than seventy-five. All had known Tolosa, his wife, their children, and the husbands of the two daughters for a long time. These elderly *testigos* provide valuable firsthand information. They give much credit to Tolosa for the discovery of the mountain of silver ore that brought about the quick settlement of *villa* Nuestra Señora de Zacatecas. Indeed, one of them describes him as the "first of the first" *pobladores*. All recount the risks Tolosa took in leading an *entrada* of forty men from Guadalajara into the domain of hostile Chichimec and Guachichil Indians.[23]

One witness who could speak with authority about Tolosa was Baltasar Temiño de Bañuelos, a charter member of the Big Four. Bañuelos's testimony confirmed that both the discoverer of La Bufa and his famous *mestiza* wife were dead. Bañuelos notes that Tolosa had not rested on the laurels of being the founder of an incredibly rich town that had swelled royal coffers with payments of the royal fifth, the crown's share of silver production, or the compulsory *diezmo* (tithe). Instead, his old companion had defended Zacatecas at his own expense when it was attacked by Chichimecs, Guachichiles, and other rebellious nations. More to his credit, Tolosa had then ventured forty leagues (more than one hundred miles) beyond the confines of Zacatecas, where he had discovered the mines of San Martín, Sombrerete, and Avino. After the discovery of these new veins of silver, Tolosa founded Spanish settlements at the first two mines, where pagan Indians were successfully converted to Christianity.[24]

Bañuelos emphasized, as did other witnesses, that Tolosa had crossed deserts without roads in the *tierra adentro* at great risk to his life. On one of his *entradas* he discovered rich salt deposits known as the Salinas de Santa María. From these salines came salt that was measured in *fanegas*. Salt not only was crucial to the diet of Spaniards on the mining frontier, but it also was vital in extracting silver from ore. As an elderly Vicente de Zaldívar remarked, these salines "were very beneficial because silver cannot be removed by using mercury without salt." Furthermore, "the ocean was too far from the settlements, making it prohibitively expensive to transport salt from the coast."[25]

Each witness stressed Tolosa's signal contributions on the northern frontier. Unfortunately, his discoveries and the expenses associated with them, as well as boom-and-bust economic cycles, had made him a poor man at his death, and they had left his children "without means and in need." Therefore, according to repeated arguments and testimony, it was incumbent on the crown to provide financial relief to his children and their spouses. This was especially appropriate, because King Philip II had recognized the importance of Zacatecas by granting it a coat of arms on July 20, 1588.[26]

The *escudo* contains representations of the sun and the moon in the upper field, with a cross between them. A portrait of a crowned Our Lady of Zacatecas is the central figure. More significantly, four *retratos* (likenesses)—of Baltasar de Bañuelos, Juan de Tolosa, Diego Ibarra, and Cristóbal de Oñate—flank Our Lady of Zacatecas, two on each side.[27] The depiction of these men bears witness to their importance as the founders of Zacatecas.

All witnesses in Tolosa's *probanza* of merits and services testified at length about the importance of family on the northern frontier of New Spain. They recounted that Moctezuma II was the *rey natural* of Mexico, that his eldest daughter and principal heir was Isabel Moctezuma, and that Leonor Cortés Moctezuma was the daughter of Isabel and the granddaughter of the Aztec emperor. Next came a discussion of doña Leonor's famous father, Fernando Cortés, referred to as the first Marqués del Valle de Oaxaca.[28] Several of the deponents noted that Leonor's half-brother Luis Cortés accompanied her on the trip to Zacatecas and that after her wedding don Luis remained in the town. For a brief time, young Cortés joined his brother-in-law on a number of *entradas* before returning to Mexico City.[29]

These same witnesses, some of whom had been present at the wedding of Leonor Cortés Moctezuma and Juan de Tolosa, some of whom had attended the christening or baptism of the couple's three children, and some of whom had been present at their daughters' weddings, lend insight into what are likely the most complex family relationships in the

Figure 5.1. Coat of arms of Nuestra Señora de Zacatecas. (Adapted from AGI, Patronato, 80, N. 5, R. 1, fol. 90. Center for Media Production, University of North Texas.)

history of Spain in America. Underlying these intricate intermarriages of families was a powerful common bond: all were Basques. It is likely, in fact, that they spoke their native tongue in their homes and in discussions relating to the business of mining.[30]

The two daughters of Juan de Tolosa and Leonor Cortés Moctezuma are identified by the substantial names of Isabel de Tolosa Cortés Moctezuma and Leonor de Tolosa Cortés Moctezuma. Their brother, Juan de Tolosa Cortés Moctezuma, was a vicar. Isabel married Juan de Oñate, the future *adelantado* of New Mexico and son of Cristóbal de Oñate.[31]

Around 1550, Catalina de Salazar, a widow with three children, married Captain Cristóbal de Oñate and the couple began a second family. Catalina's daughter from her first marriage, Magdalena de Mendoza y Salazar, wed Vicente de Zaldívar, a witness in the 1594 *probanza* of merits and services. From their marriage came three sons: Vicente de Zaldívar Mendoza, Juan de Zaldívar Mendoza, and Cristóbal de Zaldívar Mendoza. The last would marry Leonor de Tolosa Cortés Moctezuma.[32]

The family ties of the Oñates and the Zaldívars began in Spain with the marriage of Cristóbal de Oñate's sister María Pérez de Oñate, to Ruy Díaz de Zaldívar. Their sons, Juan and Vicente, were important personages in their own right. Juan figured prominently in the conquest and settlement of Nueva Galicia under the command of Guzmán. He was a *poblador* of Guadalajara and built the first windmill in that town.[33] Shortly thereafter, Juan joined the rush of prospectors and miners who relocated in Zacatecas. Brother Vicente arrived on the mining frontier a bit later. He would figure importantly as a military commander in Indian wars that came hard on the heels of Zacatecas becoming a mining boomtown by 1550.

By midpoint of the sixteenth century, roads from established towns and cities to the south began to traverse the unconquered vastness of Gran Chichimeca to reach New Spain's mining frontier. The mines and

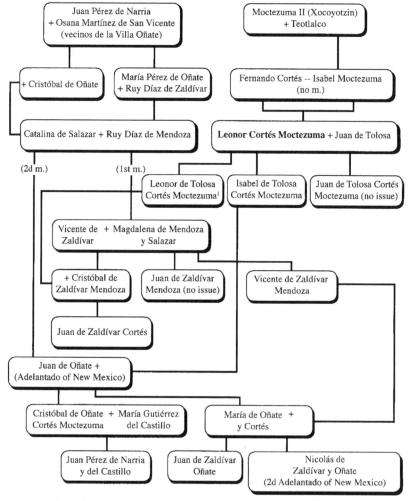

Figure 5.2. Genealogy of Leonor Cortés Moctezuma, the Oñates, and the Zaldívars. (Center for Media Production, University of North Texas.)

settlements had to have supplies, and extracted silver and rich ore had to arrive safely "at southern smelters and royal counting houses."[34]

The main highways to the north linked Guadalajara and Mexico City to Zacatecas and its environs. In late 1550, Zacateco Indians killed a group of Hispanicized Purepechas bound for the mining frontier with merchandise. This incident was the opening salvo of a war with the Chichimec nations that would engulf the mining frontier for nearly half a century. From 1550 to 1585, Spanish policy quickly evolved into a contest labeled "guerra a fuego y sangre" (war by fire and blood).[35]

Concerted military pressure was used against the offending Chichimecs. Overall, however, this intense struggle failed to pacify them. The nation that defeated with comparative ease the highest Indian civilizations in Mexico and Peru had little success with the Chichimecs. In addition to their deadly proficiency with bows and arrows, these frontier cultures were decentralized and did not depend on agriculture for their sustenance. So control of native food sources, a powerful tool in controlling sedentary cultures, was not effective against the Chichimecs. The Indians were also advantaged by their knowledge of terrain; by their difficult languages, which impeded communication by Franciscan missionaries and therefore delayed their efforts as agents of pacification; and by Spain's wide-ranging commitments in Europe and the Americas during the second half of the sixteenth century, a circumstance that often limited troop strength in any one theater of engagement.[36]

The expense of defending roads, mines, and settlements, coupled with overexpansion and failed enterprises, sapped the financial resources of Juan de Tolosa. He died at the mines of Pánuco near Zacatecas, leaving three children without an inheritance. He did not draft a will, perhaps because death came suddenly or because he had nothing of value to leave.[37]

Baltasar Temiño de Bañuelos and Diego de Ibarra fared no better than Tolosa. Bañuelos was the youngest of the Big Four and only a teenager when he arrived at Zacatecas in 1548. By 1560 he shared the misfortunes of others, because there was not a single mine, settlement, or ranch in the Zacatecas district that had not been hit by Chichimec raids. Similar attacks had struck his mines at San Martín and Avino in 1572, leaving him bereft of funds.[38] Diego de Ibarra also suffered heavy losses on the mining frontier. For example, in the 1560s Chichimecs raided one of his estancias, resulting in the death of his manager, a nephew, and many Indian workers.[39]

Having fared somewhat better than Tolosa, Bañuelos, and Ibarra—primarily because he was not in the business of mining—an elderly Vicente de Zaldívar was a key witness in the 1594 *probanza*. When asked the obligatory question about whether he knew the children of Juan de Tolosa and Leonor Cortés Moctezuma, he likely had a wry smile on his face. The sexagenarian recounted the parentage of doña Leonor and stressed his familial ties to her two daughters and their husbands. Isabel de Tolosa Cortés Moctezuma was married to Juan de Oñate, who was both Zaldívar's brother-in-law (actually the half-brother of don Vicente's wife) and his first cousin (Oñate and Zaldívar were children, respectively, of Cristóbal de Oñate and his sister, María Pérez de Oñate). A second son, Cristóbal de Zaldívar Mendoza, was married to Leonor de Tolosa Cortés Moctezuma.[40]

No one but the most dedicated of genealogists would attempt a complete understanding of the labyrinthine ties of the Moctezuma-Zaldívar-Oñate families of northern New Spain. What is important to remember is that the natural daughter of Fernando Cortés and Isabel Moctezuma married a Basque. Their daughters married an Oñate and a Zaldívar, likewise Basques. On a dangerous frontier where no one was more reliable than family members, and given the incredible difficulty of learning the Basque language, surely the Basque tongue was the vital "glue" of important people who would look beyond Zacatecas and its environs toward the land of the Pueblo Indians.

By 1585 it was clear that war by fire and blood had failed. As a consequence, Spanish policy aimed at pacifying the Chichimecs evolved over the next fifteen years. This shift in tactics has been labeled "peace by purchase," and it was instituted by the seventh viceroy of New Spain, Álvaro Manrique de Zúñiga. Manrique began the practice of providing food and clothing for Chichimecs in exchange for their promises of good behavior. He then moved colonies of Hispanicized and Christianized Indians from Central Mexico to the frontier, where they served as models of desirable conduct. Perhaps more important, Manrique's successors continued this approach, so that by 1600 "it could be said that the Spanish-Chichimeca War had come to an end."[41]

By then, thanks to the relative calm that benefited the advance of mining and cattle enterprises toward the present-day tier of northern states in Mexico, Juan de Oñate, the son-in-law of Leonor Cortés Moctezuma, had been in New Mexico for two years. In many respects, don Juan was the most notable success story of anyone in New Spain who could claim either blood or marital ties to descendants of Moctezuma II.

Juan de Oñate was one of seven children, five boys and two girls, born to Cristóbal de Oñate and Catalina de Salazar. His date of birth in Zacatecas is probably around 1552. Marc Simmons postulates that as an adult don Juan possessed both a bright and a dark side, and that his personality was a mix between that of his father and an uncle who was also named Juan.[42]

Both of the older Oñates fulfilled important roles under Guzmán in the conquest of New Galicia, yet they seemingly could not have been more different in character. In the lengthy *residencia* of Guzmán's governorship in western New Spain, witnesses praised don Cristóbal as a fine example of a conquistador–administrator who consistently respected and enforced laws that protected Indians under difficult circumstances. In contrast, these same witnesses attributed an astonishing litany of crimes to Cristóbal's brother Juan. He regularly beat and hanged Indians and fed their corpses to his mastiffs. He is portrayed in sworn testimony as a man without scruple or restraint. Recognizing that he would likely be brought before the bar of justice as a confederate of Guzmán, the elder Juan de Oñate left New Spain for Peru in 1537.[43]

Regardless of speculation about Oñate's psyche, he was certainly advantaged by birth. Cristóbal de Oñate was an important and wealthy man by the 1550s. He regularly traveled to Mexico City with his family, and it is reasonable to assume that son Juan stayed in the capital for extended periods of schooling. It was probably there that the young man picked up the social graces and command of written Spanish for which he was later noted.[44]

Mining enterprises at Zacatecas and the neighboring camp at Pánuco also became an integral part of Oñate's experience. His father, his brothers, and their associates immersed themselves in silver production. The Oñates lived in a home that was opulent enough to contain its own chapel. They were also surrounded by the bustle and noise of hammer mills and smelters used in ore processing.

Young Juan was certainly no stranger to the exploitation and abuse of the lower classes. His father owned approximately one hundred huts that housed slaves, and workers in don Cristóbal's mines included free blacks, black slaves, and underclass Indians.[45]

Oñate's formative years also coincided with the time of war by fire and blood. For some thirty-five years after his birth, the Chichimecs of northern New Spain unleashed their fury on Europeans who had invaded their homeland. These natives were highly skilled with bows with arrows that could easily penetrate Spanish armor. Spaniards experienced in foreign campaigns regarded the Zacatecos "as the best archers in the world." One observer remarked that these natives could "kill hares which, even though running, they pierce with arrows; also deer, birds, and other little animals of the land, not even overlooking rats . . . and they fish with the bow and arrow." From the time they could walk, their children practiced with this weapon by shooting at insects and small animals.[46]

The Chichimecs regularly tortured and scalped captives before cutting off their heads. They disemboweled others and forced children to drink the blood of their murdered parents. It is certainly reasonable to conclude that the horrific casualties inflicted by these Indians on Oñate's fellow miners and merchant friends colored his attitudes toward Indians. And those views were greatly intensified by the future *adelantado*'s experiences as a soldier.[47]

By his early twenties, Oñate had led campaigns against Indians, paying all expenses out of family monies. His forays against natives went on for more than two decades. As don Juan explained, he was simply emulating his ancestors, who had always volunteered their services to the king. He also had the example of an illustrious father who had fought many battles in Nueva Galicia. On a number of occasions, Oñate campaigned with his future father-in-law, Juan de Tolosa, and with Francisco de Ibarra, the youthful nephew of Diego de Ibarra.[48]

As Oñate campaigned, he kept a sharp eye out for veins of ore that promised riches. He is credited with finding, around 1574, a mining site named Charcas, some one hundred miles beyond Zacatecas. This locale was the domain of particularly fierce Chichimecs known as Guachichiles, and for several years the Spanish presence there was hotly contested. Permanent occupation of Charcas was not assured until 1582. By then Oñate was about thirty years of age and still single, but during the latter part of the 1580s he married Isabel de Tolosa Cortés Moctezuma. His marriage was little more than a brief interlude for a man who spent much of his adult life marching, fighting, and prospecting. Those experiences served to toughen his body and further mold his personality. Without doubt, they prepared him for a career in New Mexico that would secure his name in the annals of the Spanish Southwest.[49]

Prior to Oñate's discovery of Charcas, other Spaniards in the late 1560s had leapfrogged farther north to set up the settlement of Santa Bárbara near the headwaters of the Río Conchos in southern Chihuahua. This *villa* and a nearby community named Valle de San Bartolomé (present-day Valle de Allende) turned out to be logical gateways to Texas and New Mexico, especially after an Indian captive in the late 1570s spoke of populous settlements to the north wherein the people had abundant food and raised cotton for clothing.[50]

This information jogged memories of Pueblo country, not visited by Spaniards since Coronado had returned from there in the early 1540s. Fray Agustín Rodríguez, a Franciscan lay brother stationed at Valle de San Bartolomé, successfully petitioned the viceroy for permission to visit the land of the Pueblos. Joining Fray Agustín were Francisco López as his religious superior and another Franciscan, Juan de Santa María. The military commander of the expedition was an aged veteran, Francisco Sánchez de Chamuscado, who departed from Santa Bárbara in early June 1581.[51]

The *entrada* descended the Río Conchos to its junction with the Río Grande and then followed the larger stream northward to the environs of present-day Santa Fe. At that point, Father Santa María chose to leave the expedition and return alone to Santa Bárbara. Unfortunately, a war party followed him for three days, overtook him, and crushed his skull with a rock. After exploring extensively in New Mexico, Chamuscado announced his decision to return to his base near the upper Río Conchos. The two remaining friars, however, insisted on staying in what they regarded as a fertile field of missionary endeavors—a decision that would prove fatal.[52]

The second party of Spaniards to explore New Mexico left from Valle de San Bartolomé in late 1582. Led by Antonio de Espejo, it explored parts of New Mexico, where Espejo learned with certainty that López and Rodríguez had been martyred, and then probed westward to the environs of present-day Flagstaff, Arizona. After some ten months, the expedition returned to its point of departure.[53]

While Espejo was in the field, the crown, on April 19, 1583, authorized the pacification of Pueblo country. Applicants had to provide their own financing, be approved by the Council of the Indies, and agree to observe new ordinances concerning the good treatment of natives. For complex reasons that involved Juan de Oñate, no patent to colonize and pacify New Mexico would be forthcoming for a dozen years.[54]

The crown's impetus to reach an agreement with a rich Spaniard was spurred by two illegal expeditions into New Mexico in the early 1590s. But even so, finding an acceptable aspirant turned out to be agonizingly slow and Byzantine. It is apparent that Oñate was not at the top of the short list of hopefuls.

One of the richest men in New Spain was Juan Lomas y Colmenares. His properties in Nueva Vizcaya included mines, tilled fields, vineyards, and enormous pastures for thousands of cattle. Lomas y Colmenares's demands, however, were so outlandish—civil and military authority to expand New Mexico to both oceans, forty thousand Indian vassals in perpetuity, and a personal grant of land entailing more than sixty square miles—that it must have seemed as though he was the king rather than the petitioner. Additionally, Lomas asked for perpetual titles of *conde* or *marqués* and *adelantado* for him and his family. As Marc Simmons has commented, "No one since Columbus had dared ask for so much."[55] Not surprisingly, the Spanish crown did not rush to approve such an outrageous proposal.

Five years went by, and then a second petition came from Francisco de Urdiñola, another Basque with impressive credentials. Urdiñola had likewise fought Chichimecs, discovered mines, and acquired considerable wealth. Regarded as one of the most capable leaders on the northern frontier, by 1591 Urdiñola held the title of lieutenant governor of Nueva Vizcaya. At the urging of Viceroy Luis de Velasco II, in 1594 the lieutenant governor threw his hat in the ring. Consideration of his bid had scarcely begun before he was indicted on charges of "poisoning his wife and murdering several servants." Those charges were leveled by none other than a jealous and vindictive Lomas y Colmenares. In defending himself against such serious accusations, Urdiñola had little time to pursue a royal appointment in New Mexico.[56]

With Urdiñola's arrest, Viceroy Velasco turned to Juan de Oñate. Although the Oñates were the most successful of the original Big Four, there is little doubt that their resources had dwindled by the mid-1590s. Oñate was certainly far less wealthy than Lomas y Colmenares or Urdiñola but he nonetheless signed a formal contract with the viceroy on September 21, 1595. In the following month, just before being replaced as

Figure 5.3. Towns, mines, and physical features of northern New Spain and New Mexico. (Center for Media Production, University of North Texas.)

viceroy, Luis de Velasco appointed Oñate as governor and captain general of New Mexico.[57]

Oñate's choice of agents and participants in the proposed *entrada* into New Mexico again underscores the importance of family ties. His four brothers took on the responsibility of raising money and representing him before the viceroy in Mexico City. One nephew, Cristóbal de Zaldívar Mendoza, also remained in the heartland of New Spain. Two other nephews, Juan de Zaldívar Mendoza and Vicente de Zaldívar Mendoza, became, respectively, second-in-command of the expedition (field marshal) and lieutenant field marshal.

Initial preparations for the occupation of New Mexico began in Zacatecas, but by spring 1596, Oñate had begun to move his base of operations some four hundred miles north, to Santa Bárbara. However, any thoughts he may have entertained of a quick departure for the land of the Pueblos were soon dashed. For nearly two years, Oñate had to endure efforts to discredit him and replace him with another commander. During this time, his financial resources drained and discipline eroded. As a final obstacle, the expedition had to undergo a detailed inspection to determine whether Oñate had fulfilled the terms of his contract.[58]

Although Oñate did not have as many men and supplies as his original contract called for, the inspector signed off on the expedition, but only after Oñate signed a second, more restrictive, agreement and provided a bond that covered the deficiencies. At last, on January 26, 1598, the *entrada* left Santa Bárbara and Valle de San Bartolomé and began the long journey to New Mexico. Oñate reached San Juan de los Caballeros, just north of present-day Santa Fe, in July.[59]

For the next decade, Juan de Oñate served a much-troubled term as governor and captain general of New Mexico. Although his contract specified that he also receive the honorific designation of *adelantado*, the king did not confer that title until the early 1600s.[60]

Oñate's handling of affairs in New Mexico has been the subject of numerous scholarly works, so I shall emphasize the long-term impact of his governorship on the husband of Isabel Moctezuma's granddaughter and his and his wife's legacy. The most controversial matter during Juan de Oñate's residence in New Mexico was the native uprising at Ácoma Pueblo—more specifically, its suppression and the harsh punishment inflicted on the Ácomans. This revolt in late 1598 cost the lives of thirteen

Spaniards, including the governor's young nephew and second-in-command, Juan de Zaldívar Mendoza.

Under Oñate's orders, Vicente de Zaldívar Mendoza marched on Ácoma to crush the rebellion and avenge the death of his brother. On January 22 and 23, 1599, don Vicente accomplished his goal. The surviving adult males were taken as prisoners to Santo Domingo Pueblo, where their three-day trial began on February 9. Found guilty of killing Juan de Zaldívar Mendoza and twelve others, males over twenty-five years of age received Oñate's judgment on February 12. Twenty-four of them would have a foot cut off, followed by twenty years of servitude. Males between the ages of twelve and twenty-five, as well as women and girls older than twelve, were likewise sentenced to twenty years of servitude. Two Hopi Indians who were at Ácoma and fought against the Spaniards were to have their right hands amputated. Those natives condemned to have an appendage struck off received the horrific penalties in nearby towns by February 15.[61]

Oñate also employed a heavy hand with regard to four Spaniards who stole horses and dared leave New Mexico without his permission. He termed them "evildoers" and sent out a detachment to execute them as soon as they were apprehended. The fugitives made it deep into Nueva Vizcaya before being overtaken. The two ringleaders were beheaded on the spot; the right hands were chopped from the corpses, salted, and returned to Oñate as proof of death.[62]

The harshness of Juan de Oñate's decisions reflects the previously mentioned duality of his personality. Just as day-to-day life on a distant frontier without readily exploitable wealth lessened the enthusiasm of his colonists, circumstances likewise eroded don Juan's initial "largeness of spirit mixed with flexibility and enthusiasm for diplomacy." As a result, the governor's mood soured and he became suspicious of his followers. He showed favoritism toward a few and inflicted brutal punishment on others. For his merciless attitude toward real and imagined offenders, whether Indian or Spaniard, Oñate would later pay a substantial price.[63]

Marc Simmons's biography of Juan de Oñate provides evidence that the beginnings of *villa* Santa Fe precede by about two years the customarily accepted founding date of 1610, and that Oñate deserves credit for its founding. More important, Oñate laid the foundations of a new kingdom, of the Franciscan missionary program, and of European agricultural and stock-raising enterprises. He also established the northern segment of a *camino real* (royal road or principal highway) that ran from Chihuahua to Santa Fe. Despite his shortcomings and much to the displeasure of many Indians, historians have added another title to his name: the Father of New Mexico.[64]

Simmons also notes that after Oñate left New Mexico and returned to Zacatecas at the beginning of the second decade of the seventeenth century, he found the family mines in disrepair. With typical energy and expertise he brought in new equipment and restored productivity within three years. In fact, he recouped much of the family wealth that had been expended in New Mexico. This refutes a common assertion that Oñate's troubled governorship resulted in his family's financial ruin.[65]

By 1614 Oñate had been ordered to Mexico City to undergo *residencia* proceedings. Although the trial record has not come to light, his sentence and its subsequent appeal indicate that the former governor faced thirty charges of misconduct. He was cleared of eighteen counts but found guilty on twelve. The most serious of those charges involved his unjust hanging of two Indians, his use of excessive force in suppressing the revolt at Ácoma, and his orders to execute two Spanish captains who had fled beyond his jurisdiction as governor of New Mexico. Lesser charges included committing adultery, thereby setting a bad moral tone for his soldiers and colonists.

The viceroy sentenced Juan de Oñate on May 13, 1614. Punishment was far from a mere slap on the wrist, although not as punitive as one might suspect: permanent banishment from New Mexico; four years' exile from Mexico City; loss of titles; a fine of six thousand Castilian ducats; and payment of court costs.[66] There is little doubt that the name Oñate and the notable accomplishments of his forebears, as well as the prestige of his wife, ameliorated the judgment.

During his post–New Mexico residence in Zacatecas, Oñate and Isabel de Tolosa Cortés Moctezuma lost their only son, Cristóbal de Oñate Cortés Moctezuma, at age twenty-two. The death of his principal heir fell heavily on don Juan, and it appears that he never completely recovered.[67] The couple's only other child, María de Oñate y Cortés, married her cousin, Vicente de Zaldívar Mendoza, who had avenged his brother's death at Ácoma. This marriage further tightened the intricate knot of Oñates and Zaldívars, making don Vicente the second cousin, nephew, and son-in-law of the *adelantado*. This marriage occurred at about the time Oñate appealed to the king in an attempt to reverse the judge of *residencia*'s sentence.

In 1617 Oñate sent documentation to Spain to support his contention that testimony during his *residencia* had been unfair to him. He argued, for example, that the charge of adultery was absolutely false, insisting that he had always remained faithful to his wife. However, doña Isabel's whereabouts during her husband's governorship in New Mexico are uncertain. It seems unlikely that she never joined him, but in the documentation contained in a two-volume compilation by George P. Hammond and Agapito Rey, there is only one intriguing clue that Isabel may have been in New Mexico. In a list of items being sent to the province in 1600, there is this notation: "Further, there are in these wagons six boxes of gifts which Doña María de Galarza is sending to the wife of the adelantado, Don Juan de Oñate."[68] In any event, the charge of adultery was minor compared to the more serious charges from which Oñate was never entirely absolved.

Around 1619 or 1620, Oñate's wife of roughly thirty years died. Following her burial at Zacatecas, Oñate left for Spain, where he again attempted to clear his name. He aimed his petitions at restoring lost titles and receiving reimbursement for his six thousand-ducat fine. Twice he won favorable judgments from the Council of the Indies, and twice King Philip IV rejected the council's decision. Oñate's persistence, however, brought partial vindication in August 1623: repayment of the fine and restoration of his title as *adelantado* for two lives. Permanent banishment from New Mexico, however, remained in effect.[69]

Evidence of Oñate's improved standing with the king is reflected in his appointment as mining inspector for all of Spain in 1624. The former governor obviously brought superb qualifications to the post. He had grown up on New Spain's mining frontier, and he "had been closely associated with every phase of mineral assaying, extraction, smelting, and refining." In the following year, he successfully sought admission to the prestigious military Order of Santiago by filing a lengthy *prueba de caballero* (proof of eligibility)—still further evidence of Oñate's restored reputation in the eyes of the king.[70]

In June 1626 Juan de Oñate collapsed and died after inspecting a flooded mine. Given the nature of much of his life's work, the circumstances surrounding his death seem appropriate. At that time, he was probably in his mid-seventies. His will provided for a Jesuit chapel and church in Madrid, where he was to be buried. Oñate also provided a substantial bequest for his son-in-law and daughter in New Spain, but in the long run even that "great fortune" did not keep them from financial disaster.[71]

After returning to Zacatecas, Vicente de Zaldívar Mendoza had thrown himself into mining with the same enthusiasm that marked his service in New Mexico, and he was initially even more successful than his father-in-law. During one five-month period, his mines yielded 150,000 pesos' worth of silver. These riches made him and his wife well accepted into the highest circles of colonial society and, like Oñate, he, too, became a knight of Santiago.

Given the cyclical vicissitudes of silver mining in New Spain, however, don Vicente should have taken lessons from others, such as Juan de Tolosa, who saw their wealth disappear in astonishingly quick fashion. During the 1630s he lost virtually all of his vast estates and died poor around 1650. His widow, María de Oñate y Cortés, faced abject poverty. By some accounts, her sustenance depended on the sale of bedding straw from a vending cart in the streets of Zacatecas. Her son Nicolás de Zaldívar y Oñate succeeded his grandfather as the second *adelantado* of New Mexico.[72]

The other daughter of Leonor Cortés Moctezuma and Cristóbal de Zaldívar (María de Oñate y Cortés) gave birth to a son named Juan de Zaldívar Oñate. Likely encouraged by the successes of Juan de Oñate and Vicente de Zaldívar Mendoza in achieving status as knights of Santiago, young Juan filed a *prueba de caballero* in 1627. That effort apparently failed, because two years later the Council of the Indies urged the king to proceed with caution in making additional concessions of knighthood to aspirants in New Galicia. It would appear that Philip IV accepted the recommendation of his council.[73]

Overall, the descendants of Leonor Cortés de Moctezuma reprised the financial shortcomings of most descendants of Moctezuma II who remained in the New World. Those who fared best had to cross the Atlantic Ocean, where they eventually entered the ranks of the Spanish peerage. Through marriage, one of them helped secure her husband's appointment to the highest position in the government of New Spain.

Six

The Peerage and the Viceroyalty of New Spain

THROUGHOUT MUCH OF THE SIXTEENTH CENTURY, the three principal heirs of Moctezuma II and their descendants stressed that the Aztec emperor had been a *rey natural* who, if left in power, would have passed on to them legacies of great value.[1] That did not happen, because the Spanish conquest of New Spain radically altered their inheritances. These points were repeated hundreds of times in lawsuits and other legal instruments such as *memoriales* (briefs) and *probanzas* of merits and services. Crucial to the eventual success of Moctezuma II's descendants in obtaining even a diminished inheritance was whether Moctezuma had freely handed over his rights as a natural ruler to the king of Spain.

In his presidential address to the American Historical Association (1978), Charles Gibson stressed the absence of treaties between Spaniards and Indians. Contributing to this circumstance were total and comprehensive conquests in many areas of the Indies. Accordingly, "the freedom of the Indian in the Spanish colony became, as everyone knows, severely limited." Natives were then obliged to accept Spanish norms of behavior, to convert to Christianity, and to become subjects of the Spanish king.[2]

Especially important was how Spaniards viewed the status of defeated native peoples. They often thought of them as "free vassals" of the crown, which clearly implies that the Indians had had an opportunity to make this decision for themselves. Free vassalage in Spain itself "depended upon agreement, fealty, homage, honor, a sense of duty, willing service—in short attitudes incapable of being coerced." Indeed, the infamous

Requirement (*Requerimiento*, 1512), which Lewis Hanke calls "a most remarkable document," emphasized the importance of voluntarism. Succinctly stated: native acceptance of "voluntary vassalage will bring good results; continued resistance will bring slavery."[3]

The *Requerimiento* was to be read to Indians before any hostilities could legally be undertaken. It called on the natives to accept the Roman Catholic Church and its "high priest called the Pope" and to acknowledge that the kings and queens of Spain had authority over them by virtue of Alexander VI's papal bull of 1493. The Indians must also allow the Catholic faith to be preached among them, whereupon they would be accepted as free vassals. If the natives agreed, "well and good." But if not, punitive measures would follow: "We shall take you and your wives and your children, and shall make slaves of them . . . and we shall take away your goods, and shall do all the harm and damage that we can, as to vassals who do not obey, and refuse to accept their lord, and resist and contradict him; and we protest that the deaths and losses which shall accrue from this are your fault, and not that of their Highnesses."[4]

When one considers the manner in which Spanish captains often used the *Requerimiento*, it will likely tax the credulity of some readers: they read it *in Spanish* "to trees and empty huts when no Indians were to be found"; they muttered it into their beards and recited its provisions to rocks and mountains—at times more than two miles away—before beginning an attack; and they mumbled its complex verbiage from ships approaching an island. The most scathing condemnation of the *Requerimiento* came from Bartolomé de las Casas, who called it "unjust, scandalous, irrational, and absurd." Indeed, the Dominican friar summed up his feelings by remarking that he did not know whether it was better to laugh or cry about such a ridiculous document.[5]

The *Requerimiento* is well known to most students of the Spanish experience in America. I discuss it here because it was so supremely important to the children of the emperor. As Patricia Seed has noted, with the reading of the *Requerimiento*, "what is at stake is not simply . . . control over a region, but the legitimate government of an entire state. To omit the rituals would be to jeopardize the establishment of legitimate dominion." Accordingly, Cortés was at pains to state categorically that Moctezuma had freely and voluntarily ceded the Aztec empire to Charles V. Missing entirely is any mention of Moctezuma's opposition to Spaniards as they advanced from Villa Rica de la Vera Cruz to Tenochtitlan. Equally suspect are the primary sources of evidence for the emperor's donation: Cortés himself and Bernal Díaz.[6]

Cortés maintained that the conquest of the Aztec empire was legal under the umbrella of the *Requerimiento*. At the same time, Moctezuma was the legitimate ruler of his own lands. Resolution of these contradictory premises was not easily or speedily resolved. The eventual solution was one that was most acceptable within the confines of the European mentality of those times. In Cortés's view, Moctezuma had collaborated in furthering the goals of Spain and its most Catholic emperor. Once the Aztec ruler accepted obedience to Charles V, he never deviated from fealty. The rebellion that preceded La Noche Triste arose against his wishes, and in attempting to restore his subjects' loyalty to the Spanish crown, he was mortally wounded. Furthermore, Cortés referred to Moctezuma with titles that were troublesome to the crown: "señor de Tenochtitlan," "vassal of the king," "defender of Spaniards," and "sympathizer with the Catholic faith."[7]

The important thing to remember is that Charles V and Philip II accepted Cortés's claims and the validity of Moctezuma's concession. Accordingly, the dire consequences so forcibly spelled out in the *Requerimiento* could not legally be applied to the Aztec emperor or his descendants. As proof of royal assent, it will be remembered that Charles V authorized a coat of arms for Pedro Moctezuma that recognized his lineage with gold crowns—one for each of his father's thirty-two kingdoms. Philip II acknowledged the Aztec emperor's concession in 1567 by stating that Moctezuma "had voluntarily placed himself under the authority of the crown."[8]

Sir John H. Elliott has noted the irony of Cortés's actions by pointing out that the conqueror was a "natural rebel." Nevertheless, Cortés was quick to see the possibilities "of enhancing the prestige and power of his prince." He shrewdly pointed out the coincidence of the conquest of New Spain with King Charles I's accession as Holy Roman Emperor. And he suggested that Charles also call himself Emperor of New Spain, the former realm of Moctezuma II, "with no less reason and title than he did of Germany, which by the grace of God Your Majesty possesses." To strengthen his proposal, Cortés arranged "an 'imperial donation' by Moctezuma, although he conveniently lost the papers recording this singular act of state."[9]

Charles V rejected the notion of assuming still another title, as

Emperor of the Indies or of New Spain, because his view of empire was decidedly European. That the Hapsburg prince did not see himself as emperor of the entire world was consistent with the position of Francisco de Vitoria, the great Spanish political theorist who held the Prime Chair of Theology at the University of Salamanca (1526–1546). Vitoria argued that the emperor "could make no claim to exercise either sovereignty . . . or dominion over peoples who lie outside the jurisdiction of the former Roman Empire."[10] Furthermore, as Elliott notes, Charles had a pragmatic disinclination to view the Indies as an important star in the imperial crown. Between 1521 and 1544, mines in the hereditary land of the Hapsburgs produced four times as much silver as all mines in the Indies.[11]

For these reasons, Cortés's claim of Moctezuma's alleged donation did not strike a responsive chord with Charles V, apparently because he viewed New Spain as being relatively unimportant. However, with the development of silver mining in New Spain, Peru, and Bolivia by the mid-sixteenth century, followed by the coronation of Philip II in 1556, the situation changed. The matter of Moctezuma's "natural rights" became an increasingly more urgent and nagging question in a decidedly tiered world of Spaniards. The persistence and energy with which the Aztec emperor's descendants, spurred in many cases by their Spanish spouses, sought hereditary rights in New Spain made the issue even more pressing. All of this prompted Philip II to arrange a settlement with many Moctezuma family claimants in 1590. By this time, Philip primarily sought resolution with the great-grandchildren of the former Aztec emperor.

In retrospect, Philip II's attempt to reach an accord with the heirs of Moctezuma—albeit a decision delayed for the better part of a century—was consistent with norms of both Spanish and Indian society in the sixteenth century. As James Lockhart has observed, Spaniards found the indigenous system in New Spain, whereby essentially the entire population could be divided into nobles and commoners, "remarkably like their own."[12] And although Fernando Cortés and Juan Cano regarded Isabel Moctezuma as a pioneer of *mestizaje* and model of Hispanization, the granting in perpetuity of Tacuba and Ecatepec, respectively, to Isabel and Mariana Moctezuma, as well as the later concession of Tula as an entailed estate of the heirs of Pedro Moctezuma, came about because the recipients were Indian royals.[13] Reflective of the unique status of these children of the emperor was a mandatory disclaimer of any future rights as sovereigns of Mexico in exchange for specific remuneration.

Philip II granted *mercedes* to the descendants of Juan Cano, Juan de Andrade, Pedro Moctezuma, and their wives but not to the offspring of Juan de Tolosa and Leonor Cortés Moctezuma—perhaps because of Leonor Cortés's unusual birth and upbringing. Some concessions came as reward for services rendered, additional ones for recognition of Moctezuma's capitulation, and still others in exchange for *encomienda* relinquishment. Compensation took the form of one-time monetary grants, annuities from the royal treasury, and royalized *encomiendas* (granted for a specified number of lives or in perpetuity). Additional awards included unassigned vacant *encomiendas*.[14]

The multiple briefs and lawsuits filed by Juan Cano in the 1530s and the 1540s contended that revenues from Tacuba were but a fraction of what was due Isabel Moctezuma as the foremost heir of the Aztec emperor. As a case in point, Isabel's son Gonzalo requested the enormous sum of fifty thousand ducats. The overall settlement ordered by Philip II specifically mentions that the decision was in response to "these importunities" of Moctezuma's heirs.[15]

The specifics of the 1590 settlement, like many things related to the Moctezuma heirs, are complicated. Two folios containing a family tree and accompanying information are preserved in the Archivo General de Indias. One of the folios is broken on both sides, and the other is damaged in the middle, resulting in missing information. The first contains a marginal notation that Moctezuma's descendants were awarded a total of 7,400 pesos in rents, all of which were perpetual. Of those monies, the children of Juan de Andrade and María Iñiguez each received grants ranging from 500 to 650 pesos, totaling 2,100 pesos; two of their grandchildren were to divide the sum of 1,300 pesos. Pedro Moctezuma's son Diego Luis garnered 3,000 pesos; the son of Juan Cano de Moctezuma received 2,000 pesos.[16]

The sources of income for some children of the emperor varied, as described above. Since all recipients had to renounce any further rights of inheritance, Philip viewed the settlement of 1590 as ending all claims based on the donation of Moctezuma II; but this did not end the matter. For example, four years later the daughters of Juan de Tolosa and Leonor Cortés Moctezuma, who had learned of the settlement in Spain (see Figure 3.1) with other grandchildren and great-grandchildren of the Aztec emperor, sought *mercedes* for themselves, and both were willing to sign documents renouncing any hereditary rights in New Spain.[17] There is no evidence that they were successful, but, as noted in the previous chapter, the son of Vicente de Zaldívar Mendoza and María de Oñate y Cortés (the daughter of Isabel de Tolosa Cortés Moctezuma) did gain admission to the prestigious military Order of Santiago (see Figure 5.2).

In Spain, claims of descent from Moctezuma II would play an important part in continued efforts to gain admission into the ranks of the nobility and the military orders. Entry into the peerage was undeniably important. As Doris M. Ladd has noted, a Spanish noble was a "king's man whose wife and wealth were beyond reproach and whose ancestors were 'pure Christians' unsullied by the 'taint' of Moorish, Jewish, pagan, or heretical devotions." Elite noblemen were the grandees who also carried titles such as duke and count. After 1631 if a person acquired the rank of marquis or count, that individual also received and paid for the title of viscount.[18]

• • •

The extended families of Pedro Moctezuma, Gonzalo Cano de Moctezuma, Juan Cano de Moctezuma, and their wives eventually entered the rarefied atmosphere of the titled nobility or knighthood. The patterns of their successes and failures during the last hundred years of the Hapsburg era reveal just how deeply these descendants of Aztec royalty had woven themselves into the fabric of the dominant Spanish culture.

At first glance, Diego Luis, Pedro Moctezuma's principal heir, appears to have been financially secure by the 1590s. He had profited from Philip II's general settlement with many of the Moctezuma heirs; he had married the granddaughter of the powerful Duke of Alburquerque, a Spanish grandee with a sizable annual income; and he had won a judgment in 1590 amounting to twenty thousand pesos for tribute payments in New Spain that had accrued since the death of his half-brother Martín. However, it was one thing to win the promise of dependable income but quite another to collect it (see Figure 4.2).

After marriage, Diego Luis and his wife, Francisca de la Cueva, settled into a residence at Guadix near the city of Granada and began a family, which by the early years of the 1600s had grown to include four sons and a daughter. Their eldest son and principal heir was Pedro Tesifón.[19] Unfortunately, Diego Luis and his descendants were often at the mercy of

events beyond their control. Annual payments for *mercedes* granted in perpetuity were seldom received in full or in liquid form; instead, all too
often they trickled in as *juros*. All too often, promised income from
encomiendas in New Spain was not realized, and all too often, national or
international affairs meant no income whatsoever for extended periods
of time.[20]

Because Diego Luis had difficulty collecting his allotted *mercedes*, he
sought additional ones from the crown in 1603. In this petition, he admitted that he was the natural son of Pedro Moctezuma and doña Catalina,
herself a descendant of the native nobility of Tula and Tenochtitlan. In
addition to insisting that his parents were persons of quality, Diego Luis
spun out the then-established position that his grandfather Moctezuma II
had performed a great service for Charles V by becoming the emperor's
subject and by handing over his own rights as a natural king. These claims
were preparatory to Diego Luis's request for royal concessions to support
himself, his wife, and their five living children.[21]

Diego Luis asked for more extensive *mercedes* than he had ever before
requested: the three thousand pesos in tribute from New Spain's *encomiendas* should be increased to four thousand; his four sons should be admitted to military orders; the title of Marqués de Tula should be granted him;
a gift of royal lands within the province of Tula that would yield an
annual income of three hundred pesos should be made; and all income
produced by *repartimientos de trabajos* (forced labor for wages) performed
by natives on crown properties in the province of Tula should go to
him.[22]

The petitioner was particularly insistent on admission to military
orders for his four sons. This concession would guarantee them some
income, would free them from Inquisitorial investigations into their
limpieza de sangre (literally, "cleanness of blood"), and would give them
status as hidalgos. The title of *marqués* would likewise establish the family's
dignity and bring with it admission to the Spanish peerage.[23]

It seems likely that Diego Luis decided to test Philip III, the new king
of Spain, who had a reputation for being more generous than his austere
father, Philip II. Unfortunately for the petitioner, the king's advisory
council recommended against making such generous concessions. On
May 4, 1604, the council agreed to only one of Diego Luis's requests by
giving him title to small royal properties in Tula.[24]

Not satisfied, Diego Luis renewed his petitions in Valladolid on the very day he learned of the council's decision, and he did so by asking for even greater *mercedes*, amounting to fifty thousand ducats. He reiterated the request that his sons be granted admission to military orders, and he repeated his request that the title of Marqués de Tula be conferred on him. As before, his entreaties brought little by way of compensation. Philip III's advisory council recommended no increase in *encomienda* revenues from Tula. It did agree, and the king accepted the recommendation, that one military order habit would be awarded to the eldest son, Pedro Tesifón.[25]

On May 31, 1606, Diego Luis set forth the provisions of his will in Valladolid and later died in that city. The fact that he had continued to live near the court of Philip III rather than reside in Guadix certainly suggests his persistence in seeking additional *mercedes*. Each petition gained something, and at the time of his death, Diego Luis enjoined his wife, Francisca de la Cueva, and Pedro Tesifón to seek further concessions. It was a task that they readily accepted, apparently out of necessity.[26]

With the exception of Pedro Tesifón, who was twenty-one, Diego Luis's children were minors when their father died. Accordingly, the burden of providing for these youngsters fell on their mother. Her efforts were made more difficult by Spain's declining economy. Heavy taxes levied on those classes least able to pay them and depopulation occasioned by a plague in 1599 and 1600 coupled with precipitous inflation and a weak-willed monarch combined to spell trouble for anyone who depended on annuities or interest on bonds paid by the royal treasury.[27]

Philip II recognized the weaknesses of his successor by lamenting that "God, who has given me so many kingdoms, has denied me a son capable of ruling them." In support of this harsh judgment is John H. Elliott's devastating description of the new king: "Philip III, twenty years old at the time of his accession, was a pallid, anonymous creature, whose only virtue appeared to reside in a total absence of vice."[28]

Lacking the talent or energy to rule, Philip III chose to separate himself from the problems of his subjects, entrusting affairs of state to a *valido* (favorite), Francisco de Sandoval y Rojas, Marqués de Denia, better known as the Duke of Lerma. The duke's principal concern was promoting his and his family's financial interests. He also set an example of ostentation and disdain for work or commerce. The Spanish nobility, essentially exempted by law from having to pay taxes, followed suit. This made things even more difficult for Diego Luis's family, with its pretensions to nobility. They were expected to display a certain savoir vivre, made much more difficult by the uncertainty of receiving revenues from New Spain.[29]

Francisca de la Cueva's financial resources were stretched even thinner by the necessity of having to pay legal fees associated with validating her husband's will. In doing so, she had to borrow money to secure the family's entailed estate. On March 13, 1609, doña Francisca also began legal proceedings to increase her sources of income. It was a familiar scenario, harking back to the donation of Moctezuma II and the benefits thereof to the Spanish crown.[30]

Doña Francisca was particularly sensitive about confirming the legitimacy of her children—especially given the lengthy travails of her husband to establish his rights of inheritance. She emphasized that she and Diego Luis had married in the Roman Catholic Church with the blessings of the king, and that all of her offspring were the product of that union. Stressing her own *limpieza de sangre* as a granddaughter of the Duke of Alburquerque, she moved on to specific requests.[31]

The widow of Diego Luis asked once again that income from the family's *encomiendas* in New Spain be increased from three thousand to four thousand pesos; she repeated the request that the younger sons and her daughter's future husband be admitted to military orders; she sought an outright grant of four thousand pesos to be divided equally among her younger children; and she beseeched the crown to set aside part of any increased income for her own support.[32]

Unfortunately for doña Francisca, her agent, charged with collecting rents in New Spain, informed her that Tula could no longer provide the promised income, much less any increase. Any additional sources of tribute payments to the family would have to come from the allocation of vacant *encomiendas*, which only the crown could order. Doña Francisca then threw herself on the mercy of the king, declaring that since the death of her husband the family had lived in abject poverty.[33]

This petition struck a responsive chord when a royal tribunal agreed to hear the case on December 3, 1609, although it took slightly more than two years to hammer out the details. During this time, Pedro Tesifón took an active part in representing the family. In a formal legal compact, the crown signed off on concessions, which, if honored, amounted to a significant victory for this branch of the Moctezuma family.[34]

The settlement stated specifically that none of Pedro Moctezuma's descendants could ever again make claim to political authority in New Spain. In exchange, the following concessions would be made: Pedro Tesifón and doña María's future husband would receive the habits of military orders, thereby providing her a dowry; Pedro Tesifón would inherit the entailed estate granted to his grandfather plus an additional one thousand ducats—both awarded in perpetuity; the three younger sons and their sister won yearly stipends of fifteen hundred ducats—with the stipulation that they and their eldest brother were each to provide their mother with three hundred ducats yearly for the rest of her life.[35]

The family accepted the terms and in doing so won awards amounting to seven thousand ducats in excess of the original amount granted to Pedro Tesifón. However, a stipulation that all monies must come from vacant *encomiendas* in New Spain significantly undercut the value of this contract. Terms of the agreement also set the stage for legal maneuvers by the family for decades to come. As a final gesture and show of good faith on the part of the crown, a special one-time *merced* of six thousand ducats was given to don Pedro with the proviso that he use it to support the family until the promised income could be realized. As it turned out, this stipend was much needed.[36]

Having issued a judgment favorable to Diego Luis's widow and her children, the crown sent orders in April 1612 to the viceroy of New Spain, commanding him to collect annually tribute from vacant *encomiendas* amounting to approximately seven thousand silver pesos. Three years later, Viceroy Diego Fernández de Córdoba, Marqués de Guadalcázar, insisted that he had not been able to comply with the directive.[37]

In the meantime, monies from the royal treasury helped support the family while it awaited income from New Spain, but it was not enough. Pedro Tesifón and a younger brother enlisted as captains in the Spanish infantry. The former served for a time in North Africa and Italy. Although military service brought some compensation, Pedro Tesifón admitted that the obligation of providing his own equipment and retainers made it an unprofitable undertaking.[38]

Desperate for income, doña Francisca filed one petition after another with the crown. The official response was to send new and more urgent directives to the viceroy of New Spain. The family also employed an agent to represent it before the viceroy and Audiencia in Mexico City— all to no avail. As mentioned, in 1615 the Marqués de Guadalcázar acknowledged his inability to comply with repeated royal directives.

Only a small amount of tribute could be collected from vacant *encomien-das*, and the amount of unpledged monies in the treasury of New Spain was minuscule.[39]

By late 1616 Pedro Tesifón had probably been informed by the family's agent of the dismal prospects for income from New Spain. He once again beseeched the crown to provide direct payments from the royal treasury in lieu of unrealized tribute income. On this occasion, as before, the crown responded by sending yet another *cédula* to the viceroy. However, rather than leave the matter to the discretion of the Marqués de Guadalcázar, fifteen *pueblos* located in various parts of New Spain were specifically awarded to the Moctezumas.[40]

Although tribute from these *encomienda* towns was considerably lower than in previous years, it did provide a source of income that helped the family. And with the premature death of Philip III on March 31, 1621, hope for additional concessions came in the person of the new king.

Philip IV was only sixteen years of age when he ascended the Spanish throne. Given his youth, it was natural that supplicants for royal favors would test his mettle. However, petitioners also had to win favor with Philip's *privado* (counselor), Gaspar de Guzmán, Count Duke of Olivares, the young monarch's childhood mentor.[41]

Shortly after Philip IV's coronation, Cristóbal Moctezuma, Pedro Tesifón's younger brother, died without direct heirs. The crown ordered that his income be divided among his siblings and his mother. Even so, the family continued to protest the lack of promised income from its *encomiendas* in New Spain.[42]

In the mid-1620s, Pedro Tesifón married Gerónima de Porras y Castillo, a daughter of the Marqués de Castro Nuevo. Thus, he became linked by marriage to a noble house in Spain. On February 24, 1627, Philip IV granted him the title of Viscount of Ilucan. In September 1627 Pedro Tesifón drafted a communication to Philip IV in which he indicated that his preference for a title was Count of Moctezuma de Tula y Tultengo. In doing so, he acknowledged that his ancestry sprang not only from the former Aztec emperor but also from prominent native nobles associated with those Toltec cities. On December 14 of the same year he received the more prestigious title of Count of Moctezuma. Philip stated that these honors were bestowed in recognition of the great service that Moctezuma II had rendered to Charles V, as well as for Pedro Tesifón's service to the crown. In late summer of that same year, Philip approved entry into military orders for Pedro Tesifón, his younger brother, and his sister's future husband.[43] But just as matters had taken such a favorable turn, disaster lay in the near future.[44]

As an example of this family's vulnerability to events beyond its control, in 1628 Dutch warships commanded by Piet Heyn captured the annual Spanish treasure fleet that transported gold, silver, and spices from the Indies. Although Spain in the sixteenth century had instituted a convoy system that had successfully protected the shipment of such valuable New World shipments from its foreign enemies for many decades, security failed in this instance. The loss of the entire fleet and its cargo produced a financial crisis of major proportions. Among the many who suffered were Pedro Tesifón and his family.[45]

In 1629 Pedro Tesifón sought once again to alleviate the family's financial plight. He asked the king to grant him an expanded inheritance in the province of Tula, arguing that this was due him because the full possessions of his great-grandmother (María Miahuaxochitl) had been unfairly awarded to others. He also asked permission to move his family to New Spain, where he could take personal control of his diverse properties. Both requests were denied, but the petitioner did not come away empty-handed. An additional *merced* of three thousand ducats in annual revenues from vacant properties in New Spain rewarded his efforts. However, this did not translate into immediate benefits, because the promised revenue was not forthcoming.[46]

Two years later, on July 16, 1631, Pedro Tesifón sent a brief to the crown. In it he stated that the loss of the treasure fleet denied him three years' income, and he had not received any of the three thousand ducats offered as compensation. Furthermore, he had been apprised that various persons had illegally settled on some of his properties. He again asked permission to relocate to New Spain, where he could protect his interests, and again his request was denied. However, in the following year he was awarded an additional grant of one thousand ducats per year for two lives—the monies to come from tribute payments in New Spain.[47]

Not surprisingly, Pedro Tesifón then adopted a different approach. Given that income from New Spain had proved so disappointing and that the king and the Council of the Indies would not acquiesce to his request to move to the Indies, he next sought dependable assets in Spain itself. He offered to exchange his promised stipend of one thousand ducats for the right to acquire income from Villa de Peza near the family home in Guadix.[48]

The Council of the Indies studied this proposal for about two years. On January 22, 1634, it advised the king that it would be prudent to let the petitioner have the Peza concession, but a commissioner would have to go there and assess the town's true value. The council's appointee reported that rents came from some twenty thousand vassals, as well as from various taxes.[49]

Because income from Peza had traditionally gone into the royal coffers, the Council of the Indies appointed two of its members to meet with an equal number from the treasury. This junta met in January 1635, but it decided not to make any recommendations until word arrived from the viceroy of New Spain concerning income due the Moctezumas from their New Spain *encomiendas*. This delayed a definitive decision for another three years. Finally, in 1638 the crown awarded Peza to Pedro Tesifón, but he had little time to enjoy the fruits of this hard-won victory. Recognizing that death was near, he executed his will on November 10, 1639.[50]

Pedro Tesifón's will reflects a number of titles that the crown had bestowed on him: Count of Moctezuma de Tula y Tultengo, Viscount of Ilucan, Knight of Santiago, Señor (Lord) of Tula, Lord of Peza, and Perpetual Regidor of Guadix. The count declared that he and his wife had two surviving children: Diego Luis Tesifón Moctezuma (second Count of Moctezuma) and Theresa Francisca de Moctezuma. His widow was to receive income from her dowry and one thousand ducats annually from the grant of 1632 until her death. At that juncture, doña Gerónima's income should devolve to their daughter, as well as fifteen hundred ducats from the estate of a deceased brother of her husband. The daughter should also receive income from timber harvested in the woods of Peza. In his will, Pedro Tesifón acknowledges another son, (Pedro) Diego Luis de Moctezuma, who was born out of wedlock and was at the time a member of the Jesuit Order. A small bequest also went to a woman presumed to the mother of this Diego Luis.[51]

It is obvious that the Spanish crown recognized an obligation to provide for the welfare of this extended branch of the Moctezuma family. But it is equally apparent that it pushed much of this responsibility onto the viceroys of New Spain. When Pedro Tesifón died in 1639, promised but uncollected thousands of pesos and ducats were still in arrears. His heirs would have to assume the difficult and thankless task of trying to rectify that situation.[52]

Don Pedro Tesifón's widow, Gerónima de Porras, proved to be a determined and resolute champion of these Moctezumas. She, like other family members, pointed out the 1612 agreement and its unfilled provisions. But the relatively young widow faced almost insurmountable obstacles.

What followed in the wake of doña Gerónima's repeated entreaties were *cédulas* followed by more *cédulas*, all commanding the viceroys of New Spain to forward income from the Moctezuma *encomiendas*. The results were no different from before.[53] In fact, matters had worsened by the 1640s.

In 1640 the treasure fleet from the Indies did not sail. Three years later, near the end of the Thirty Years' War, Spain, weakened by a host of problems, suffered a humiliating defeat at Rocroi. It was the first head-to-head loss for a Spanish army in Europe in nearly a century and a half. The Count Duke of Olivares, Philip IV's trusted *privado*, resigned in 1643. That same year, doña Gerónima declared that the sum owed her for unpaid *mercedes* amounted to 13,740 silver pesos.[54]

Unfortunately, matters did not improve for Philip IV. In the following year, his wife, Isabel de Borbón, died on June 6. His only son, youthful Baltasar Carlos, followed his mother in death on September 10, 1646. In 1649 Philip married a second time. Several years later, Mariana of Austria gave the king another male heir—the tragic Charles II.[55]

Diego Luis Tesifón Moctezuma, the second Count of Moctezuma, probably married in the late 1640s. His bride was Isabel Ana de Loaysa y Ovalle, and from this union came one child, a daughter, Gerónima María de Moctezuma. Don Diego's sister, Theresa Francisca de Moctezuma, married Diego de Cisneros y Guzmán, a distant relative of Cardinal Francisco Jiménez de Cisneros, who served as inquisitor general of Spain, archbishop of Toledo, and regent after the death of Ferdinand the Catholic in 1516. From this marriage came descendants who would later enter the ranks of the Spanish peerage as the Marqueses de Tenebrón.[56]

With the death of Philip IV in September 1665, Diego Luis Tesifón Moctezuma renewed his requests for dependable income. These entreaties were directed to Mariana of Austria, the king's widow, who served as regent for her sickly four-year-old son, Charles II. In this instance, Diego Luis Tesifón sought an exemption from all taxes on the family's properties. The queen regent refused to abrogate all taxes but did order a 10 percent reduction in the future.[57]

In fairness to the Spanish crown, the national economy in the last quarter of the 1600s, especially during what has been called the "tragic decade" (1677–1687), was a disaster. Castile in particular was hit with calamities of "biblical proportions," including drought, crop failures, decimation of herds, a sharp rise in agricultural prices, and epidemic disease. This, coupled with the expense of Spain's involvement in the wars of Louis XIV, meant that the national treasury was often devoid of funds and in no position to fulfill promises of payments to Moctezuma families from its own coffers.[58]

Mariana of Austria apparently accepted in good faith the obligation to pay all monies outstanding to the Moctezuma family, but because of the disastrous circumstances herein described, this responsibility fell on the viceroys of New Spain. However, as before, those payments did not arrive in Spain. Frustrated, Diego Luis Tesifón placed his hope in Charles II's accession, which came in November 1675. Known in Spanish history as "el hechizado" (the bewitched) or the imbecile king, Charles was the product of six generations of intermarriage between the Spanish and Austrian Hapsburgs.[59]

The second Count of Moctezuma's strategy for winning concessions from Charles II was never successful. When he died on January 15, 1680, Diego Luis Tesifón left his estate solely in the hands of his daughter, the third Countess of Moctezuma. As with her predecessors, collecting what she felt was due her under contractual agreements with the crown would be a seemingly never-ending struggle.[60] By this time, the daughter of Diego Luis Tesifón carried the formidable name of Gerónima María de Moctezuma Loaysa de la Cueva. Her titles included Countess of Moctezuma, Viscountess of Ilucan, and Señora de (Lady of) Tula and Tultengo. She married Joseph Sarmiento de Valladares, a man of prominence in his own right.[61]

Like his father, Joseph Sarmiento was a knight of Santiago. He was also a judge of the Audiencia of Granada, and, by virtue of his marriage, Count of Moctezuma. The new count's prestige and experience in the workings of the Spanish government made him a formidable advocate for his financially troubled wife. And it did not take him long to swing into action.

Just eight days after the death of his wife's father, Joseph Sarmiento dispatched a letter to the crown. In it he declares doña Gerónima to be the sole heir of the second Count of Moctezuma. His father-in-law, however, had died deeply in debt, because officials in New Spain had steadfastly refused to remit what the crown had awarded him.[62]

To illustrate his points, Sarmiento followed his letter of January 23, 1680, with a second, dated March 23. In this letter he enumerates one particular *merced* of two thousand ducats, awarded to Diego Luis Tesifón in December 1662, that had never been paid. The king, attempting to rectify the situation, sent a report to the Council of the Indies commanding those officials to pay this amount in full and guarantee its collection for one life beyond the countess. The council did this. In June of the same year, Sarmiento sought tax relief for the Moctezuma estates, although this matter was not immediately resolved.[63]

Sarmiento then turned his attention to litigation pending before the Audiencia of New Spain that involved Moctezuma properties in the province of Tula. In 1681 Francisco de Orduña appeared before the Audiencia, maintaining that his inheritance had been unfairly claimed by the Moctezumas. As an example of legal matters that seemingly never reached final resolution, this case made reference to a decision made by Viceroy Marqués de Falces in 1567. Some 114 years earlier, the viceroy had awarded a piece of land in Tula to an Indian ancestor of Orduña. Succeeding members of don Francisco's family had enjoyed the fruits of this property, but agents of the Moctezumas had repeatedly challenged their rights of ownership.[64]

The Audiencia sequestered the disputed land and then sent its agent to Tula to investigate. The official reported that the property in question, as well as other towns in the province that had since been claimed by Indians and Spaniards, had indeed been an original grant to the Moctezumas. While this case dragged on in New Spain for a number of years, the countess's mother, Isabel Ana de Loaysa, petitioned the crown in her own behalf on November 13, 1682.[65]

Doña Isabel repeated a familiar refrain. Her husband, because he had been denied monies due him, had spent her entire dowry of fifty thousand ducats and left her with debts in excess of sixty thousand ducats. She insisted that her daughter was unable to help her. In seeking a stipend, the supplicant ran through a number of favors awarded by the crown to other family members. Her efforts bore some fruit in that she was paid fifteen hundred ducats to relieve her immediate lack of funds.[66]

Sarmiento continued to press the issue of unfulfilled contractual obligations to the Moctezuma family. As a result, the king issued a strongly worded *cédula* on June 9, 1684, which was sent to the viceroy of New Spain. This directive outlined every royal concession from the three thousand pesos granted to Pedro Moctezuma in 1567 to the drafting of this document. It also noted that illegal taxes had been collected on tribute payments to the family. The *cédula* concluded with a demand that all monies in arrears be paid in full. One can judge its effectiveness by the crown's having to send a similar *cédula* to New Spain on June 14, 1685, and yet another one in October.[67]

In 1686 a new viceroy, the Conde de Monclova, arrived in Mexico City. On September 2, 1687, the crown sent specific instructions to the count to confiscate without fail one-half of the incomes from all *encomiendas* in New Spain for four years. Those monies were to be placed in the royal treasury as an emergency fund. This would also have halved income from the Moctezuma *encomiendas*, but their properties were exempted—thanks to the efforts of Joseph Sarmiento.[68]

By now it should be clear that nothing moved expeditiously in matters relating to the financial well-being of this branch of the Moctezuma family. For example, an audit of its *encomiendas* was ordered in 1683. It was completed in 1685, but the data were not forwarded to Spain until May 1690. Contained in the report were dramatic numbers: the family had lost 47,294 pesos in illegally imposed taxes; its tributary units had decreased by 57,523 pesos since the *encomiendas* were first assigned; and, given nonpayment of grants over the years, the family had been denied income amounting to an astonishing total of 163,481 silver pesos.[69] Nothing could have more dramatically illustrated the righteousness of the petitions made by this branch of the Moctezumas in the 1600s.

Despite admitting the validity of the Moctezuma family's claims, the Conde de Galve stated that funds were not available to pay the required amount. This, however, did not stop the drafting of additional royal *cédulas*, sent in June and August of 1691, which demanded that the viceroy cover the entire deficit.[70]

The countess, doña Gerónima, died in February 1692, leaving her husband with two young daughters—Fausta Dominga, not yet three years of age, and Melchora, aged ten and half months. Her husband filed Gerónima's will in Granada and asked to be appointed guardian of his daughters. He also requested that the title of countess be given to his eldest daughter. The crown agreed on June 4, 1692. At that time, Fausta Dominga's yearly income was set at 8,500 ducats, and her *encomiendas* were extended for two lives. As usual, officials in Mexico could not pay this amount in full, nor could they pay anything toward the sum of 163,481 pesos in arrears.[71]

Sarmiento soon remarried. He then asked that the crown permit him and his family to move to New Spain, where he could personally look after the collection of monies owed to his widow's family. Although the crown had consistently denied previous requests by this family to relocate to the Indies, circumstances were then different. In the late 1600s, government offices—including that of viceroy of New Spain—were sold to the highest bidder by a revenue-desperate crown.[72]

It appears that the Count of Moctezuma offered a substantial amount of money for the post of viceroy. He no doubt felt that if he held the highest office in New Spain, his chances of collecting money due his late wife would be greatly improved. With his appointment, the Council of the Indies ordered the Audiencia in Mexico City to remit 163,481 pesos and expenses incurred in moving the count and his family across the Atlantic. This, however, did not happen.[73]

The new viceroy, accompanied by the two daughters born to doña Gerónima, his second wife, María Andrea de Guzmán Dávila, and their daughter, Bernarda Sarmiento Guzmán y Moctezuma, sailed from Cádiz on July 28, 1696. They arrived at Veracruz on October 3, 1696, and reached Mexico City on February 2, 1697, whereupon the count inaugurated New Spain's thirty-second viceregal administration.[74]

In many respects, the Conde de Moctezuma's viceroyalty marks the end of an era. The inaugural entrance of a viceroy into Mexico City traditionally touched off the greatest secular festival under the Hapsburg kings. These ostentatious celebrations included "mock battles, jousts, masked parades, dances, bullfights, dramatic performances, artillery and marching demonstrations, banquets, . . . public speeches, . . . all with elaborate costuming, reflecting months of planning and organization." These events on average lasted for three weeks. As Linda A. Curcio has remarked, "the entrance of a new viceroy in Mexico City was the pre-

miere event during most of the colonial period."[75] The celebrations associated with it were intended to underscore the power and authority of
government and demonstrate "a measure of legitimacy in a less than sta-
ble world." Nonetheless, these extravaganzas were exceedingly expensive,
requiring the Mexico City *cabildo* to borrow large sums of money to
underwrite them. However, with the coming of Bourbon officials, who
took control of Spain and its empire in the early 1700s, royal decrees
greatly reduced authorized spending for viceregal entries.[76]

Joseph Sarmiento de Valladares, Conde de Moctezuma, headed the
government of New Spain until November 4, 1701. It would be gratify-
ing to state that a descendant of Moctezuma II, albeit by virtue of marriage to the Countess of Moctezuma, had a record of distinguished
accomplishments in office, but such was not the case. With few exceptions, notably, the second viceroyalty of Luis Velasco II, the same could be
said about the count's twenty-five predecessors from 1595 to 1701. As
Lewis Hanke has remarked about the administration of Sarmiento de Valladares, "during this period of time nothing extraordinary occurred."
This is certainly true regarding domestic issues. Although riches from
New Spain, Peru, and the Philippines continued to flow into the royal
coffers, the general populace in Mexico suffered serious food shortages
resulting from poor harvests throughout much of the 1690s, some of
which prompted revolts.[77]

The new viceroy's instructions from the crown are also singularly
unremarkable. For example, he was to look into the refusal of some
encomenderos to allow priests to reside in their subject towns, which had
led to the mistreatment of Indians; he was to promote the conversion of
natives by making sure that missionaries were assigned to frontier regions,
such as Nueva Galicia and Nueva Vizcaya; he was to ensure that no new
monasteries were founded without express license from the king, which
occurred under former viceroys; and he was to make sure that the clergy
did not discuss any matters relating to public affairs from the pulpit,
which had the potential of creating dissatisfaction or anxiety among
parishioners.[78]

In a broader sense, events of some importance did occur during the
count's administration: Father Juan de Salvatierra and fellow Jesuits
departed for missions in northwest New Spain (1697); in Europe the War
of the League of Augsburg (known as King William's War in the Ameri-

cas) ended with the Peace of Ryswick (1697); the French established a permanent colony near the mouth of the Mississippi River (1699); Franciscan missions in northern New Spain expanded to the Río Grande with the founding on January 1 of Mission San Juan Bautista (1700); and in Spain death claimed Charles II on November 1 at the age of thirty-nine (1700). Thus, with the passing of the king and the coronation of the French Bourbon, Philip V, the Conde de Moctezuma would be the last Hapsburg-appointed viceroy of New Spain.

During his five-year administration, the count assuredly did not fare well in matters relating to his family or its attempts to collect unpaid *mercedes*. Less than a year after his arrival in New Spain, his eldest daughter, the young Countess Fausta Dominga, died, on July 16, 1697. She was laid to rest in the chapel of the Santo Domingo monastery near Pedro Moctezuma, an ancestor who had died in 1570. A few months later, on October 16, 1697, came the bad news that the Council of the Indies had abrogated the responsibility of paying the 163,481 pesos owed to the estate of the viceroy's first wife.[79]

When Sarmiento de Valladares left office in 1701, he faced the inevitable *residencia*. Resulting from it were only four charges of consequence: first, that he had failed to implement seven royal *cédulas* sent to him; second, that he had failed to collect sufficient royal revenues on the cargo of a ship (the *Nuestra Señora de Rosario*) that had arrived at Acapulco from the Philippines; third, that he had failed throughout his administration to apprise the Council of the Indies of the arrival of the *flota* (the fleet sent to New Spain annually), which for many months denied this vital information to the council; fourth, that he had not corrected a situation wherein an *alcalde mayor* had without legal authority collected more than 2,214 silver pesos from towns in cash tribute, which he had failed to turn over to the provisional general accountant. In all four instances, the Conde de Moctezuma was absolved.[80]

Following the conclusion of his *residencia*, the Conde de Moctezuma departed New Spain with his family, leaving the office of viceroy in the hands of an interim successor, Juan de Ortega y Montañez, the archbishop of Mexico City. Shortly after the count's arrival in Spain, Philip V indicated approval of his service to the crown by appointing him to the prestigious position of president of the Council of the Indies. On November 17, 1704, the king granted the title of first Duke of Atrisco to the former viceroy, making him a grandee of Spain.[81]

When the duke died in 1708, he left his entire estate in the hands of Melchora, his surviving daughter. The new countess, however, died prematurely and without direct heirs on August 15, 1715. In her will she left the Moctezuma inheritance and the title of Countess of Moctezuma to a distant cousin, Teresa Nieto de Silva y Moctezuma, Marquesa de Tenebrón. Doña Melchora bequeathed the Atrisco properties to her half-sister, Bernarda Sarmiento, who became the third Duchess of Atrisco. The provisions of this testament were approved by the Spanish crown but contested by lawsuits that are beyond the scope of this work.[82]

• • •

The roads to knighthood and to the peerage for the descendants of Gonzalo Cano de Moctezuma and Juan Cano de Moctezuma, sons of Juan Cano de Saavedra and Isabel Moctezuma, were far less tortuous than the one traveled by Pedro Moctezuma's heirs (see Figure 3.1). This is primarily because they did not face the same number of problems stemming from absenteeism that plagued Pedro's offspring. Furthermore, with the death in 1577 of their half-brother, Juan de Andrade (Gallego) Moctezuma, the Tacuba *encomiendas* were entirely within the Cano branch of the family.[83]

Gonzalo, who married Ana de Prado Calderón, and his family chose to remain in New Spain, where they could more closely supervise their *encomienda* properties. Gonzalo won a *mayorazgo* for his family in 1571. When he drafted his will in Mexico City on January 3, 1597, he acknowledged two legitimate children—Juan Cano Moctezuma y Prado and María Cano Moctezuma. Juan received the *mayorazgo*.[84] It appears that only one member of Gonzalo's progeny gained admission to a military order. His grandson, Diego Cano Moctezuma, became a knight of Santiago in 1620. His daughter, María Cano Moctezuma married twice. From her first marriage, to Gerónimo Agustín de Espinosa, came the Raza Cano Moctezuma family; from the second marriage, to Antonio Andelo, came another branch known as the Andelo (Augdelo) Cano Moctezuma family. The Raza Cano Moctezuma and Andelo Cano Moctezuma families and their descendants became the chief beneficiaries in Mexico of a portion of the Tacuba *encomienda*.[85] As noted in the Introduction, payments from the Mexican government continued into the 1930s.

Juan Cano de Moctezuma, as mentioned in Chapter 3, accompanied his father to Spain. There he married Elvira de Toledo and inherited Cano properties in Cáceres, Spain. The crown formalized his *mayorazgo* in

Figure 6.1. Palacio de los Toledo-Moctezuma, Cáceres, Spain, prior to restoration. (Photo courtesy of Ida Altman.)

Granada on February 22, 1577. The entailed estate specifically included his share of the revenues from Tacuba and its *sujetos*.[86] As an example of this family's financial successes, after Juan Cano de Moctezuma died, his widow brought suit against the royal *fiscal* for payment of 1,327 *marcos* and 5 *reales* of fine silver, revenue from Tacuba that had been encumbered by the Casa de Contratación. The Council of the Indies, which reviewed the case, ordered that these monies be paid to Elvira de Toledo on January 16, 1581.[87] Juan de Toledo Moctezuma, the eldest son of Juan Cano de Moctezuma, was the eventual heir of the *mayorazgo*. He married Mariana Carbajal de Toledo, and from this union came twelve children. Their eldest son, Juan Moctezuma Carbajal y Toledo, gained admission to the military Order of Alcántara and became a perpetual *regidor* of the Cáceres *cabildo*.[88]

From the descendants of Juan Cano de Moctezuma and Elvira de Toledo came a line of Spanish peers, which, beginning in the late 1600s, carried the titles of Counts of Enjarada and Fuensalida and Dukes of Abrantes and Linares. The Toledo-Moctezuma palace is a magnificent structure, reminding citizens of Cáceres of a native son's ties to the Aztec emperor.[89]

Thus, some descendants of Pedro and Isabel Moctezuma attained noble status. Pedro's progeny became Dukes and Duchesses of Atrisco, Counts and Countesses of Moctezuma, as well as Marques and Marquesas of Tenebrón and Viscounts and Viscountesses of Ilucan (see Figure 4.2).[90] Their primary source of income was the ancient city and province of Tula, as well as the town of Tultengo.

Juan de Andrade (Gallego) Moctezuma, Isabel Moctezuma and Pedro Gallego de Andrade's son, married María Iñíguez. This union produced four sons and a daughter. None of the sons gained entry to a military order.

Pedro Cano de Moctezuma, Isabel's eldest son by Juan Cano, is identified as a bachelor or priest without heirs in some sources, but that was clearly not the case.[91] He married Ana de Arriaga, who bore him one child, María Cano. She married Gonzalo de Salazar, but their offspring did not attain military knighthood or noble status.

Two sons of Juan Cano and Isabel Moctezuma, Gonzalo Cano Moctezuma and Juan Cano de Moctezuma, did have descendants who became knights of Santiago and Alcántara, respectively, and the latter's heirs joined the ranks of Spanish nobility as counts and dukes.

Conclusions

THE RISE OF HUMAN POPULATIONS in the Central Valley of Mexico, a matter addressed in this book's first chapter, explains how the Aztecs came to have a ruling family whose members, including Moctezuma II and his heirs, could claim the status of *reyes naturales*. Spaniards ranging from Cortés to the kings of Spain in the sixteenth and seventeenth centuries would respond to this claim in ways that permitted these heirs of defeated and deposed forebears to play a significant role in Mexico and Spain for many years following the Conquest.[1] In particular, three children of the emperor—two daughters and a son, whom the Spaniards christened Isabel, Mariana, and Pedro—benefited from their status as "natural monarchs." The emperor's granddaughter Leonor Cortés Moctezuma was the offspring of Cortés and Isabel Moctezuma. Doña Isabel (Tecuichpotzin) was clearly recognized as the surviving principal heir of Moctezuma by both Aztecs and Spaniards. In spite of seemingly never-ending legal battles and the frustrations of promised income that did not materialize, the accomplishments of these children of the emperor were remarkable and deserve examination. Over the course of nearly two centuries, from the mid-1520s to the early 1700s, they demonstrated what Susan Schroeder has called "a complex of resistance attributes—alliance, accommodation, self preservation."[2]

In granting *encomiendas* to Isabel and Mariana Moctezuma and confirming the Tula properties of Pedro Moctezuma, Cortés acknowledged their unique position as Indian royals in the postconquest society of New

Spain. Throughout most of the sixteenth century, no one other than the conqueror and his descendants as Marqueses del Valle de Oaxaca and two daughters of the emperor and their heirs became possessors of tribute payments by Indian vassals in perpetuity. The fact that these Indian and mestizo elites held rights of inheritance comparable to those of the *marqueses* and that these same rights extended into the 1930s under first Spain and then Mexico is truly remarkable.

Cortés and Juan Cano, the third Spanish husband of Isabel Moctezuma, also saw this Aztec princess as a pioneer of *mestizaje* and Hispanization. And if a model of acculturation to Spanish societal and religious norms was needed, they could hardly have chosen a better subject.[3]

As Princess Tecuichpotzin, she arguably was one of the three most prominent women in Aztec history. Ilancueitl as the wife of the first Aztec emperor, Acamapichtli, gave the Mexica an indisputable tie with Culhuacan and provided nobility to a fledgling dynasty (see Figure 1.6). As Susan Gillespie notes, Ilancueitl had a dual persona (Atotoztli) as the female creator of half of the Tenochtitlan dynasty.[4] Following the death of Moctezuma Ilhuicamina, his daughter, also named Atotoztli, provided a vital link with the sixth Aztec emperor and perhaps served as interim ruler. So, it was not without precedent that Tecuichpotzin occupied a place of prime importance, perhaps being the second woman to serve as interim empress, in her case, following the death of Moctezuma II in late June 1520.

At this time, Tecuichpotzin was the widow of Atlixcatzin, son of Ahuitzotl, who had been Moctezuma II's most likely successor. She married her uncle Cuitlahuac, who died of smallpox eighty days later, following which she wed her cousin Cuauhtemoc, a union that lasted for about four years. All of these nuptials were intradynastic—that is, "marriages in which both parties are descendants of a ruler of the dynasty"—as opposed to the Aztecs' more commonly arranged interdynastic matrimonies. And since only males occupied the office of emperor for extended periods of time, "marriages within the dynasty turn out to be marriages among agnates."[5]

Similarly, Tecuichpotzin would become perhaps the most important Indian woman in sixteenth-century New Spain.[6] In her second and third marriages to Spaniards, she bore six children, four of whom had children of their own, as did Leonor Cortés Moctezuma, who was born out of wedlock. When doña Isabel drafted her will in 1550, she demonstrated a degree of Hispanization and independence that clearly displeased Juan Cano and ran against his monetary interests, as well as those of the three sons she bore him.[7] Bequeathing property as she saw fit appears to have been a privilege of noble Aztec women before the Spaniards came, and it was assuredly a right of women under Castilian law.[8]

Had Isabel's will gone uncontested, her son by Pedro Gallego de Andrade would have fared best of all. But Isabel was hardly in her tomb before the intrafamily lawsuits began. After bitterly contested litigation, the Tacuba *encomienda* was divided six ways but remained that way for only a short time, because the nuns, doñas Isabel and Catalina, renounced their shares in favor of their father and full brothers. With the deaths of Juan Cano, Pedro Cano de Moctezuma, and Juan de Andrade (Gallego) Moctezuma, the primary *encomenderos* of Tacuba became Gonzalo Cano de Moctezuma and Juan Cano de Moctezuma. These sons and their descendants in Mexico and Spain, respectively, are present-day claimants to Moctezuma properties. Those in Spain eventually achieved the ultimate in the peerage as Dukes of Abrantes and Linares, but those in Mexico did not become titled.

It would be of great interest to know what the natives of Tacuba, the source of wealth and accompanying success for Isabel Moctezuma and her descendants, thought of their *encomendera*, but the apparent lack of evidence on this matter strongly suggests that there was no significant opposition. Had there been, as was the case with the Indians of Tula, the Spanish would have had no reason to cover it up.[9]

Mariana Moctezuma was a second principal heir of the Aztec emperor. Despite the circumstances of her birth to a secondary wife or consort of Moctezuma II, Spaniards regarded her as legitimate. She, like Isabel, received the revenues of her *encomienda*, Ecatepec, in perpetuity. However, the involvement of Diego Arias Sotelo, a grandson-in-law of the emperor, in the Ávila-Cortés conspiracy in the 1560s cast doubt over this continuing inheritance. By the seventeenth century, the grandchildren of Diego Arias Sotelo had allowed the Ecatepec properties to pass from this branch of Moctezuma's heirs in exchange for a cash settlement (see Figure 4.1).

Pedro Moctezuma, the male heir of the emperor, did not receive a formal grant of *encomienda* from Cortés that included specific *estancias* in Tula, and his inheritance was the most bitterly contested by Indians in New Spain. *Principales* of Tula filed complaint after complaint, lawsuit after lawsuit, against him, and they did so with a fair degree of success. In particular, during a two-year absence from New Spain (1528–1530), don Pedro was unable to prevent significant erosion of his income and property. In attempting to recoup his losses, he ran into an aspect of Spanish judicial procedure that constantly frustrated him. The Audiencia in Mexico City was the supreme court of New Spain, but its decisions were final only in criminal cases. In matters involving property of significant value, the Audiencia's rulings could be appealed to the Royal Council of the Indies in Spain.[10] This caused adjudication delays that went on for decades.

Don Pedro was also the least Hispanicized of Moctezuma's principal heirs. He was about ten years older than his half-sisters, Isabel and Mariana, which perhaps made learning Spanish more difficult for him. More important, his wives and consorts were all Indians. In this regard, Pedro's choice of mothers for his children fits the pattern of marriages between Indian men and Spanish women in the early colonial period: they were extremely rare. As Pedro Carrasco observes, Spaniards subordinated the indigenous population as conquered people; accordingly, few Spanish women chose to marry men below their class. Second, there was an overall scarcity of Spanish women; the few who were present in New Spain usually came as wives of Spanish officials or colonists.[11]

Perhaps the most revealing evidence of Pedro's lack of *hispanismo* lies in the circumstances of his last will and testament. He dictated its provisions in Nahuatl, and an interpreter of the Audiencia of New Spain translated them into Spanish. The dying man also appointed a guardian for his adult son and heir, Martín, who did not understand Spanish law.

When Martín died without heirs, the most important factor favoring Pedro Moctezuma's descendants was a proviso in his will that addressed this eventuality by passing rights of inheritance in Tula to Diego Luis, an illegitimate son, and don Diego's presence in Spain, where he could more easily petition the Council of the Indies (see Figure 4.2). Diego Luis fell on hard times and spent two years in the public jail of Seville. After he gained his release, he won a hard-fought victory when the Council of the Indies declared him legitimate. Legitimacy meant that Diego Luis could inherit Tula properties as an entailed estate—a significant victory had he and his heirs been able to collect in full. But such was not the case.

This indigenous son of Pedro Moctezuma married a Spanish noblewoman, the granddaughter of the Duke of Alburquerque. Diego Luis's prospects for income and his status as a Hispanicized Indian royal made it an acceptable marriage for his bride. This couple's principal heir, Pedro Tesifón, would enjoy some success in the seventeenth century and acquire the titles of viscount and count, still claimed by his descendants.

Perhaps the crowning achievement of Pedro Moctezuma's heirs was appointment of the third Countess of Moctezuma's husband to the office of viceroy in New Spain. Nearly two centuries after the death of the Aztec emperor, in a sense, things had come full circle. The spouse of initially disinherited native royalty came to New Spain as its highest official. Through the Conde de Moctezuma, last viceroy during the Hapsburg dynasty, came the titles of Duke of Atrisco and Count of Moctezuma.

The descendants of Leonor Cortés Moctezuma, natural daughter of Fernando Cortés and Isabel Moctezuma, made their lives and fortunes (both won and lost) on the silver frontier of northern New Spain (see Figure 5.2). Somewhat out of the mainstream of life in New Spain and certainly in Spain itself, these children of the emperor did not achieve titles of nobility. Nonetheless, Juan de Oñate, a great-grandson-in-law of both Cortés and Moctezuma, became a high-profile personage on the northern frontier of New Spain. Marc Simmons calls this first governor of New Mexico the "Last Conquistador." Oñate was also the last Spanish official in New Spain to acquire the title of *adelantado*.

Moctezuma II's heirs provide an excellent example of Indian accommodation and Hispanization. Unfortunately, much of their monetary success came at the expense of other Indians in New Spain who paid tribute to them as absentee *encomenderos*. At the same time, the European world of Spaniards provided the social and legal environment that permitted a conquered people to use its courts and laws and at times receive fair and equitable treatment. Again, as Lucas Alamán notes, there are few examples in history where the victors have granted so many rights and privileges to the defeated.[12]

Notes

Abbreviations

AGI =   Archivo General de Indias, Seville
AGN =   Archivo General de la Nación, Mexico City
AHN =   Archivo Histórico Nacional, Madrid
DII =   *Colección de documentos inéditos relativos al descubrimiento, conquista y organización de las antiguas posesiones españolas en América y Oceanía.* 42 vols.
DIU =   *Colección de documentos inéditos relativos al descubrimiento, conquista y organización de las antiguas posesiones de Ultramar.* 25 vols.
ENE =   *Epistolario de Nueva España, 1505–1818.* 16 vols.

Introduction

1. Kroeber, *Nature of Culture*, 79.

2. "In This Issue."

3. Augustinians, like the other early orders, manned parishes in Central Mexico. They also founded hospitals for indigenous people.

4. Durán, *History*, xxvii.

5. Preconquest techniques for writing in Central Mexico included direct depiction, ideograms, and phonetic transcription. For a discussion of these methods, see Lockhart, *Nahuas after the Conquest*, 327–330.

6. Thomas, *Conquest*, xv.

7. Schroeder, "Introduction," 5.

8. Lockhart, *Nahuas after the Conquest*, 4–5, quotation on 4. See also Sweet and Nash, eds., *Struggle and Survival*, for other examples of this interaction in colonial America.

9. Lockhart, *Nahuas after the Conquest*, 94, 102.

10. Alamán, *Disertaciones*, 1: 132.

Chapter 1

1. Sanders, "Natural Environment," 59.

2. Ibid., 60. Each of the three major lakes later incorporated lesser bodies of water formed by artificial dikes or dams; thus, some colonial sources refer to six lakes within the basin.

3. De Terra, Romero, and Stewart, *Tepexpan Man*, 61–62.

4. Sanders, "Natural Environment," 60–61; MacNeish, *Origins of Agriculture*, 329.

5. MacNeish, *Origins of Agriculture*, 3.

6. León-Portilla, *Aztec Image*, 19. Some anthropologists and archeologists regard Cuicuilco, which predates Teotihuacan, as having seminal importance in the Central Valley.

7. Ibid., 20–21.

8. Ibid., 21, first quotation; Carrasco, *Quetzalcoatl*, 2, second and third quotations.

9. León-Portilla, *Aztec Image*, 21.

10. Millon, ed., *Urbanization*, 45; Carrasco, *Quetzalcoatl*, 110, 118.

11. Gordon Brotherson refers to *this* Tula as Mexquital Tula, associating it with the name of the highland valley in which it is located. See "Tula" for a discussion of textual references to earlier places with this name.

12. León-Portilla, *Aztec Image*, 22.

13. Ibid.; Davies, *Toltecs*, 64–65. Davies notes that Quetzalcoatl is also associated with the Huastecs to the east, with Mixtec codices in the south, and with other regions of Mexico.

14. Carrasco, *Quetzalcoatl*, 4, first quotation; Townsend, "Burying the White Gods," 668, second quotation.

15. Brotherson, "Tula," 22.

16. León-Portilla, *Aztec Image*, 27–28.

17. Ibid., 28–29, quotation on 29.

18. Durán, *History of the Indies*, xxv.

19. Ibid., xxi.

20. Ibid., 13–19; Davies, *Aztecs*, 8. The seven tribes in order of their appearance are Xochimilcas, Chalcas, Tepanecs, Culhuas, Tlahuicas, Tlaxcalans, and Aztecs.

21. James Lockhart prefers the term "Nahuas," partly because of its currency in Mexico today. See *Nahuas after the Conquest*, 1.

22. Davies, *Aztecs*, 8–10.

23. Ibid., 10.

24. Ibid., 11.

25. Brundage, *Rain of Darts*, xi.

26. Ibid., 24.

27. Ibid., 25–26; León-Portilla, *Aztec Image*, 29, quotation. As in Teotihuacan, a small number of people still lived at or near Tula. Its population had increased considerably by the 1500s.

28. León-Portilla, *Aztec Image*, 29–31; Smith, *Aztecs*, 40.

29. León-Portilla, *Aztec Image*, 31.

30. See Peterson, *Ancient Mexico*, 88, for a drawing that depicts the Aztecs' role in this war, during which they kept track of their prisoners by cutting off ears.

31. León-Portilla, *Aztec Image*, 31–32.

32. Peterson, *Ancient Mexico*, 88.

33. Ibid.

34. León-Portilla, *Aztec Image*, 33. The year 1325 is often presented as the date of origin for Tenochtitlan, but a more likely date is 1345. See Davies, *Aztecs*, 37, 316–317n37.

35. With few exceptions, it is difficult to single out important wives of Aztec rulers, because "polygyny prevailed among [them]. . . . Wives were of different rank, according to their status at birth and the type of marriage contracted." For a discussion of such unions, especially the ancestry of Acamapichtli and his wife, see Carrasco, "Royal Marriages," 44.

36. Davies, *Aztecs*, 41–43. This first king of Tlatelolco was named Cuacuapitzhuac. See Chapter 2 for a discussion of Acamapichtli's wife and her dual importance in linking the Aztecs to Culhuacan.

37. León-Portilla, *Aztec Image*, 33–34. It is possible that the Aztecs later manufactured the account of the heron and duck hatchlings to illustrate the rank arrogance of the Tepanecs or to justify rebellion against them, but these tribute demands are recounted by Durán, *History*, 56.

38. León-Portilla, *Aztec Image*, 34.

39. Brundage, *Rain of Darts*, 51.

40. Ibid., 51–52; Smith, *Aztecs*, 50. Smith notes the widespread use of *chinampas* by 1430. At times of severe drought, the lake surface receded, leaving the artificial islands on dry land.

41. Brundage, *Rain of Darts*, 52.

42. Ibid.

43. León-Portilla, *Aztec Image*, 36; Durán *History*, 69.

44. Nezahualcoyotl, the king of Texcoco, had seen his father, Ixtlilxochitl, murdered on orders of Tezozomoc, thus prompting the young king's desire for revenge. See Davies, *Aztecs*, 57–58; León-Portilla, *Aztec Image*, 34–35; Durán, *History*, 73–80. Durán discusses a failed attempt, prior to this war, by Tlacaelel Cihuacoatl to arrange an acceptable peace with the Tepanecs.

45. Brundage, *Rain of Darts*, 80.

46. Durán, *History*, 80. The fate of Maxtlatzin is uncertain. León-Portilla believes that he escaped to Coyoacan, where he suffered a second defeat by the Aztec army. Nigel Davies presents evidence that the Tepanec king was clubbed in the head and later executed by Nezahualcoyotl, who cut out Maxtlatzin's heart and scattered his blood at Azcapotzalco. See León-Portilla, *Aztec Image*, 97; Davies, *Aztecs*, 76–77.

47. León-Portilla, *Aztec Image*, 98.

48. Much of Tlacaelel's alleged influence on several Aztec monarchs derives from one source, *La crónica X*. Robert Barlow has given this title to an early pictorial chronicle, written in Nahuatl in the late 1530s, which is no longer extant. This chronicle was apparently used by Diego Durán, Tezozomoc, and others in the sixteenth century. See Barlow, "La crónica X"; and Durán, *History*, 569–574.

49. Those who think history is at best "worthless" should perhaps consider examples of evidence to the contrary. If history has no value, why have regimes from the Aztecs to the

Bolsheviks and Nazis in the twentieth century tried to change it by burning books? One should also add Spaniards in New Spain to this list, for they were equally guilty of destroying preconquest codices. If history is nothing more than a "pack of lies played on the dead," try telling a Scot that centuries-old feuds between the Campbells and the McDonalds mean nothing today. Joanne Pope Melish, in *Disowning Slavery*, "explores the process by which New England, despite a century and a half of the enslavement of Africans," created a "mythic history" that disavows the existence there of human bondage—how convenient for New Englanders who wished to differentiate themselves from the slave-holding South (reviewed by Margaret M. R. Kellow in *Reviews in American History* 27 [1999]: 527).

50. Sahagún, *Florentine Codex*, Bk. 1, Pt. II: 1.

51. León-Portilla, *Aztec Image*, 99–100, quotation on 100.

52. Brotherson, "Tula," 20.

53. León-Portilla, *Aztec Image*, 100–101.

54. Davies, *Aztec Empire*, 232. The five cities were Tepeaca, Calpan, Tecalli, Cuauhtinchan, and Cuauhquechollan.

55. León-Portilla, *Aztec Image*, 103.

56. Ibid., 104.

57. Davies, *Aztec Empire*, 232–234, quotation on 234. It should be noted that Tlacaelel did not rekindle the flower wars until near the end of the long reign of Moctezuma I.

58. Ibid., 117–118; Davies, *Aztecs*, 91–93.

59. Work on the great aqueducts began around 1453 but took thirteen years to complete. See Brundage, *Rain of Darts*, 152, 157.

60. Hassig, *Aztec Warfare*, 162–175.

61. León-Portilla, *Aztec Image*, 106; Davies, *Aztecs*, 94–95. One of the most complete discussions of the Aztecs' ancient calendar may be found in Durán, *Book*, 388–470. For the alleged significance of Ce Acatl (One Reed) in the conquest, see note 1 in the Conclusions.

62. León-Portilla, *Aztec Image*, 107, as quoted. For a depiction of Tlacaelel as "the power behind the throne," see p. 37.

63. Durán, *History*, 249.

64. Ibid.

65. Ibid., first quotation on 259; second quotation on 257.

66. Ibid. The Tlatelolca leaders were their new king, Moquihuix, and his military commander, Teconal.

67. León-Portilla, *Aztec Image*, 108–109.

68. Durán, *History*, 307. Durán states that Tlacaelel attended Tizoc's funeral and lived into the 1480s. For a discussion of the possible roles and disputed life span of Tlacaelel, see Davies, *Aztec Empire*, 47–50.

69. In all, the Templo Mayor underwent "seven major stages of construction." From a common platform, two bases supported shrines to Huitzilopochtli and Tlaloc. See Broda, Carrasco, and Matos Moctezuma, *Great Temple*, 57, quotation; León-Portilla, *Aztec Image*, 111. The difficulties of capturing an individual in battles fought in distant lands and then marching that same person to Tenochtitlan for sacrifice are discussed in Davies, *Aztec Empire*, 228–230.

70. Brundage, *Rain of Darts*, 104.

71. See Davies, *Aztecs*, 167, for a brief analysis of the number of sacrificial victims.

72. Davies, *Aztec Empire*, 219–220.

73. Ibid., 221, quotation. See Harner, "Ecological Basis"; and Harris, *Cannibals and Kings*, 108–110.

74. See Sahagún, *Florentine Codex*, Bk. 3, Pt. IV, 11–14, for the importance of Tezcatlipoca (whom he calls Titlacauan) and Quetzalcoatl.

75. Davies, *Aztec Empire*, 248–263, 286, quotations on 286.

76. Ibid., 287.

77. Nigel Davies speculates that this postconquest account of Ahuitzotl's death was influenced by the similar manner in which Charles VIII of France died at the Château of Blois in 1501. See *Aztec Empire*, 7.

78. Durán, *History*, 382.

79. León-Portilla, *Aztec Image*, 112. Moctezuma II was also the nephew of Ahuitzotl.

80. Ibid.

81. Durán, *History*, 394.

82. León-Portilla, *Aztec Image*, 113.

83. Davies, *Aztecs*, 209.

84. Ibid., 210; Durán, *History*, 398, quotations.

85. At this juncture many accounts of the conquest of Mexico mention the occurrence of omens at Tenochtitlan that seemed to presage impending disaster for Moctezuma II and the Aztecs. For an enumeration of these omens, see Sahagún, *Florentine Codex*, Bk. 12, Pt. 13, 1–3. See Townsend, "Burying the White Gods," 667, for a discussion of the Florentine omens and parallels to them in Greek and Latin texts that were known to have been available to Sahagún's informants. See also Lockhart, ed. and trans., *We People Here*, 17, for his speculation that the omens are typical "after the fact" explanations of a defeated people and ought not to be ascribed to fatalism and superstition.

86. Davies, *Aztecs*, 230–232, quotations on 232.

87. Hassig, *Aztec Warfare*, 234–235, quotation on 235.

88. Durán, *History*, 495, first quotation; Townsend, "Burying the White Gods," 681, second quotation

89. Sahagún, *Florentine Codex*, Bk. 12, Pt. 13, 19–20.

CHAPTER 2

1. Cortés, *Letters from Mexico*, xi–xii.

2. Hassig, "Collision of Two Worlds," 81–82.

3. Ibid., 84.

4. Given the manner in which Cortés departed Cuba and his problems with Diego de Velázquez, the former obviously could not count on outside support from that quarter; however, he did benefit from three ships and crews sent out by Francisco de Garay, the governor of Jamaica, which failed in their primary mission but wound up at Vera Cruz, where they bolstered his army. For details, see Chipman, *Nuño de Guzmán*, 51–52.

5. Recounting the Spaniards' technological superiority over the Aztecs must not be construed as extending beyond this comparison. As Camilla Townsend points out, "one

group can be better equipped technically without being better equipped morally or intel-
lectually." For example, the Aztecs had developed an accurate calendar, they wrote beautiful poetry, and they produced outstanding works in gold and stone. Unlike the Incas, who
were a paperless culture, Aztec pictograph books are expertly drawn. See Townsend,
"Burying the White Gods," 661.

6. Hassig, "Collision of Two Worlds," 84, first quotation; idem, *Mexico and the Spanish
Conquest*, 57–58, 72, second quotation.

7. Thomas, *Conquest*, 222–223.

8. Ibid., 172, 222–223. For a discussion of doña Marina's incredible command of
Nahuatl and Maya, as well as of Spanish, see Karttunen, "Rethinking Malinche," 299–301.
Jerónimo de Aguilar's facility with Chontal Maya, which he learned on Cozumel and
used to communicate with doña Marina when she joined the Cortés expedition at
Potonchan (Villa de Tabasco), indicates the widespread use of that language. It is well
established that Aguilar did not understand Nahuatl; consequently, his communication
with doña Marina had to be in Maya. See Scholes and Roys, *Maya Chontal Indians*, 36–37.

9. Sahagún, *Florentine Codex*, Bk. 12, Pt. 13: 21–23; see also Hassig, "Collision of Two
Worlds," 82, sidebar depiction.

10. Hassig, "Collision of Two Worlds," 86–88.

11. Thomas, *Conquest*, 258.

12. Durán, *History*, 528–529, quotations; Thomas, *Conquest*, 256–261.

13. Hassig, *Aztec Warfare*, 242–243, quotation on 242.

14. Cortés, *Letters from Mexico*, 84, 109, quotation on 109.

15. Hassig, *Aztec Warfare*, 244.

16. Cortés, *Letters from Mexico*, xii.

17. Ibid., xii–xiii.

18. Ibid., xxii. If Cortés wrote a First Letter to the king, as he claimed, it has never
come to light.

19. As mentioned earlier, Scholes did not live long enough to write what he envi-
sioned as a comprehensive three-volume biography of Cortés. There is no reliable evidence that Cortés attended the University of Salamanca, as asserted by some historians.
Student records for that era are missing. The year 1485 is frequently given as Cortés's birth
year, but a plaque above the baptismal font in a reconstructed chapel in Medellín lists
1484.

20. Cortés, *Letters from Mexico*, xv.

21. This missive from the new municipality is included in publications of Cortés's five
major letters to the king.

22. Cortés, *Letters from Mexico*, xix.

23. Ibid., xxiv–xxv.

24. Ibid., xxv.

25. Elliott, *Imperial Spain*, 141–149.

26. Thomas, *Conquest*, 365–368.

27. Hassig, "Collision of Two Worlds," 95. This settlement was Segura de la Frontera,
also known as Tepeaca.

28. Thomas, *Conquest*, 378–381.

29. Sahagún, *Florentine Codex*, Bk. 12, Pt. 13: 55–56, quotation on 56. Alvarado appar-

ently feared that the gathering of so many Mexica nobles was preliminary to their capture and sacrifice of all Spaniards in the city.

30. Thomas, *Conquest*, 394–396.

31. Ibid., 397, as quoted.

32. Cortés, *Letters from Mexico*, 48.

33. Moctezuma offered Tecuichpotzin (Isabel) in marriage to Cortés. The conqueror declined, because he was already married and because Tecuichpotzin was too young. See Manero Suárez, *Doce generaciones*, 17. The offer of a child in marriage, traditional practice in Aztec diplomacy, may have been an attempt to secure an alliance with the Spaniards against Tlaxcala. See Hassig, *Aztec Warfare*, 244.

34. Cortés, *Letters from Mexico*, 91.

35. Thomas, *Conquest*, 392.

36. Ibid., 394–398; Hassig, "Collision of Two Worlds," 96.

37. Thomas, *Conquest*, 398.

38. Ibid.

39. Sahagún, *Florentine Codex*, Bk. 12, Pt. 13: 57–58, quotations on 57. Durán does not relate the rooftop exchange, saying only that Moctezuma "wept bitterly" and requested that "he and all the others who were prisoner . . . be slain, and their wishes were to be granted later." See *History*, 538.

40. A lengthy footnote in Sahagún's *Florentine Codex* (Bk. 12, Pt. 13: 65n1) sums up the controversy over the manner in which Moctezuma II died: "Concerning the death of Moctezuma various versions exist, but all of them may be included in two large groups: those emanating from the natives and those emanating from the Spaniards. The former maintains that Moctezuma was killed by the Spaniards, and the latter that his death was due to being struck by a rock as he tried to calm his subjects."

41. Thomas, *Conquest*, 404–407.

42. Sahagún, *Florentine Codex*, Bk. 12, Pt. 13: 67.

43. Díaz del Castillo, *Discovery and Conquest of Mexico*, 314.

44. Sahagún, *Florentine Codex*, Bk. 12, Pt. 13: 66; *Colección de documentos inéditos relativos al descubrimiento, conquista y organización de las antiguas posesiones españolas en América y Oceanía* (hereafter, *DII*), 26: 423; Thomas, *Conquest*, 411, 412. For varying estimates of Spanish deaths, see idem, *Conquest*, 734–753n63.

45. Gillespie, *Aztec Kings*, 21–26, quotation on 26. For an explanation of Atotoztli and Ilancueitl's being substitutable for each other, see 25–56.

46. See Carrasco, "Royal Marriages," 44.

47. There is some evidence that "if there were no males who were close relations and most worthy, females could succeed to rulership." See ibid., as quoted.

48. Ibid., 62.

49. See Chapter 6 for discussion of legitimacy as it relates to the heirs of Moctezuma II.

50. Fernández de Oviedo, *Historia general*, 4: 260.

51. Cano erred in reporting the name of his wife's brother as Asupacaci. See Brundage, *Rain of Darts*, 282.

52. Clavigero, *Historia antigua de México*, 3: 309 (all translations are mine unless otherwise noted). There is evidence that Cuauhtemoc and Isabel continued to live as husband

and wife until October 1524. See Manero Suárez, *Doce generaciones*, 17.

53. Thomas, *Conquest*, 538.

54. Ibid., 550.

55. Ibid.

56. Ibid., 550–552.

57. Ibid., 552–553.

58. Chipman, *Nuño de Guzmán*, 59–65.

59. Chipman, "Alonso Alvarez de Pineda," 377–378; *DII*, 26: 71–76.

60. Elliott, *Imperial Spain*, 148.

61. Thomas, *Conquest*, 572.

62. Ibid., 573.

63. Ibid., 584.

64. Ibid., 576.

65. Chipman, *Nuño de Guzmán*, 91–92.

66. AGN, Hospital de Jesús, 265–5.

67. Reference here is to the revolt against royal authority by Gonzalo Pizarro in Peru and the Ávila-Cortés conspiracy in New Spain.

68. Chipman, *Nuño de Guzmán*, 85–86.

69. Gibson, *Aztecs*, 155.

70. AGN, Hospital de Jesús, 265–5; Warren, *Conquest*, 104–105.

71. Bancroft, *History of Mexico*, 2: 234–236.

72. Chipman, *Nuño de Guzmán*, 131–132.

73. Ibid., 86–87.

74. Cortés, *Cartas y documentos*, 361.

75. Prescott, *History*, 3: 448–449. See *DII*, 26: 32, for testimony relating the arrival of the Narváez expedition and the Aztecs' rebellion in Tenochtitlan.

76. *DII*, 1: 168; 26: 394.

77. Díaz del Castillo, *Historia verdadera*, 1: 298–300.

78. Ibid., 300; *DII*, 26: 395; 27: 14; 35: 436–437. Bernal Díaz states that Grado remained in the stocks for only two days.

79. *DII*, 27: 217–218, 359, 495; Zavala, *Esclavos indios*, 7–8.

80. Díaz del Castillo, *Historia verdadera*, 2: 50; 1: 414.

81. Chipman, *Nuño de Guzmán*, 132. It will be remembered that Cortés had conquered Pánuco in 1523, and that he had granted *encomiendas* there to his partisans.

82. Ibid., 144–172.

83. López de Meneses, "Tecuichpotzin," 475–477, quotation on 475. See ibid. for Cortés's sexual relations with other Indian women.

84. Chipman, "Isabel Moctezuma," 221.

85. Cline, "Hernando Cortés," 71; Thomas, *Conquest*, 596–597.

86. AGI, Justicia 181, 5v–10.

87. Burkett, "Indian Women," 106. Burkett notes that Spaniards married every daughter of Huayna Capac, the Inca emperor who died just prior to the Spanish conquest.

88. Chipman, "Isabel Moctezuma," 221–222.

Chapter 3

1. Peter Gerhard states that a small *estancia* (Tuchitlapilco) in Oaxaca "seems to have been assigned to an Indian governor, Juan Sánchez." Whatever the facts of the matter, this *estancia* had escheated to the crown by 1568. See *Guide*, 131.

2. Cortés, *Cartas y documentos*, 358–362. See Chapter 6 for a brief discussion of these *encomienda* grants as appropriate concessions to Indian royals.

3. Gibson, *Aztecs*, 32, first quotation; second quotation, as quoted.

4. Ibid., 32–33. This mixing of concepts is clearly reflected in Spanish sources used by Gibson. A corrective, however, comes from Nahuatl documents studied by James Lockhart, who uses the indigenous word "*altepetl*" for what native people viewed as the entire "ethnic state" of equal, distinct, independent components (*calpolli*). There is, however, no Nahuatl word for a dominant unit that ruled over the *calpolli*. In short, the pre-Spanish structure did not contain the concept of *cabecera*. Still, for purposes of this study, "the mental organizations of the indigenous world" are unimportant. As Lockhart admits, "generally speaking, Gibson's accounts of events and trends are unaffected"; see *Nahuas after the Conquest*, 14–15; and *Nahuas and Spaniards*, 180–181, quotations on 181.

5. Gibson, *Aztecs*, 32–33.

6. Ibid., 33. See note 4 above for Lockhart's corrective on the arrangement of the ethnic state in Central Mexico.

7. Ibid., 194–195.

8. Similarly, Francisco Pizarro and his brothers claimed for themselves the richest *encomiendas* in postconquest Peru. See Gabai and Jacobs, "Peruvian Wealth," 659–663.

9. The Spanish used two pesos of differing value. The *peso de oro de minas* (gold peso) was valued at 450 *maravedís*; the *peso de oro común* (silver peso) was valued at 272 *maravedís*. The silver peso contained eight *reales*, each valued at thirty-four *maravedís*. The *maravedí*, also a coin, was the smallest unit of currency. Often, the value of an item would be given in hundreds of thousands of *maravedís*, rather than in pesos. A *ducado*, or ducat, equaled 375 *maravedís*.

10. Cortés, *Cartas y documentos*, 360–361; Chipman, "Judicial Proceedings," 31–33.

11. AGI, Justicia, 165, N. 2; Gibson, *Aztecs*, 427–428.

12. Gibson, *Aztecs*, 196; Chipman, "Judicial Proceedings," 27–35.

13. Chipman, *Nuño de Guzmán*, 221–225.

14. Ibid., 231–232; idem, "Judicial Proceedings," 28.

15. Chipman, "Judicial Proceedings," 31–33. Huejotzingo was a major town located northwest of Cholula in the present-day state of Puebla.

16. AGI, Justicia, 226, fols. 417–418v. Unfortunately, the sworn testimony of Isabel Moctezuma is extremely brief, and she offers only corroborative evidence that Delgadillo and Matienzo seized a number of *encomiendas*, including hers.

17. Scholes, "Last Days," 183.

18. Cline, "Hernando Cortés," 70–71.

19. Ibid., 71; Cortés, *Cartas y documentos*, 596–599.

20. Cortés, *Cartas y documentos*, 599–600.

21. Bancroft, *History of Mexico*, 2: 317.

22. Ibid., 2: 321–322.

23. López de Meneses, "Tecuichpotzin," 479; AGI, Justicia, 181, fols. 26v–27.

24. Gruzinski, *Mestizo Mind*, 49–51, first quotation on 49, second quotation on 50–51.

25. Juan Cano was a native of Cáceres in western Spain. He was the son of Pedro Cano and Catalina Gómez de Saavedra. Both of his grandparents, Juan Cano and Gonzalo de Saavedra, served the Catholic monarchs in the reconquest of Granada. See Icaza, *Diccionario*, 1: 22.

26. Gibson, *Aztecs*, 124.

26. Doña Isabel, whose namesake had been the most Catholic queen of Castile, probably had little choice but to embrace completely Christianity and *hispanismo*.

28. Konetzke, "Mestizaje," 7.

29. Ibid., 9.

30. Quitt, "Trade and Acculturation," 231, first quotation; 238, second quotation. Quitt also documents that only two English women can be identified among the 445 persons who arrived at Jamestown in 1607 and 1608. Accordingly, heterosexual contact between Europeans was essentially not an option.

31. Konetzke, "Mestizaje," 28.

32. Ibid., 14; Díaz del Castillo, *Historia verdadera*, 2: 113. See Burkett, "Indian Women," 105, for comments on the Spaniards' rape of Indian women as "an integral part of the drive for submission that characterizes all conquest."

33. Díaz del Castillo, *Historia verdadera*, 1: 413.

34. Konetzke, "Mestizaje," 25, quotation on 27.

35. Fernández de Oviedo, *Historia general*, 4: 260.

36. López de Meneses, "Dos nietas," 82; idem, "Tecuichpotzin," 484; Gibson, *Aztecs*, 425.

37. AGI, Patronato, 245, R. 5, fol. 2v; Gibson, *Aztecs*, 425. For an incomplete list of *sujetos* and examples of variant spellings, see Cortés, *Cartas y documentos*, 360–361.

38. Ortega y Pérez Gallardo, *Historia genealógica*, 3: 41.

39. Ibid.

40. Sahagún, *Florentine Codex*, Bk. 10, Pt. 11: 45.

41. Ortega y Pérez Gallardo, *Historia genealógica*, 3: 42. The text of doña Isabel's testament also appears in AGI, Justicia, 181, 203v–210v. Josefina Muriel regards Isabel's personal possessions as prime examples of a life-style that blended Hispanic and indigenous elements; see *Mujeres de Hispanoamérica*, 54–55.

42. Lavrin, "Women in Convents," 252.

43. Gibson, *Aztecs*, Table 3, 64.

44. Speculation that Juan Cano objected to his stepson's rights of inheritance over Cano's biological offspring is supported by the promptness of his challenges to the provisions of Isabel Moctezuma's will.

45. Gerhard, *Guide*, 271.

46. It appears that the fifteen hundred *doblas* had already been awarded to the Canos by the viceroy and Audiencia of New Spain. So the decision of the council served only as a reaffirmation of the lower court's decision. See AGI, Patronato, 275, R. 36.

47. Ortega y Pérez Gallardo, *Historia genealógica*, 3: 42. Tepexoyuca is not identifiable as a *sujeto* included in the 1526 grant. Its possession by Isabel Moctezuma in 1550 may have

resulted from yet another successful petition. See Gerhard, *Guide*, 271. The fact that Isabel's eldest son by Juan Cano, Pedro Cano de Moctezuma, did not figure more prominently in her bequests may be explained by Pedro's rights of inheritance in Spain, which were later confirmed in his father's will.

48. Ortega y Pérez Gallardo, *Historia genealógica*, 3: 42–43. Isabel Moctezuma was buried in the Monastery of San Agustín, which had profited immensely from her largess. The monastery was destroyed by fire in 1676. See López de Meneses, "Dos nietas," 85–86.

49. Ortega y Pérez Gallardo, *Historia genealógica*, 3: 48–49.

50. Muriel, *Conventos*, 32; Lavrin, "Women in Convents," 255.

51. Muriel, *Conventos*, 37; AGI, Justicia, 181, fols. 321–326.

52. Gibson, *Aztecs*, 235, 423. See also Lockhart, *Nahuas and Spaniards*, 172.

53. The rapidity of Cano's challenges to his wife's testament immediately after her death supports this assertion.

54. Kellogg, "Tenocha Mexica Women," 126–127, quotation on 126; *Siete Partidas*, Pt. IV, Title XI, Law VII, 938.

55. Kellogg, "Tenocha Mexica Women," 126–127, quotation on 127; see also idem, *Law*, 126.

56. AGI, México, 1088; López de Meneses, "Tecuichpotzin," 489–494.

57. Although Susan Kellogg does not cite Isabel Moctezuma's will in her excellent chapter "Wills, Property, and People," doña Isabel's testament is consistent with Kellogg's findings with regard to fourteen wills executed by Mexica women between 1546 and 1581. Doña Isabel disposed of residential property, land, and movables, and she left bequests to both sons and daughters. See Kellogg, *Law*, 138.

58. AGI, Justicia, 181, fols. 202vff.; López de Meneses, "Tecuichpotzin," 489–494.

59. AGI, Justicia, 181, fols. 202vff.

60. Gibson, *Aztecs*, 423–424.

61. See Chapter 4, note 3, for a discussion of inconsistencies in sources referring to Mariana/Leonor Moctezuma.

62. Juan Paz's surname is frequently recorded in documentation as Páez.

63. Gibson, *Aztecs*, 424. The question of Mariana's legitimacy is addressed in Chapter 4.

64. AGI, Justicia, 181, fols. 202vff.

65. AGI, Contratación, 209, N. 1, R. 7, fols. 7–14v. In his will, drafted in Seville and dated September 3, 1572, Juan Cano enumerates his assets in Seville and Cáceres and asks that his eldest son, Pedro, either come to Spain and assume control of the *mayorazgo* or send an agent.

66. AGI, Justicia, 181, fols. 202vff.

67. For names of the five grandchildren of Isabel Moctezuma, see Fig. 3.1. When the elder Juan de Andrade died around 1577, the Tacuba *encomienda* became the sole inheritance of the Cano Moctezuma family. See Gibson, *Aztecs*, 425.

68. Ana's parents were Rodrigo Calderón of Mérida and Josefa Núñez de Prado of Badajoz.

69. Gibson, *Aztecs*, 424. The house has been renamed the Palacio de los Toledo-Moctezuma.

70. AGI, Justicia, 181, unnumbered folios following 503.

71. Ibid.

72. Ibid.

73. Ibid.

74. Ibid.; Muriel, *Conventos*, 160n31. This information is at variance with Charles Gibson's statement regarding the resolution of this case. See *Aztecs*, 424. I have been unable to trace the subsequent history of this small portion of the Tacuba *encomienda*, which remained with Pedro Cano de Moctezuma's daughter.

75. Fernández de Recas, *Mayorazgos*, 158–165. More detailed information about these families may be found in Chapter 6.

76. AGI, Patronato, 59, N. 3, R. 6. The third brother was Antonio Andelo Cano Moctezuma.

Chapter 4

1. Henry R. Wagner argues that Cortés did not speak to Moctezuma after the latter was allegedly injured. See *Rise of Fernando Cortés*, 306–307.

2. Cortés, *Cartas y documentos*, 359, 361. Fernando Alvarado Tezozomoc, the son of a half-sister of Isabel Moctezuma, states that María died young (*Crónica*, xx, 155–156).

3. Cortés, *Cartas y documentos*, 362. There is confusion about the Christian name given to the *encomendera* of Ecatepec. Early documents, including Cortés's original grant, refer to her as Mariana. However, by the 1530s she was invariably called Leonor. One explanation is copyists' mistakes, unlikely except that this woman's only child, a daughter fathered by Cristóbal de Valderrama, was named Leonor. Amada López de Meneses suggests that Mariana referred to herself as Leonor after that name was given to her during the sacrament of confirmation, and evidence supports her conclusion. Diego Arias Sotelo would surely have known the preferred name of his mother-in-law. He refers to her as Leonor in a lawsuit concerning the revenues from Tacuba. Because I discuss many other women named Leonor in this book, I shall refer to her throughout as Mariana.

4. Gibson, *Aztecs*, 38.

5. Cortés, *Cartas y documentos*, 362; Gibson, *Aztecs*, 418.

6. Icaza, *Diccionario*, 1: 115–116; López de Meneses, "Tecuichpochtzin," 477n16.

7. The wills of both Isabel Moctezuma and Fernando Cortés include bequests to Leonor Cortés Moctezuma, and it was common for Spaniards to name natural children as heirs.

8. López de Meneses, "Tecuichpochtzin," 477n16; Gibson, *Aztecs*, 419.

9. Gibson, *Aztecs*, 74.

10. Ibid.

11. Ibid.

12. Ibid., 74–75.

13. Ibid., 75.

14. In the 1560s Tacuba ranked first; Coyoacan, a perpetual holding of Cortés's son Martín, ranked second. See Gibson, *Aztecs*, Table 3, 64.

15. As the Ávila-Cortés conspiracy was brewing, Leonor de Valderrama y Moctezuma died. Following her death, Diego Arias Sotelo married María Tramuel. See Orozco y Berra, *Noticia histórica*, 248.

16. Scholes and Adams, *Documentos*, 7: 7; *Diccionario Porrúa*, 2: 2212.

17. Bancroft, *History of Mexico*, 2: 602.

18. Ibid., 609.

19. Ibid., 613–617.

20. Martín Cortés embarked for Spain in April 1567, where the Council of the Indies conducted his trial. He was found culpable, fined, permanently banished from the Indies, and exiled to North Africa. However, the sentence was never implemented. In 1574 don Martín received a pardon from the council and the restoration of the *marquesado* in New Spain, but he remained in Spain, where he died in 1589. See *Diccionario Porrúa*, 1: 534.

21. Lockhart, *Men of Cajamarca*, 222, 254; Orozco y Berra, *Noticia histórica*, 243n2. Valderrama refers to Baltasar as the brother of Diego Arias Sotelo, noting that he had "recently come" to New Spain. See Scholes and Adams, *Documentos*, 7: 226.

22. Orozco y Berra, *Noticia histórica*, 247. Diego Arias Sotelo also held the *encomienda* of Tarímbaro and others in Michoacán (Gerhard, *Guide*, 345). During his two years of incarceration, he underwent cord and water torture in the manner of the Spanish Inquisition, leaving him "very frail and sick from many infirmities." See AGI, Patronato, 217, R. 3.

23. Historians have failed to find credible evidence of treasonous intent on the part of those charged in the so-called Ávila-Cortés conspiracy. Rather, they blame youthful foolishness, on one hand, and an overzealous crown prosecutor, on the other.

24. Orozco y Berra, *Noticia histórica*, 277; Bancroft, *History of Mexico*, 2: 618, 626n35–627, 628n40. Diego Arias Sotelo was transported to Oran in North Africa. For additional information on Martín Cortés and his half-brothers, Luis and Martín (the mestizo son of doña Marina), in the aftermath of the Ávila-Cortés *conjuración*, see Orozco y Berra, *Noticia histórica*.

25. In the context of the Valderrama visitation, there is an interesting petition filed by the cacique and *principales* of Tacuba in 1566. The Indians asserted that the visitor-general had seized revenues from the Tacuba *encomienda* and assigned them to the crown. The matter had to be referred to the Council of the Indies, because no official in New Spain had the authority to override a decision of the visitor-general. See AGI, Justicia, 1029, fols. 1–37. This document does not contain the council's decision, but it obviously rescinded the sequestration because of Tacuba's status as a perpetual holding.

26. AGI, Escribanía de Cámara,, 178A, Exp. 12, fols. 7v, 62–65.

27. Alvarado Tezozomoc, *Crónica*, 126–127,

28. AGI, Escribanía de Cámara,, 178A, Exp. 12, fols. 48–51v, 66, 131.

29. Ibid., fols. 1–13.

30. Gibson, *Aztecs*, 419.

31. Davies, *Toltecs*, 42; Barlow, "Anales." Variant spellings of Tula include Tullan and Tulan.

32. Brundage, *Rain of Darts*, 230; Davies, *Toltecs*, 42.

33. Hollingsworth, "Pedro de Moctezuma," 22. Miahuaxochitl's father was Ixtlilcuexhuaca.

34. Thomas, *Conquest*, 562, 577. There is no evidence that Cortés granted Tula as an *encomienda* to Pedro Moctezuma. Documentation contained in AGI, México, 764, suggests that Pedro's *estancias* were those that accompanied his mother as dotal property when she married Moctezuma II. However, Pedro's descendants did not receive hereditary rights to

these revenues until this income was included in an entailed estate. See this chapter, below.

35. Thomas, *Conquest*, 587.

36. Cline, "Hernando Cortés," 85. Cline lists three of Moctezuma's sons (don Martín Cortés Nezahualtecolotl, don Pedro Gutiérrez Aculan, and don Juan Covamitle) who accompanied Cortés on his first return to Spain in 1528. Don Juan remained in Spain and may have died there; don Martín returned to New Spain but died on the road from Veracruz to Mexico City; and don Pedro returned to New Spain, where he received honors from the crown.

37. AGN, Tierras, 1529, fols. 102–103v, 112.

38. Hollingsworth, "Pedro de Moctezuma," 31.

39. Villar Villamil, *Cedulario*, núm. 141; AGI, México, 764, Reflexiones sobre la Tabla VI. The *privilegio de armas* and its design were not sent from Spain until September 11, 1570.

40. AGN, Tierras, 1529, fol. 96v; Hollingsworth, "Pedro de Moctezuma." After she was baptized, the Christian name María was regularly used with Miahuaxochitl.

41. AGN, Tierras, 1529, fols. 94–94v. These municipalities included Ystla, Xitomatla, Tolpa, Tepetlapa, Tlatilco, Coyagualco, Techichilco, Saavestepan, Tepeytique, Tecoquipan, Tultengo, Xicocac, Tecontepeque, Yztaque, Zaquala, Milpa, Coculco, Ilucan, Tlazongo, and Tlapan. The spellings of these twenty *estancias* varies with virtually every repetition by the same scribe in the same document. This is not an unusual circumstance in that *escribanos* had to render toponyms spoken in native languages into Spanish orthography. See Gerhard, *Guide*, 35. The spellings used here appear to be those that are used most consistently.

42. Hollingsworth, "Pedro de Moctezuma," 33–34. Fourteen years later, the stipend was increased to one hundred pesos.

43. AGN, Mercedes, 1, fols. 10–10v, 51–51v; AGN, Tierras, 1529, fols. 97–98.

44. James Lockhart notes that in areas outside the cities of the Aztec Triple Alliance individual *altepetl* were largely left intact and self-contained. This was apparently the situation in Tula, and it explains why Indians there were "fully aware of their heritage and eager to cast off tribute obligations and other ties at the first opportunity." See *Nahuas after the Conquest*, 27; Hollingsworth, "Pedro de Moctezuma," 34.

45. Simpson, *Encomienda*, 129–132; Haring, *Spanish Empire*, 56–57.

46. Haring, *Spanish Empire*, 57.

47. In the interim, on October 19, 1550, Pedro Moctezuma won a stipend of five hundred silver pesos per year, payable from the treasury of New Spain. See *Colección de documentos inéditos relativos al descubrimiento, conquista y organización de las antiguas posesiones de Ultramar* (hereafter *DIU*), 18: 76.

48. Hollingsworth, "Pedro de Moctezuma," 34–35; AGN, Tierras, 1529, fols. 100v–101.

49. Barlow, "Anales"; Hollingsworth, "Pedro de Moctezuma," 36–37; AGN, Tierras, 1529, fol. 101.

50. Hollingsworth, "Pedro de Moctezuma," 37; AGN, Tierras, 1529, fol. 101.

51. AGN, Tierras, 1529, fols. 104–107v.

52. Hollingsworth, "Pedro de Moctezuma," 39; *ENE*, 9: 53: AGN, Tierras, 1529, fols. 105–128. The *ENE* citation contains only the date of Pedro's request (June 30, 1560).

53. Carrasco, "Indian-Spanish Marriages," 93. Carrasco maintains that don Pedro and

doña Inés were not allowed to marry formally. As Pedro's cousin, Inés could not obtain the necessary dispensation, and she later married Rodrigo Irés. Nevertheless, Spaniards viewed Pedro and Inés's son, don Martín, as the legitimate heir of Pedro Moctezuma.

54. Pedro had more children by four Indian women, from Tenayuca, Tula, and Tenochtitlan: Bartolomé, Lorenzo, María, and Magdalena. All received the Moctezuma surname. See AGI, México, 764, Tabla II and Reflexiones sobre la Tabla VI. The names of the mothers are found in Tabla II. Pedro Carrasco notes that very few marriages occurred between Indian men and Spanish women in New Spain. See "Indian-Spanish Marriages," 90.

55. AGN, Tierras, 1529, fols. 112–123v.

56. Mentioned as contested *estancias* in the case are Tecontepeque, Coculco, Techichilco, Xicocac, Tepeytique, Zaquala, Tlazongo, Tequipa, Ystla, Tlapan, Tultengo, Ilucan, and Ahuehuepan. See Hollingsworth, "Pedro de Moctezuma," 41. Tequipa and Ahuehuepan are not identifiable as being among the original twenty *estancias* that were awarded to Pedro Moctezuma in 1540.

57. Hollingsworth, "Pedro de Moctezuma," 41–42.

58. Ibid., 43–44.

59. *ENE*, 16: 81–82.

60. AGI, Patronato, 245, R. 4, fols. 1–5.

61. Ibid.; AGI, México, 764, Reflexiones sobre la Tabla VI; AGN, Vínculos, 69, fols. 9–10. The date of Philip II's *cédula* (March 23, 1577) in *DII*, 6: 68, is incorrect. The king's orders were sent to Viceroy Marqués de Falces, who was in office from 1566 to 1567.

62. AGN, Vínculos, 76, fols. 5v–29. The copy of Pedro's will in AGN, Vínculos, 69, fols. 9–24, is badly deteriorated, with broken folios and missing information in the first half. A printed version of his testament in *DII*, 68–94, indicates missing information.

63. Hollingsworth, "Pedro de Moctezuma," 50–52; AGN, Vínculos, 76, fols. 5v–29; AGI, México, 764, Tabla II.

64. AGN, Vínculos, 69, fols. 24–25; *DII*, 6: 93, 102.

65. Hollingsworth, "Pedro de Moctezuma," 54; AGN, Vínculos, 69, fol. 27; AGN, Vínculos, 76, fols. 30v–32; AGI, México, 764, Tabla XI.

66. Hollingsworth, "Pedro de Moctezuma," 54–55; AGN, Vínculos, 69, fol. 27; AGN, Vínculos, 76, fols. 30v–32; AGI, Indiferente General, 1615, fol. 78.

67. AGI, México, 764, fols. 51–51v.

68. Ibid., Tabla IX.

69. AGI, Patronato, 245, R. 6, fols. 4–5.

70. López de Meneses, "Un nieto," 2: 568–570.

71. Juan de Andrade, María de Iñíguez's husband, had been ordered by royal *cédula* to return to New Spain and resume marital life, but he died in Seville in late 1577.

72. Hollingsworth, "Pedro de Moctezuma," 57–58; AGI, Patronato, 245, R. 6, fols. 4–5.

73. Hollingsworth, "Pedro de Moctezuma," 58–59; AGI, Patronato, 245, R. 6, fols. 10–17.

74. For a summary of these lawsuits, see Hollingsworth, "Pedro de Moctezuma," 59–64. For information on still another claimant to the *mayorazgo*, see a letter (dated October 9, 1587) from Pedro Enrique Moctezuma to his relatives in Iztapalapa in Lock-

hart and Otte, eds., *Letters*, 161–162. As noted earlier in this chapter, Inés Tiacapan married after being separated from Pedro Moctezuma, so Pedro may not have had information about her whereabouts.

75. *DII*, 6: 109; AGN, Vínculos, 69, fols. 34v–35; AGI, México, 764, Tabla IX; AGI, Patronato, 245, R. 15, fols. 35–38.

76. Hollingsworth, "Pedro de Moctezuma," 65–66; AGI, Patronato, 245, R. 15, fols. 35–38; AGI, México, 764, Tabla IX.

77. Hollingsworth, "Pedro de Moctezuma," 66–67; AGI, Patronato, 245, R. 15, fol. 10; AGI, Indiferente General, 1615, fol. 79.

78. Lynch, *Spain*, 1: 134.

CHAPTER 5

1. Himmerich y Valencia, *Encomenderos*, 160; Gerhard, *Guide*, 44. The name of the *encomienda* was Iscuincuitlapilco,

2. Chipman, "Isabel Moctezuma," 220–221. Altamirano was from the province of Ávila. He conducted the *residencia* of Governor Diego de Velázquez in Cuba before arriving in New Spain.

3. Warren, *Conquest*, 42.

4. Ibid. It will be remembered that Cuauhtemoc and the kings of Texcoco and Tacuba were forced to accompany Cortés on the trek to Honduras, during which they were executed.

5. Ibid., 102.

6. Chipman, "Nuño de Guzmán," 206.

7. Ibid., 206–207.

8. Warren, *Conquest*, 221–236. Additional charges against the Tarascan king included performing homosexual acts (sodomy), ordering the death of Spaniards in Michoacán, and engaging in idolatrous practices after accepting Christianity. See Scholes and Adams, eds. *Proceso*.

9. Chipman, "Nuño de Guzmán," 210–211, 215–216.

10. Ibid., 212–213.

11. Chipman, *Spanish Texas*, 45.

12. Chipman, *Nuño de Guzmán*, 245–249.

13. Chipman, *Spanish Texas*, 42.

14. Bakewell, *Silver Mining*, 4–6.

15. Chipman, *Spanish Texas*, 46.

16. Powell, *Soldiers*, 11–12; Chipman, *Spanish Texas*, 46.

17. AGI, Guadalajara, 5, visitation of Alonso de Santacruz (April 16, 1550).

18. Conway, *Last Will and Testament*, Item XXXIII. For provisions in Isabel Moctezuma's will that relate to Leonor Cortés Moctezuma, see Chapter 3.

19. Liss, *Mexico*, 136.

20. Garate, "Juan de Oñate's *Prueba de caballero*," 147, 148, quotation on 148; Mecham, *Francisco de Ibarra*, 40; Bakewell, *Silver Mining*, 10; AGI, Patronato, 80, N. 5, R. 1, fols. 6–8. Garate notes that at least three Tolosa families resided in the town of Oñate in the early 1540s.

21. AGI, Patronato, 80, N. 5, R. 1, fols. 6v–7.

22. Testimony was given in both Guadalajara and Zacatecas.

23. Chichimec, or Chichimeca, was a generic term for nomadic Indians of northern Mexico who occupied the *tierra adentro*, essentially lands that by 1542 lay north of a line running from Culiacán southeastward to Lake Chapala, eastward to the environs of Querétaro, and then northeastward to present-day Tampico.

24. AGI, Patronato, 80, N. 5, R. 1, fols. 54v–55.

25. Ibid., fol. 51.

26. Ibid., fols. 51v, 90–91v, quotation on 51v. The royal *cédula* granting a coat of arms to the city of Zacatecas is printed in Dávila Garibi, *Sociedad de Zacatecas*, 105–106.

27. AGI, Patronato, 80, N. 5, R. 1, fol. 90. The colored coat of arms is preserved in AGI, Mapas y Planos, Escudos y Árboles Genealógicos, 102.

28. Leonor Cortés Moctezuma also received a coat of arms. It is reproduced in Dávila Garibi, *Sociedad de Zacatecas*, between pages 28 and 29, but this reproduction does not contain a date or a legend. My efforts to locate the original in the AGN were not successful.

29. It is worth noting that Luis Cortés, like Leonor, was a "natural" offspring of the conqueror. Initially, Luis fared quite well in his father's will, receiving an annual pension of one thousand ducats for life. But in the codicil, the old conquistador revoked, disclaimed, and annulled "altogether said command" regarding his son. See Conway, *Last Will and Testament*, Item XXIII.

30. Garate, "Juan de Oñate's *Prueba de caballero*," 148.

31. Ibid., 147. The elder Oñate was born in the town of Oñate in the present-day province of Guipúzcoa, Spain. His parents were Juan Pérez de Narria and Osana Martínez de San Vicente, natives of Narria and Oñate, respectively. Juan de Oñate's mother was Catalina de Salazar, a native of Granada. She was the daughter of Gonzalo de Salazar, one of the four treasury officials who governed New Spain during the years 1524–1526, and Catalina de la Cadena of Burgos. Narria was a *barrio* associated with the town of Oñate.

32. Ibid., 157–158; Chipman, "Oñate-Moctezuma-Zaldívar Families," 305. Catalina de Salazar's first husband was Ruy Díaz de Mendoza. The couple set out for the New World with their three children, one of whom was a girl, Magdalena de Mendoza y Salazar. En route, Díaz died.

33. Chipman, "Oñate-Moctezuma-Zaldívar Families," 304–305.

34. Powell, *Soldiers*, 16.

35. Chipman, *Spanish Texas*, 47–49.

36. Ibid., 49–50.

37. Information submitted in 1627 by Cristóbal de Zaldívar Mendoza, Juan de Tolosa's son-in-law, states that revenues from mines discovered by Juan de Tolosa between the years 1575 and 1614 amounted to 6,338,000 pesos. Royal treasury officials certified this amount as correct. See AGI, Patronato, 80, N. 5, R. 1. This income obviously failed to enrich Tolosa, who may have died before 1575.

38. Powell, *Soldiers*, 62, 75, 118. In 1572, perhaps in recompense for Bañuelos's losses, Viceroy Martín Enríquez appointed him lieutenant captain-general of New Galicia.

39. Ibid., 30, 66, 74.

40. AGI, Patronato, 80, N. 5, R. 1.

41. Powell, *Soldiers*, 186–203, quotation on 202.

42. Simmons, *Last Conquistador*, 32–34.

43. Chipman, "Oñate-Moctezuma-Zaldívar Families," 300; Dávila Garibi, *Sociedad de Zacatecas*, 15.

44. Simmons, *Last Conquistador*, 34–35.

45. Ibid., 36.

46. Powell, *Soldiers*, 47–48, as quoted on 48.

47. Simmons, *Last Conquistador*, 36–37.

48. Ibid., 38.

49. Ibid., 39.

50. Chipman, *Spanish Texas*, 56.

51. Ibid., 55–56.

52. Ibid., 56.

53. Jones, *Nueva Vizcaya*, 66,

54. Chipman, *Spanish Texas*, 58.

55. Simmons, *Last Conquistador*, 55–56, quotation on 56.

56. Ibid., 56–58, quotation on 56. Urdiñola was eventually absolved, but the trial dragged on until 1598.

57. Ibid., 60.

58. Ibid., 58–87.

59. Ibid., 87; Jones, *Nueva Vizcaya*, 67–68.

60. Beerman, "Death," 306.

61. Hammond and Rey, *Don Juan de Oñate*, 1: 477–479.

62. Simmons, *Last Conquistador*, 119–123.

63. Ibid., 119–120, quotation on 119.

64. Ibid., 194–195.

65. Ibid., 185.

66. Hammond and Rey, *Don Juan de Oñate*, 2: 1109–1113.

67. Cristóbal de Oñate Cortés Moctezuma had married María Gutiérrez del Castillo. Their son was Juan Pérez de Narria y del Castillo.

68. Hammond and Rey, *Don Juan de Oñate*, 1: 530.

69. Simmons, *Last Conquistador*, 190–192.

70. Ibid., 192, quotation; Lohmann Villena, *Americanos*, 1: 292. Also see Garate, "Juan de Oñate's *Prueba de Caballero*."

71. Beerman, "Death," 312–314; Simmons, *Last Conquistador*, 193–194.

72. Chipman, "Oñate-Moctezuma-Zaldívar Families," 307; Simmons, *Last Conquistador*, 189. Vicente de Zaldívar Mendoza was admitted to the Order of Santiago in 1626. See Archivo Histórico Nacional (hereafter, AHN), Órdenes Militares—Santiago, Exp. 9070; see also Lohmann Villena, *Americanos*, 1: 460.

73. Chipman, "Oñate-Moctezuma-Zaldívar Families," 307–308.

CHAPTER 6

1. According to an *información* (report) in 1554, the amount of yearly tribute paid by Indians to Moctezuma II was set at 1,962,450 pesos de oro común of 272 *maravedís* each

in value. Although this precise figure has been questioned, the amount of tribute was clearly impressive. See Zurita, *Life and Labor*, 285–287.

2. Gibson, "Conquest, " 12.

3. Hanke, *Spanish Struggle* (1949), 31; Gibson, "Conquest," 13, quotations. See also Liss, *Mexico*, 31–35.

4. Hanke, *Spanish Struggle*, 33, as quoted.

5. Ibid., 34, first quotation; Las Casas, *Historia*, 2: Lib. 3, Cap. 58, 583, second quotation.

6. Seed, *Ceremonies*, 70, quotation; Gibson, "Conquest," 13; Díaz del Castillo, *Historia verdadera*, 1: 315.

7. Muriel, "Reflexiones," 233. Again, Cortés's account of Moctezuma's rooftop injury, which led to the emperor's death, is at variance with native sources.

8. *DII*, 6: 67; Gibson, "Conquest," 13. Gibson uses the incorrect date of 1577, because that mistake appears in *DII*, as noted earlier.

9. Elliott, *Old World*, 84, last quotation as quoted.

10. Vitoria, *Political Writings*, xxvi. See also Hanke, *Spanish Struggle* (2002), 150–152. Students may appreciate that Vitoria published nothing in his lifetime, arguing that those who sat in his classroom had enough to read. His "writings" come from student notes, made possible by the manner in which Vitoria lectured—word by word delivered so slowly that verbatim copying was easy.

11. Elliott, *Old World*, 85.

12. Lockhart, *Nahuas after the Conquest*, 94. Some readers may be more familiar with the status of Indian elites in the British North American colonies than with those regarded as *reyes naturales* in colonial Mexico. It is interesting to note that the British applied the title "king" (rather unsuccessfully as it turned out) to four young Indians with largely fictitious ties to the Iroquois confederacy. These Indians traveled to London in 1710. Only one of the group could be classified as a sachem. These "kings" and others with the title, such as Powhatan, were never admitted to the British peerage; rather, they represented an attempt to build the empire by linking separate Indian nations to the crown, not to different colonies. See Countryman, "Indians"; Hinderaker, "'Four Indian Kings.'"

13. Spaniards attached little stigma to illegitimacy. It is significant that Mariana Moctezuma, the daughter of Moctezuma and a secondary wife, received an *encomienda* grant that is identical in language to that of her half-sister, doña Isabel. Don Pedro's heirs claimed his supremacy as an heir of Moctezuma over his half-sisters, because males had occupied the position of emperor. Legitimacy became a contested issue when attorneys introduced it into intrafamily lawsuits, and, it is important to note, in the case of Diego Luis Moctezuma, who was specifically labeled a natural son by his father. These issues are summarized near the end of AGI, México, 764, Reflexiones sobre la Tabla VI: Legitimidad de Don Pedro y Doña Isabel de Motezuma [*sic*].

14. Gibson, *Aztecs*, 424.

15. See, for example, Juan Cano's petition, dated December 1, 1547, in which he mentions other briefs sent to the crown: AGI, Patronato, 245, R. 2, fols. 1–2; Gibson, *Aztecs*, 424–425.

16. AGI, Mapas, Escudos, y Árboles Genealógicos, 212, 213. The total is 8,400 pesos, not

7,400, because the grandchildren of Juan de Andrade and María Iñiguez did not receive perpetual *mercedes*. Nevertheless, this branch's claims to *mercedes* in the seventeenth century were Juan de Andrade Moctezuma III (El Mozo, 1653), Juan de Andrade Moctezuma IV (1688), the latter's brother, Antonio Andrade Moctezuma (1688), and Felipe de Andrade Moctezuma (1695). See AGI, México, 764, Tabla VI. The documents cited above do not indicate a grant to Gonzalo Cano's heirs; Pedro Cano's offspring are not mentioned; nor, of course, is there reference to their sisters, Isabel and Catalina, who renounced all inheritances when they became nuns.

17. AGI, Patronato, 80, N. 5, R. 1, fols. 23v–27.

18. Ladd, *Mexican Nobility*, 3–4, quotation on 3.

19. AGI, Patronato, 245, R. 17, fols. 1–11. The younger sons were named Felipe and Francisco. The surviving daughter was christened María; a second daughter, Agustina, died in early childhood. See Hollingsworth, "Pedro de Moctezuma," 68.

20. Given the catastrophic decline in the Indian population of New Spain during the sixteenth century, *encomiendas* naturally lost much of their original value because of diminishing tributary units. Since all *encomiendas* granted to the heirs of Moctezuma II were situated within Central Mexico, Indian population loss there is most germane. Gibson projects a 90 percent or greater decline in numbers within the basin of Mexico from the conquest to the late 1500s and early 1600s; see *Aztecs*, 138. William T. Sanders places the Indian population loss for Central Mexico at approximately 93 percent by the late sixteenth century; see "Population," 120.

21. AGI, Patronato, 245, R. 24, fols. 1–2; Hollingsworth, "Pedro de Moctezuma," 69–71.

22. Hollingsworth, "Pedro de Moctezuma," 70–71.

23. AGI, México, 762, fols. 6–9; Hollingsworth, "Pedro de Moctezuma," 71.

24. Hollingsworth, "Pedro de Moctezuma," 71.

25. AGI, México, 762, fols. 6–9.

26. Elliott, *Imperial Spain*, 299; AGI, Indiferente General, 1615, fols. 2–3.

27. Hollingsworth, "Pedro de Moctezuma," 73; Elliott, *Imperial Spain*, 292–299.

28. Lynch, *Spain*, 2: 14, first quotation; Elliott, *Imperial Spain*, 295, second quotation.

29. Elliott, *Imperial Spain*, 295–296; Hollingsworth, "Pedro de Moctezuma," 74–75.

30. Hollingsworth, "Pedro de Moctezuma," 75.

31. Ibid.

32. Ibid., 75–76.

33. AGI, Patronato, 245, R. 15, fols. 1–11; AGN, Vínculos, 80, Exp. 1, fols. 105–109; Hollingsworth, "Pedro de Moctezuma," 76–77. It is difficult to assess the true financial circumstances facing Diego Luis's widow.

34. AGI, Patronato, 245, R. 15, fols. 11–17, 29–36.

35. AGI, Patronato, 245, R. 17, fols. 1–11; AGI, México, 762; AGI, México, 764; AGN, Vínculos, 80, Exp. 1, fols. 105–108. Somewhat later, the yearly stipends granted to the younger siblings were made renewable for three generations beyond the death of the original grantee.

36. Hollingsworth, "Pedro de Moctezuma," 78–79.

37. Ibid., 80; AGI, Patronato, 245, R. 18, fols. 1–2. The crown repeated the directive in a second *cédula*, dated September 16, 1612; see AGI, Patronato, 245, R. 16, fols. 1–2.

38. AGI, México, 762.

39. AGI, Patronato, 245, R. 18, fols. 1–2v; Lynch, *Spain*, 2: 189–202; Gibson, *Aztecs*, 136–144.

40. AGI, México, 762. The *pueblos* were Cacaotepec, Zaquala, Zoquitzingo, Tenancingo, Yoloxinecuila, Xonacatlan, Ostoticpic, Xilocingo (Xilotzingo), Taliztaca, Chachuapa, Escapuzalco, Tecomastlaguaca, Tlacotepec, Santiago Tecali, and Zumpaguacan. The orthography has been rendered consistent with the index in Gerhard, *Guide*, 445–476.

41. Lynch, *Spain*, 2: 67.

42. AGI, Indiferente General, 1615, fols. 12–15; AGI, México, 762; AGN, Vínculos, 80, fols. 3–4.

43. AGI, México, 762; Muriel, "Reflexiones," 233; Hollingsworth, "Pedro de Moctezuma," 84–84; Atienza, *Títulos*, 445, 583.

44. AGI, México, 762; AGN, Vínculos, 80, Exp. 1, fols. 105–108. The title was formalized by Philip IV on December 14, 1627. See Ortega y Pérez Gallardo, *Estudios genealógicos*, 157.

45. Lynch, *Spain*, 2: 82.

46. AGI, México, 762.

47. Hollingsworth, "Pedro de Moctezuma," 89–90.

48. AGI, México, 762; AGI, Indiferente General, 1615, fol. 5; Hollingsworth, "Pedro de Moctezuma," 90–91.

49. Hollingsworth, "Pedro de Moctezuma," 90–91.

50. Ibid., 94.

51. Ibid., 94–95. Theresa Francisca de Moctezuma's granddaughter Teresa (Theresa) Nieto de Silva y Moctezuma, would assume the title of sixth Countess of Moctezuma in the early 1700s. Thus, the Moctezuma peerage in this branch of the Moctezuma family would eventually continue through Pedro Tesifón's legitimate daughter. The natural son, (Pedro) Diego Luis Moctezuma, would later pen a curious book entitled *Corona mexicana; ó, historia de los nueve Motezumas*, a fanciful account of the first nine Aztec emperors, ending with Moctezuma II. For a more thorough description of the book, see Keen, *Aztec Image*, 201–203.

52. Hollingsworth, "Pedro de Moctezuma," 96.

53. For a summary, see ibid., 99–104.

54. Elliott, *Imperial Spain*, 337–345; Hollingsworth, "Pedro de Moctezuma," 102; AGI, México, 762.

55. Elliott, *Imperial Spain*, 354.

56. Hollingsworth, "Pedro de Moctezuma," 105–106. See Figure 4.2.

57. Elliott, *Imperial Spain*, 354; Hollingsworth, "Pedro de Moctezuma," 113.

58. Lynch, *Spain*, 2: 276–289. Lynch notes that the traditional view of Spain in this era as a corpse picked over by parasites is somewhat overdrawn, and that recovery was discernible in Castile by the end of the seventeenth century.

59. See Langdon-Davies, *Carlos*, 29.

60. Hollingsworth, "Pedro de Moctezuma," 112–116.

61. Ibid., 118–119. Joseph Sarmiento de Valladares was the son of Gregorio de Valladares y Meira, a knight of Santiago, and Juana Sarmiento de Valladares y Meira, probably a cousin. Both were citizens of Vigo, as were Joseph's paternal grandparents. See AHN, Órdenes Militares—Santiago, 5925.

62. Hollingsworth, "Pedro de Moctezuma," 119.

63. Ibid., 119–120.

64. AGN, Tierras, 2284, fols. 74–78; Hollingsworth, "Pedro de Moctezuma," 121.

65. Hollingsworth, "Pedro de Moctezuma," 122–124.

66. AGI, México, 762.

67. Hollingsworth, "Pedro de Moctezuma," 126–127.

68. AGI, México, 762, 765.

69. Ibid.

70. Hollingsworth, "Pedro de Moctezuma," 130–131.

71. AGI, México, 762; Hollingsworth, "Pedro de Moctezuma," 131.

72. Lynch, *Spain*, 2: 291.

73. Hollingsworth, "Pedro de Moctezuma," 132–133.

74. Vetancurt, *Teatro mexicano*, Tratado de la Ciudad de México, fol. 17.

75. Curcio, "Saints," 51.

76. Ibid., 71; quotation, 114–115. For additional information on ceremony and celebration in the baroque age, see Leonard, *Baroque Times*, esp. 117–144.

77. Hanke, *Virreyes*, 5: 187. For the viceroy's efforts to deal with widespread famine by ordering Indians to leave Mexico City and plant crops in their fields, see his orders of May 19, 1697, in AGI, México, 65. See also Curcio-Nagy, "Giants," 19.

78. Hanke, *Virreyes*, 5: 188–205.

79. AGI, México, 765.

80. Hanke, *Virreyes*, 5: 239–241. A silver peso consisted of eight *reales*. Later, this peso would be called the piece of eight.

81. AGI, Indiferente General, 1615, fols. 50v–51v; AGI, México, 763; Hollingsworth, "Pedro de Moctezuma," 142–144. The date of Philip V's concession of a dukedom to José Sarmiento de Valladares (April 17, 1708) in Atienza, *Títulos*, 27, is in error.

82. Hollingsworth, "Pedro de Moctezuma," 145–147. Doña Teresa, the great-granddaughter of Pedro Tesifón Moctezuma, was the sixth Countess of Moctezuma. See Figure 4.2.

83. Gerhard, *Guide*, 247; López de Meneses, "Tecuichpochtzin," 492n42. Juan de Andrade (Gallego) Moctezuma's descendants entered the peerage as Counts of Miravalle. See Figure 3.1.

84. AGI, Escribanía de Cámara, 178A. Gonzalo Cano asked to be buried in the chapel of the convent of San Agustín near his mother, Isabel Moctezuma.

85. Gibson, *Aztecs*, 424. See Lohmann Villena, *Americanos*, 1: Num. 86, for admission of Diego Cano Moctezuma into the military Order of Santiago. See also AHN, Órdenes Militares—Santiago, 1477.

86. AGI, México, 762.

87. AGI, Justicia, 938, fols. 1–78.

88. AGI, México, 764, Tabla VII.

89. Gibson, *Aztecs*, 424. For a description of the renovated Palacio de los Toledo-Moctezuma, see http://www.terra.es/personal2/joseabra/ptmocte.htm.

90. The lineage of the Marqueses and Marquesas of Tenebrón descends from Theresa Francisca de Moctezuma, the daughter of Pedro Tesifón Moctezuma. See Figure 4.2.

91. See, for example, García Iglesias, *Isabel Moctezuma*, 208; and AGI, México, 764, Tabla VIII.

CONCLUSIONS

1. This study addresses a long-standing question: How could a few hundred Spaniards triumph over vast numbers of Aztec warriors? This question, although not essential to the fate of Moctezuma's heirs, is important in the beginning of their story. Traditional accounts of the conquest have placed a priest/deity, Topiltzin Quetzalcoatl, at Tula, Hidalgo, in the twelfth century; have recounted his birth in the year Ce Acatl (One Reed) of the calendar used by the Aztecs; have credited him with opposing human sacrifice, for which in part he and his followers were driven into exile, where their influence extended from Central Mexico to Yucatán; have noted that Quetzalcoatl promised to return from the east in his birth year and bring with him better times; have suggested that Moctezuma II was frozen into inaction when Cortés—perhaps believed to be Topiltzin Quetzalcoatl—landed at Veracruz in 1519 (Ce Acatl); and have suggested that Spaniards themselves were perceived as "white gods."

A new look at Topiltzin Quetzalcoatl began with Gillespie's *Aztec Kings* in 1989 and continues with the lead article in the *American Historical Review* of June 2003, "Burying the White Gods," by Camilla Townsend. Along the way, the publications of Ross Hassig and James Lockhart, as well as of other scholars, have contributed substantially to standing the history of the conquest on its head. In short, the confusion of Cortés with Topiltzin Quetzalcoatl, the significance of Ce Acatl, and the perception of Spaniards as gods now appear as post-factum observations that entered mainstream accounts of the conquest around the middle of the sixteenth century.

It makes much better sense to attribute Spanish success to two vitally important factors: the Spaniards' superior technology and their ability to recruit Indian allies. Even if Cortés and his army had been annihilated, it would have prolonged the Aztec empire for only a brief time. European technology would have eventually prevailed over indigenous technology, and that has nothing to do with Cortés's being confused with a returning Topiltzin Quetzalcoatl, nor has it anything to do with Spaniards being viewed by the Aztecs as white gods.

2. Schroeder, "Introduction," 21. Schroeder uses these words to describe doña Marina (Malinche), but they also apply to the heirs of Moctezuma II.

3. The degree to which, by example, Isabel Moctezuma aided the Hispanization of other indigenous people in Central Mexico during her lifetime is admittedly questionable.

4. Gillespie, *Aztec Kings*, 25–26.

5. Carrasco, "Royal Marriages," 56 (quotations), 62.

6. Isabel Moctezuma's only rival in importance was doña Marina (Malinche/Malintzin). See Karttunen, "Rethinking Malinche," 290–312.

7. It must have been satisfying for Isabel Moctezuma, who had six husbands selected for her, to dispose of her estate in a manner that pleased her.

8. For a study of women's property rights in Spain and Texas, see Stuntz, "His, Hers, and Theirs." Stuntz analyzes women's property rights as defined in the *Siete Partidas*, the Laws of Toro, and the Ordenanzas Reales.

9. It may turn out that in Mexican and Spanish archives there is a corpus of formal

legal actions taken by the Indians of Tacuba against their *encomendera* but I have failed to find such materials.

10. Haring, *Spanish Empire*, 130–131. By 1542 an amount regarded as "significant" had increased from about one thousand to ten thousand or more pesos.

11. Carrasco, "Indian-Spanish Marriages," 90.

12. Alamán, *Disertaciones*, 1: 132.

Glossary

adelantado. Medieval title given to a Spanish captain who could expand the realm's frontier.

alcalde mayor. Provincial official and administrator.

aldea. Village or small town.

alguacil mayor. Chief constable.

altepetl. Ethnic unit, composed of separate, independent units. *See calpolli*.

barrio. Town subdivision or quarter.

bellaco. Rogue or villain.

cabeza/cabecera. Head town.

cabildo. Municipal council. *See also regidor*.

calmecac. Elite centers of learning.

calpixqui (pl. *calpixque*). Tax or tribute collector.

calpolli. Component units of an *altepetl*.

camino real. Royal road or principal highway.

capitán general. As used in text, supreme military commander.

Ce Acatl. Literally, "One Reed," a year on the Aztec calendar that repeated cyclically. Ce Acatl coincided with 1519 on the European calendar.

cédula. Royal order or decree.

chinampas. Aquatic fields or gardens.

ciudad. City.

ciudadela. Citadel.

contador. Accountant.

criollo/a. Spaniard born in the New World.

diezmo. Tenth, or tithe.

dobla. Castilian unit of currency of varying value.

ducado. Ducat or coin valued at 375 *maravedís*.

elotes. Ears of green corn.

"en dote y arras." As dowry and security.

encomendero/a. Possessor of an *encomienda*.

encomienda. Grant to Spaniards of specified Indians as tribute payers; also the location of Indians.

entrada. Military entry into lands not settled by Spaniards.

escribano. Scribe.

escudo. Coat of arms.

estancia. Subordinate community; also a farm.

expedientes. Files of papers relating to a specific subject.

factor. Business agent.

fanega. Unit of dry measure, about 1.6 bushels.

fiscal. Legal expert and prosecutor.

flota. Annual fleet assigned to New Spain.

gobernador. Governor or provincial official.

guerra a fuego y sangre. War by fire and blood.

guerra florida. Flower war; also *xochiyaotl*.

hechizado, el. The bewitched or possessed.

hijo/a natural. Son or daughter born out of wedlock.

hispanismo. Hispanization, or acceptance of Spanish values.

información. Report.

juros. Bonds or annuities issued by the Spanish government.

legajos. Bundles of papers or documents. *See also ramos.*

limosnas. Alms.

limpieza de sangre. Literally, "cleanness of blood," but generally meant absence of Jewish ancestry.

lugar. Place.

maravedís. A coin that was the smallest unit of Spanish currency. Thirty-four *maravedís* equaled one *real*, an eighth of a peso.

marco. Unit of weight for gold and silver; one-half of a *libra*, or old peso, in Castile.

mayorazgo. Entailed estate.

memorial. Legal brief.

merced. Grant.

mestizaje. Mixing of Spanish and Indian ancestry.

mestizo/a. Product of Spanish and Indian ancestry.

monjas profesas. Professing nuns of a convent.

mozo, el. The younger.

Noche Triste. "Sad Night"; specifically, the Spaniards' name for their retreat from Tenochtitlan, June 30–July 1, 1520.

"Obedezco pero no cumplo." Literally, "I obey but I do not comply." In practice, it meant that a Spanish official in the New World was obedient to the king but chose not to implement a royal mandate, because to do so would be injurious to the monarch's best interests.

oidor. Judge of the Audiencia.

para disimular. To dissimulate or dissemble.

peninsular. Spaniard born in Spain.

peso de oro común. Silver peso, valued at 272 *maravedís.*

peso de oro de minas. Gold peso, valued at 450 *maravedís.*

pilla (pl. *pipiltin*). Member of the Indian upper class.

poblador. Settler or populator.

primeros conquistadores, los. Honorific applied to first Spaniards in New Spain under the command of Cortés.

principales. Members of the Indian upper class.

privado. Royal favorite or counselor.

privilegio de armas. Right to a coat of arms.

probanza. Legal term for proof or evidence.

proceso. Lawsuit.

procurador. Legal representative or agent.

prueba de caballero. Proof of eligibility for knighthood.

pueblo. Town.

ramos. Sections or divisions within a *legajo.*

real. One-eighth of a silver peso.

regidor. Councilman of a *cabildo.*

repartidor. Official in charge of distribution or assignment of Indians to Spaniards.

repartimientos de trabajos. Allocations of Indians forced to labor for wages.

Requerimiento. Requirement.

residencia. Trial at the end of an official's term in office.

retrato. Portrait or likeness.

rey natural. Native lord or king.

ricos hombres. Rich or wealthy men.

señor/a. Lord/lady.

sujeto. Subject town.

techcatl. Slab used for human sacrifice.

teniente de alcalde mayor. Lieutenant of a provincial official.

teniente de alguacil mayor. Deputy constable.

testigo. Witness in a lawsuit.

tierra adentro. Unexplored territory.

tlatoani (pl. *tlatoque*). Indian ruler of a community.

toltecayotl. Quality of being Toltec.

valido. Individual in the best graces or favor of seventeenth-century Spanish monarchs.

veedor. Official in charge of extracting the king's share of precious metals, usually one-fifth.

villa. Municipality of greater importance than a *pueblo*.

visitador de indios. Inspector of matters relating to Indians.

visitador general. Visitor-general or royal inspector.

xochiyaotl. Flower war; also *guerra florida*.

Bibliography

ARCHIVAL MATERIALS

Archivo General de Indias (AGI) (Seville)
    Contratación, 209, N.1, R.7
    Escribanía de Cámara, 178A
    Guadalajara, 5
    Indiferente General, 1615
    Justicia, 165, N.2; 181; 226; 938; 1029
    Mapas y Planos, Escudos y Árboles Genealógicos, 102, 212, 213
    México, 65, 762; 763; 764; 765; 1088
    Patronato, 59, N.3, R. 6; 80, N. 5, R. 1; 217, R. 3; 245, R. 2, R. 4–6, R.
    15–18, R. 24; 275, R. 36
Archivo General de la Nación (AGN) (Mexico City)
    Hospital de Jesús 265–5
    Mercedes, 1
    Tierras, 1529; 2284
    Vínculos (y Mayorazgos), 69; 76; 80
Archivo Histórico Nacional (AHN)(Madrid)
    Órdenes Militares—Santiago, 1477; 5925; 9070

BOOKS

Alamán, Lucas. *Disertaciones.* 2d ed. 3 vols. Mexico City: Editorial Jus,
    1969.

Alvarado Tezozomoc, Fernando. *Crónica mexicano/Crónica mexicayotl.* Trans. Adrián León. 2d ed. Mexico City: Universidad Nacional Autónoma de México, 1992.

Anderson, Arthur J. O.; Frances Berdan; and James Lockhart. *Beyond the Codices.* Berkeley & Los Angeles: University of California Press, 1976.

Atienza, Julio de. *Títulos nobiliarios hispanoamericanos, con prólogo del autor y 20 reproducciones de escudos de armas.* Madrid: M. Aguilar, 1947.

Bakewell, Peter J. *Silver Mining and Society in Colonial Mexico: Zacatecas, 1546–1700.* Cambridge: Cambridge University Press, 1971.

Bancroft, Hubert H. *History of Mexico.* 6 vols. San Francisco: A. L. Bancroft & Company, 1883–1888.

Bernal, Ignacio. *Bibliografía de arqueología y etnografía: Mesoamérica y norte de México.* Mexico City: Instituto Nacional de Antropología, 1962.

Boban, Eugène. *Documents pour servir a l'histoire du Mexique: Catalogue raisonné de la collection de m. E.-Eugène Goupil.* 2 vols. Paris: Ernest Leroux, 1891.

Broda, Johanna; Davíd Carrasco; and Eduardo Matos Moctezuma. *The Great Temple of Tenochtitlan: Center and Periphery in the Aztec World.* Berkeley & Los Angeles: University of California Press, 1987.

Brundage, Burr C. *A Rain of Darts: The Mexica Aztecs.* Austin: University of Texas Press, 1972.

Burkhart, Louise M. *The Slippery Earth: Nahua-Christian Moral Dialogue in Sixteenth-century Mexico.* Tucson: University of Arizona Press, 1989.

Burland, Cottie A. *Montezuma: Lord of the Aztecs.* New York: G. P. Putnam's Sons, 1973.

Carrasco, Davíd. *Quetzalcoatl and the Irony of Empire: Myths and Prophecies in the Aztec Tradition.* Rev. ed. Boulder: University Press of Colorado, 2000.

Chipman, Donald E. *Nuño de Guzmán and the Province of Pánuco in New Spain, 1518–1533.* Glendale, CA: Arthur H. Clark, 1967.

———. *Spanish Texas, 1519–1821.* 1992. Reprint, Austin: University of Texas Press, 1994.

Clavigero, Francisco Javier. *Historia antigua de México.* 4 vols. Mexico City: Editorial Porrúa, 1945.

Clendinnen, Inga. *Aztecs: An Interpretation.* Cambridge: Cambridge University Press, 1991.

Codex Ramírez: Relación del origen de los indios que habitan esta Nueva España. Mexico City: Editorial Leyenda, 1944.

Códice Chimalpopoca: Spanish and Aztec. Trans. Primo Feliciano Velázquez. Mexico City: Universidad Nacional Autónoma de México, Instituto de Investigaciones Históricas, 1975.

Colección de documentos inéditos relativos al descubrimiento, conquista y organización de las antiguas posesiones de Ultramar, DIU). 25 vols. Reprint. Vaduz, Liechtenstein: Kraus, 1967.

Colección de documentos inéditos relativos al descubrimiento, conquista y organización de las antiguas posesiones españolas en América y Oceanía (DII). 42 vols. 1864–1884. Reprint, Vaduz, Liechtenstein: Kraus, 1967.

Conway, G. R. G. *The Last Will and Testament of Hernando Cortés, Marqués del Valle.* Mexico City: Privately published, 1939.

Cortés, Hernán. *Cartas y documentos.* Intro. Mario Hernández Sánchez-Barba. Mexico City: Editorial Porrúa, 1963.

———. *Letters from Mexico.* Trans., ed. Anthony Padgen. Intro. J. H. Elliott. New Haven, CT: Yale University Press, 1986.

Davies, Nigel. *The Aztec Empire: The Toltec Resurgence.* Norman: University of Oklahoma Press, 1987.

———. *The Aztecs: A History.* New York: G. P. Putnam's Sons, 1973.

———. *The Toltec Heritage: From the Fall of Tula to the Rise of Tenochtitlan.* Norman: University of Oklahoma Press, 1980.

———. *The Toltecs: Until the Fall of Tula.* Norman: University of Oklahoma Press, 1977.

Dávila Garibi, José Ignacio. *La sociedad de Zacatecas en los albores del régimen colonial, actuación de los principales fundadores y primeros funcionarios públicos de la ciudad.* Mexico City: Antigua Librería Robredo, 1939.

De Terra, Helmut; Javier Romero; and T. D. Stewart. *Tepexpan Man.* New York: Johnson Reprint Corp., 1949.

Díaz del Castillo, Bernal. *The Discovery and Conquest of Mexico, 1517–1521.* Ed. Genaro García. Trans. A. P. Maudslay. Intro. Irving A. Leonard. New York: Farrar, Straus, and Cudahy, 1956.

———. *Historia verdadera de la conquista de la Nueva España.* Intro., notes Joaquín Ramírez de Cabañas. 2 vols. Mexico City: Editorial Porrúa, 1955.

Diccionario Porrúa de historia, biografía y geografía de México. 3d ed. 2 vols. Mexico City: Editorial Porrúa, 1971.

Durán, Diego. *Book of the Gods and Rites and the Ancient Calendar.* Trans., ed. Fernando Horcasitas and Doris Heyden. Norman: University of Oklahoma Press, 1971.

————. *The History of the Indies of New Spain.* Trans., annot., intro. Doris Heyden. Norman: University of Oklahoma Press, 1994.

Elliott, J. H. *Imperial Spain, 1469–1716.* New York: St. Martin's Press, 1964.

————. *The Old World and the New, 1492–1650.* Cambridge: Cambridge University Press, 1972

Epistolario de Nueva España, 1505–1818 (ENE). 16 vols. Mexico City: Antigua Librería Robredo, 1939–1942.

Fernández de Oviedo, Gonzalo. *Historia general y natural de las Indias.* Ed. Juan Pérez de Tudela Bueso. 5 vols. Madrid: Ediciones Atlas, 1959.

Fernández de Recas, Guillermo S. *Mayorazgos de la Nueva España.* Mexico City: Instituto Bibliográfico Mexicano, 1965.

García Granados, Rafael. *Diccionario biográfico de historia antigua de Méjico.* 3 vols. Mexico City: Instituto de Historia, 1952–1953.

García Iglesias, Sara. *Isabel Moctezuma: La última princesa azteca.* Mexico City: Ediciones Xochitl, 1946.

Gerhard, Peter. *A Guide to the Historical Geography of New Spain.* Rev. ed. Norman: University of Oklahoma Press, 1993.

Gibson, Charles. *The Aztecs under Spanish Rule: A History of the Indians of the Valley of Mexico, 1519–1810.* Stanford, CA: Stanford University Press, 1964.

Gillespie, Susan D. *The Aztec Kings: The Construction of Rulership in Mexica History.* Tucson: University of Arizona Press, 1989.

Gruzinski, Serge. *The Mestizo Mind: The Intellectual Dynamics of Colonization and Globalization.* Trans. of *La pensée métisse*, by Deke Dusinberre. New York: Routledge, 2002.

Hammond, George P., and Agapito Rey. *Don Juan de Oñate: Colonizer of New Mexico, 1595–1628.* 2 vols. Albuquerque: University of New Mexico Press, 1953.

Hanke, Lewis. *The Spanish Struggle for Justice in the Conquest of America.* Philadelphia: University of Pennsylvania Press, 1949.

————. *The Spanish Struggle for Justice in the Conquest of America.* New intro. Susan Scafidi and Peter Bakewell. Dallas, TX: Southern Methodist University Press, 2002.

————. *Los virreyes en América durante el gobierno de la Casa de Austria.* 5 vols. Madrid: Ediciones Atlas, 1976–1978.

Haring, Clarence H. *The Spanish Empire in America.* New York: Oxford University Press, 1947.

Harris, Marvin. *Cannibals and Kings: The Origins of Cultures.* New York: Random House, 1977.

Hassig, Ross. *Aztec Warfare: Imperial Expansion and Political Control.* Norman: University of Oklahoma Press, 1988.

———. *Mexico and the Spanish Conquest.* London: Longman, 1994.

Himmerich y Valencia, Robert. *The Encomenderos of New Spain, 1521–1555.* Austin: University of Texas Press, 1991.

Icaza, Francisco A. de. *Diccionario autobiográfico de conquistadores y pobladores de Nueva España.* 2 vols. Guadalajara, Mexico: E. Arviña Levy, 1969.

Jones, Oakah L., Jr. *Nueva Vizcaya: Heartland of the Spanish Frontier.* Albuquerque: University of New Mexico Press, 1988.

Keen, Benjamin. *The Aztec Image in Western Thought.* New Brunswick, NJ: Rutgers University Press, 1971.

Kellogg, Susan. *Law and the Transformation of Aztec Culture, 1500–1700.* Norman: University of Oklahoma Press, 1995.

Klor de Alva, J. Jorge; H. B. Nicholson; and Eloise Quiñones Keber, eds. *The Work of Bernardino de Sahagún: Pioneer Ethnographer of Sixteenth-century Aztec Mexico.* Institute for Mesoamerican Studies, Studies on Culture and Society, Vol. 2. Albany: State University of New York, 1988.

Kroeber, A. L. *The Nature of Culture.* Chicago: University of Chicago Press, 1952.

Ladd, Doris M. *Mexican Nobility at Independence, 1780–1826.* Austin, TX: Institute of Latin American Studies, 1976.

Langdon-Davies, John. *Carlos: The King Who Would Not Die.* Englewood Cliffs, NJ: Prentice-Hall, 1962.

las Casas, Fray Bartolomé de. *Historia de las Indias.* Prol. Gonzalo de Reparaz (1927). 3 vols. Madrid: M. Aguilar, n.d.

Leonard, Irving A. *Baroque Times in Old Mexico: Seventeenth-century Persons, Places, and Practices.* Ann Arbor: University of Michigan Press, 1966.

León-Portilla, Miguel. *The Aztec Image of Self and Society: An Introduction to Nahua Culture.* Salt Lake City: University of Utah Press, 1992.

——— ed., *The Broken Spears: The Aztec Account of the Conquest of Mexico.* Expanded and updated ed. Boston: Beacon Press, 1992.

Liss, Peggy K. *Mexico under Spain, 1521–1556: Society and the Origins of Nationality.* Chicago: University of Chicago Press, 1975.

Lockhart, James M. *The Men of Cajamarca: A Social and Biographical Study of the First Conquerors of Peru.* Austin: University of Texas Press, 1972.

————. *The Nahuas after the Conquest: A Social and Cultural History of the Indians of Central Mexico, Sixteenth through Eighteenth Centuries.* Stanford, CA: Stanford University Press, 1992.

————. *Nahuas and Spaniards: Postconquest Central Mexican History and Philology.* Stanford, CA: Stanford University Press, 1991.

————, ed. and trans. *We People Here: Nahuatl Accounts of the Conquest of Mexico.* Berkeley & Los Angeles: University of California Press, 1993.

Lockhart, James M., and Enrique Otte, eds. and trans. *Letters and People of the Spanish Indies: Sixteenth Century.* Cambridge: Cambridge University Press, 1976.

Lohmann Villena, Guillermo. *Los americanos en las órdenes nobiliarias (1529–1900).* 2 vols. Madrid: Consejo Superior de Investigaciones Científicas, Instituto Gonzalo Fernández de Oviedo, 1947.

Lynch, John. *Spain under the Habsburgs.* 2d ed. 2 vols. New York: New York University Press, 1981.

MacNeish, Richard S. *The Origins of Agriculture and Settled Life.* Norman: University of Oklahoma Press, 1992.

Manero Suárez, Enrique. *Doce generaciones de "Manero" y sus ramas troncales (de 1360 a 1960).* Mexico City: N.p., n.d.

Martínez Cosío, Leopoldo. *Los caballeros de las órdenes militares en México: Catálogo biográfico y genealógico.* Mexico City: N.p., 1946.

Mecham, J. Lloyd. *Francisco de Ibarra and Nueva Vizcaya.* Durham, NC: Duke University Press, 1927.

Melish, Joanne Pope. *Disowning Slavery: Gradual Emancipation and "Race" in New England, 1780–1860.* Ithaca, NY: Cornell University Press, 1998.

Millon, René, ed. *Urbanization at Teotihuacán, Mexico.* Vol. 1, Pt. 1: *Text.* Austin: University of Texas Press, 1973.

Motezuma, Diego Luis de. *Corona mexicana; ó, historia de los nueve Motezumas.* Ed., prol. Lucas de Torre. Madrid: Biblioteca Hispania, 1914.

Muriel, Josefina. *Conventos de monjas en la Nueva España.* 2d ed. Mexico City: Editorial Jus, 1995.

————. *Las mujeres de Hispanoamérica: Época colonial.* Madrid: Editorial Mapfre, 1992.

Nicholson, H. B. *Topilztin Quetzalcoatl: The Once and Future Lord of the Toltecs.* Boulder: University Press of Colorado, 2001.

Nobiliario de conquistadores de Indias. Madrid: Imprenta de M. Tello, 1892.

Obras históricas de Don Fernando de Alva Ixtlilxochitl. 2 vols. Mexico City: Oficina Tip. de la Secretaría de Fomento, 1891–1892.

Orozco y Berra, Manuel. *Noticia histórica de la conjuración del Marqués del Valle: Años de 1565–1568.* Mexico City: Tipografía de R. Rafael, 1853.

Ortega y Pérez Gallardo, Ricardo. *Estudios genealógicos.* Mexico City: Imprenta de Eduardo Dublán, 1902.

———. *Historia genealógica de las familias más antiguas de México.* 3d ed. 3 vols. Mexico City: Imprenta de A. Carranza, 1908–1910.

Padden, R. C. *The Hummingbird and the Hawk: Conquest and Sovereignty in the Valley of Mexico, 1503–1541.* New York: Harper and Row, 1970.

Paz, Julián. *Catálogo de los manuscritos de América existentes en la Biblioteca Nacional.* Madrid: Tip. de Archivos, 1933.

Peterson, Frederick A. *Ancient Mexico: An Introduction to the Pre-Hispanic Cultures.* New York: G. P. Putnam's Sons, 1959.

Powell, Philip W. *Soldiers, Indians, and Silver: The Northward Advance of New Spain, 1550–1600.* Berkeley & Los Angeles: University of California Press, 1952.

Prescott, William H. *History of the Conquest of Mexico.* Ed. John Foster Kirk. 3 vols. Philadelphia: J. B. Lippincott, 1873.

Rípodas Ardanaz, Daisy. *El matrimonio en Indias: Realidad social y regulación jurídica.* Buenos Aires: Fundación para la Educación, la Ciencia y la Cultura, 1977.

Robles, Antonio de. *Diario de sucesos notables (1665–1703).* 3 vols. Mexico City: Editorial Porrúa, 1946.

Rubio Mañé, J. Ignacio. *Introducción al estudio de los virreyes de Nueva España, 1535–1746.* 2d ed. 4 vols. Mexico City: Universidad Nacional Autónoma de México, Instituto de Investigaciones Históricas, 1983.

Sahagún, Bernardino de. *Florentine Codex: General History of the Things of New Spain.* Trans. Arthur J. O. Anderson and Charles E. Dibble. 12 bks., 13 pts. Santa Fe, NM: School of American Research and the University of Utah, 1950–1982.

Scholes, France V., and Eleanor B. Adams, eds. *Documentos para la historia del México colonial.* 7 vols. Mexico City: José Porrúa e Hijos, 1955–1961.

———. *Proceso contra Tzintzicha Tangaxoan el Caltzontzin, formado por Nuño de Guzmán, año de 1530.* Mexico City: N.p., 1952.

Scholes, France V., and Ralph L. Roys. *The Maya Chontal Indians of Acalan-Tixchel: A Contribution to the History and Ethnography of the Yucatan Peninsula.* Washington, DC: Carnegie Institution of Washington, 1948.

Schroeder, Susan; Stephanie Wood; and Robert Haskett, eds. *Indian*

Women of Early Mexico. Norman: University of Oklahoma Press, 1997.

Seed, Patricia. *Ceremonies of Possession in Europe's Conquest of the New World, 1492–1640*. Cambridge: Cambridge University Press, 1995.

Las Siete Partidas. Trans., notes Samuel P. Scott. Chicago: Commerce Clearing House, 1931.

Simmons, Marc. *The Last Conquistador: Juan de Oñate and the Settling of the Far Southwest*. Norman: University of Oklahoma Press, 1991.

Simpson, Lesley B. *The Encomienda in New Spain: The Beginning of Spanish Mexico*. Berkeley & Los Angeles: University of California Press, 1950.

Smith, Michael E. *The Aztecs*. Oxford: Blackwell, 1996.

Sweet, David G., and Gary B. Nash, eds. *Struggle and Survival in Colonial America*. Berkeley & Los Angeles: University of California Press, 1981.

Thomas, Hugh. *Conquest: Montezuma, Cortés, and the Fall of Old Mexico*. New York: Simon & Schuster, 1993.

Torres Lanzas, Pedro. *Relación descriptiva de los mapas, planos, etc., de México y Florida existentes en el Archivo General de Indias*. 2 vols. Seville: Imprenta de Mercantil, 1900.

Vetancurt, Agustín de. *Teatro mexicano: Descripción breve de los sucesos ejemplares, históricos y religiosos del Nuevo Mundo de las Indias*. 1st facs. ed. Mexico City: Editorial Porrúa, 1971.

Villar Villamil, Ignacio de. *Cedulario heráldico de conquistadores de Nueva España*. Mexico City: Talleres Gráficos del Museo Nacional de Arqueología, Historia y Etnografía, 1933.

Vitoria, Francisco de. *Political Writings*. Ed. Anthony Padgen and Jeremy Lawrance. Cambridge: Cambridge University Press, 1991.

Wagner, Henry R. *The Rise of Fernando Cortés*. 1944. Reprint, New York: Kraus, 1969.

Warren, J. Benedict. *The Conquest of Michoacán: The Spanish Domination of the Tarascan Kingdom in Western Mexico, 1521–1530*. Norman: University of Oklahoma Press, 1985.

Zavala, Silvio. *Los esclavos indios en Nueva España*. Mexico City: Colegio Nacional, 1967.

———. *Las instituciones jurídicas en la conquista de América*. 3d ed. Mexico City: Editorial Porrúa, 1988.

Zurita, Alonso de. *Life and Labor in Ancient Mexico: The Brief and Summary Relation of the Lords of New Spain*. Trans. Benjamin Keen. New Brunswick, NJ: Rutgers University Press, 1963.

ARTICLES, CHAPTERS, COLLECTIONS, AND UNPUBLISHED
WORKS

Barlow, Robert. "Anales de Tula, Hidalgo, 1361–1521." *Tlalocan: A Journal of Source Materials on the Native Cultures of Mexico* 3 (1949): 2–13.

———. "La crónica X: Versiones coloniales de la historia de los Mexica Tenocha." *Revista Mexicana de Estudios Antropológicos* 7 (1945): 65–87.

Beerman, Eric. "The Death of an Old Conquistador: New Light on Juan de Oñate." *New Mexico Historical Review* 54 (October 1979): 305–319.

Brotherson, Gordon. "Tula: Touchstone of the Mesoamerican Era." *New Scholar* 10 (1986): 19–39.

Burkett, Elinor C. "Indian Women and White Society: The Case of Sixteenth-century Peru." In *Latin American Women: Historical Perspectives*, ed. Asunción Lavrin. Westport, CT: Greenwood Press, 1978.

Carrasco, Pedro. "Indian-Spanish Marriages in the First Century of the Colony." In *Indian Women of Early Mexico*, ed. Susan Schroeder, Stephanie Wood, and Robert Hasket. Norman: University of Oklahoma Press, 1997.

———. "Royal Marriages in Ancient Mexico." In *Explorations in Ethnohistory: Indians of Central Mexico in the Sixteenth Century*, ed. H. R. Harvey and Hanns J. Prem. Albuquerque: University of New Mexico Press, 1984.

Chipman, Donald E. "Alonso Álvarez de Pineda and the Río de las Palmas: Scholars and the Mislocation of a River." *Southwestern Historical Quarterly* 98 (January 1995): 369–385.

———. "Isabel Moctezuma: Pioneer of *Mestizaje*." In *Struggle and Survival in Colonial America*, ed. David G. Sweet and Gary B. Nash. Berkeley & Los Angeles: University of California Press, 1981.

———. "Judicial Proceedings in New Spain: An Addendum to the Harkness 1531 Huejotzingo Codex." *Quarterly Journal of the Library of Congress* 35 (January 1978): 27–35.

———. "Nuño de Guzmán and His 'Grand Design' in New Spain." In *Homenaje a Don José María de la Peña y Cámara*, Madrid: Ediciones José Porrúa Turanzas, 1969.

———. "The Oñate-Moctezuma-Zaldívar Families of Northern New Spain." *New Mexico Historical Review* 52 (November 1977): 297–310.

Cline, Howard F. "Hernando Cortés and the Aztec Indians in Spain." *Quarterly Journal of the Library of Congress* 26 (April 1969): 70–90.

Countryman, Edward. "Indians, the Colonial Order, and the Social Significance of the American Revolution." *William and Mary Quarterly* 53 (April 1996): 342–386.

Curcio, Linda A. "Saints, Sovereignty, and Spectacle in Colonial Mexico." Ph.D. dissertation, Tulane University, 1993.

Curcio-Nagy, Linda A. "Giants and Gypsies: Corpus Christi in Colonial Mexico." In *Rituals of Rule, Rituals of Resistance: Public Celebrations and Popular Culture in Mexico*, ed. William H. Beezley, Cheryl English Martin, and William E. French. Wilmington, DE: Scholarly Resources, 1994.

Gabai, Rafael Varón, and Auke Pieter Jacobs. "Peruvian Wealth and Spanish Investments: The Pizarro Family during the Sixteenth Century." *Hispanic American Historical Review* 67 (November 1987): 657–695.

Garate, Don T. "Juan de Oñate's *Prueba de Caballero*, 1625: A Look at His Ancestral Heritage." *Colonial Latin American Historical Review* 7 (Spring 1998): 129–173.

Gibson, Charles. "The Aztec Aristocracy in Colonial Mexico." *Comparative Studies in Society and History: An International Quarterly* 2 (1959–1960): 169–196.

———. "Conquest, Capitulation, and Indian Treaties." *American Historical Review* 83 (February 1978): 1–15.

Harner, Michael. "The Ecological Basis for Aztec Sacrifice." *American Ethnologist* 4 (February 1977): 117–135.

Hassig, Ross. "The Collision of Two Worlds." In *The Oxford History of Mexico*, ed. Michael C. Meyer and William H. Beezley. Oxford: Oxford University Press, 2000.

Hinderaker, Eric. "The 'Four Indian Kings' and the Imaginative Construction of the First British Empire." *William and Mary Quarterly* 53 (July 1996): 487–526.

Hollingsworth, Ann P. "Pedro de Moctezuma and His Descendants, 1521–1718." Ph.D. dissertation, North Texas State University, 1980.

"In This Issue." *American Historical Review* 108 (June 2003): xiv.

Karttunen, Frances. "Rethinking Malinche." In *Indian Women of Early Mexico*, ed. Susan Schroeder, Stephanie Wood, and Robert Haskett. Norman: University of Oklahoma Press, 1997.

Kellogg, Susan. "Tenocha Mexica Women, 1500–1700." In *Indian Women of Early Mexico*, ed. Susan Schroeder, Stephanie Wood, and Robert Haskett. Norman: University of Oklahoma Press, 1997.

Konetzke, Richard. "El mestizaje y su importancia en el desarrollo de la población hispano-americana durante la época colonial." *Revista de Indias* 7 (1947): 7–44.

Lavrin, Asunción. "Women in Convents: Their Economic and Social Role in Colonial Mexico." In *Liberating Women's History: Theoretical and Critical Essays*, ed. Bernice Carroll. Urbana: University of Illinois Press, 1976.

López de Meneses, Amada. "Dos nietas de Moteczuma, monjas de la Concepción de México." *Revista de Indias* 12 (1952): 81–100.

———. "Un nieto de Moctezuma en la cárcel de Sevilla." In *Erudición ibero-ultramarina.* 5 vols., 2: 562–572. Madrid: V. Suárez, 1932.

———. "Tecuichpotzin, hija de Moteczuma (1510?–1550)." *Revista de Indias* 9 (1949): 471–495.

Muriel, Josefina. "Reflexiones sobre Hernán Cortés." *Revista de Indias* 9 (1949): 229–245.

Quitt, Martin H. "Trade and Acculturation at Jamestown, 1607–1609: The Limits of Understanding." *William and Mary Quarterly* 52 (April 1995): 227–258.

Sánchez, Joseph P. "Juan de Oñate and the Founding of New Mexico, 1598–1609." *Colonial Latin American Historical Review* 7 (Spring 1998): 89–107.

Sanders, William T. "The Natural Environment of the Basin of Mexico." In *The Valley of Mexico: Studies in Pre-Hispanic Ecology and Society*, ed. Eric R. Wolf. Albuquerque: University of New Mexico Press, 1976.

———. "The Population of the Central Mexican Symbiotic Region, the Basin of Mexico, and the Teotihuacan Valley in the Sixteenth Century." In *The Native Population of the Americas in 1492*, ed. William M. Denevan. 2d ed. Madison: University of Wisconsin Press, 1992.

Scholes, France V. "The Last Days of Gonzalo de Sandoval: Conquistador of New Spain." In *Homenaje a Don José María de la Peña y Cámara.* Madrid: Ediciones José Porrúa Turanzas, 1969.

Schroeder, Susan. "Introduction." In *Indian Women of Early Mexico*, ed. Susan Schroeder, Stephanie Wood, and Robert Haskett. Norman: University of Oklahoma Press, 1997.

Stuntz, Jean A. "His, Hers, and Theirs: Domestic Relations and Marital Property Law in Texas to 1850." Ph.D. dissertation, University of North Texas, 2000.

Townsend, Camilla. "Burying the White Gods: New Perspectives on the Conquest of Mexico." *American Historical Review* 108 (June 2003): 659–687.

CD-Rom

Family Search: Pedigree Resource File, Disc 14. The Church of Jesus Christ of Latter-day Saints.

World Wide Web

http://www.almanach.be/search/m/mexicomoctezuma.html
http://www.geocities.com/revista_conciencia/zacatecas
Palacio de los Toledo-Moctezuma:
   http://www.terra.es/personal2/ joseabra/ptmocte.htm

Index

Yetepec, 64
Yoloxinecuila, 169n40
Ystla, 162n41, 163n56
Yucatán, 25, 28, 33, 34
Yztaque, 162n41

Zacatecas, xix, xxii, 68, 100, 101, 102, 103, 106–108, 110, 114, 116–118
Zacateco Indians, 101, 107, 110
Zacatula, 76
Zaldívar, Ruy Díaz de, 105
Zaldívar, Vicente de, 104–106, 108, 115
Zaldívar Cortés, Juan de, 106
Zaldivar Mendoza, Cristóbal de, 105, 106, 109

Zaldívar Mendoza, Juan de, 105, 106, 114, 115
Zaldívar Mendoza, Vicente de, 105, 106, 114, 116, 118, 124
Zaldívar Oñate, Juan de, 106, 118
Zaldívar y Oñate, Nicolás de, 106, 118
Zaquala, 162n41, 163n56, 169n40
Zaragosa, Juan de, 74
Zaragosa, Miguel de, 74
Zoquitlan, 10
Zoquitzingo, 169n40
Zumárraga, Juan de, 51, 55
Zumpaguacan, 169n40

Milton Keynes UK
Ingram Content Group UK Ltd.
UKHW030740040924
447866UK00001B/7